STRENGTHENING TI._ CONNECTIONS BETWEEN LEADERSHIP AND LEARNING

Examining a decade of research and practice, this book makes the case for a radical reappraisal of leadership, learning, and their interrelationship in educational policy. Discussing whether policy direction is progressively constraining the professionalism and initiative of teachers and school leaders, it challenges conventional understanding and argues the case for thinking differently about the way to lead learning.

Based on the Leadership for Learning (LfL) Project, the book clarifies, extends, and refines LfL principles and practices, and their contribution to ameliorating some of the difficult conditions encountered in the contemporary educational policy environment. It starts by discussing the direction and influence of current education policy and its subsequent consequences; chapters then move on to explore the framing values informing the LfL Projects, particularly focusing on what they imply for commitments to social justice, children's rights and breadth in student learning, and considering how to create favourable conditions for learning.

Identifying a disconnect between seminal principles and the nature of day-to-day practice, *Strengthening the Connections between Leadership and Learning* challenges school policy and practice at national and local levels. It is an essential read for postgraduate students, especially those studying leadership in education, as well as for teachers and policymakers in schools.

John MacBeath is Emeritus Professor at the University of Cambridge, UK, co-founder of Leadership for Learning: the Cambridge Network, and Fellow of Hughes Hall.

Neil Dempster is Emeritus Professor at Griffith University and former Dean of the Griffith University Faculty of Education, Australia.

David Frost was a member of the Faculty of Education, University of Cambridge, UK, for 20 years. He was one of the co-founders of Leadership for Learning: the Cambridge Network and the founder of the HertsCam Network.

Greer Johnson is Director of the Griffith Institute for Educational Research at Griffith University, Australia, and was previously a member of the Australian team on the Leadership for Learning Project.

Sue Swaffield teaches and researches in educational leadership and school improvement at the Faculty of Education, University of Cambridge, UK. Sue is a co-founder of Leadership for Learning: the Cambridge Network.

STRENGTHENING THE CONNECTIONS BETWEEN LEADERSHIP AND LEARNING

Challenges to Policy, School and Classroom Practice

John MacBeath, Neil Dempster, David Frost, Greer Johnson and Sue Swaffield

Routledge
Taylor & Francis Group

LONDON AND NEW YORK

First published 2018
by Routledge
2 Park Square, Milton Park, Abingdon, Oxon OX14 4RN

and by Routledge
711 Third Avenue, New York, NY 10017

Routledge is an imprint of the Taylor & Francis Group, an informa business

British Library Cataloguing-in-Publication Data
A catalogue record for this book is available from the British Library

Library of Congress Cataloging-in-Publication Data
A catalog record has been requested for this book

ISBN: 978-0-8153-4914-3 (hbk)
ISBN: 978-0-8153-4915-0 (pbk)
ISBN: 978-1-351-16532-7 (ebk)

Typeset in Bembo
by Deanta Global Publishing Services, Chennai, India

CONTENTS

List of illustrations   *viii*
Acknowledgements   *ix*

Introduction   **1**

1   The policy challenge   **5**

Eight policy consequences   6
Productive failure   13
From dutiful compliance to rule breaking   14
The policy dilemma space   15
Conclusion   17
References   19

2   The backdrop to policy reform   **21**

Global policy trends and the policy dilemma space   21
*The global policy backdrop and flirtation with
    managerialism   24*
Global policy effects in Carpe Vitam *Project countries   25*
Change without improvement   34
Conclusion   35
References   35

3 **Leadership for Learning: An essential narrative
   in a challenge to policy** 37

   Millennium change 37
   The Carpe Vitam *Leadership for Learning Project 38*
   Leadership for Learning: Principles for practice 41
   A challenge to policy 49
   Conclusion 53
   References 55

4 **Professional integrity** 58

   Moral purpose 59
   Professional integrity 59
   Test-driven narrowness versus a broad education 61
   *The rights of the child, moral purpose, and
       professional integrity 63*
   *Social justice dimensions as a further test for
       professional integrity in education 67*
   *Testing integrity questions for school leaders
       implementing projects and programs 68*
   *Two illustrative international Leadership
       for Learning cases 69*
   A final word on critical friendship 80
   Conclusion 81
   References 83

5 **Leadership as practice** 87

   Towards understanding leadership as practice 88
   The leader-practitioner 90
   Leadership as a set of practices 90
   Summary 95
   Leadership in the flow of practice 96
   Summary 97
   Vignette 1 98
   Vignette 2 101
   Conclusion 105
   References 106

6   **Thinking differently about learning and teaching**   109

Case study: The Learning School   112
What we have learnt   114
Modes of knowing and being   118
Storyline: Telling and creating stories   127
Conclusion   130
References   131

7   **Enhancing teacher professionality**   133

Teacher quality, effectiveness, and standards   133
Professionalism, professionality, and professional identity   135
What counts as knowledge   136
The Leadership for Learning alternative   136
Case 1: The Teacher Leader Fellowship
  in Florida   138
Case 2: The HertsCam Network approach
  to teacher leadership   141
Individual and collective agency in enhancing professionalism   147
Conclusion   148
References   149

8   **Challenging policy, school, and classroom practice**   154

What we have argued in this book   156
The four fields of endeavour – key points   159
Continuing the struggle   163
Inherited intelligence or hard work?   165
Autonomy and the dark side   166
The inertia of change   168
Conclusion   169
References   170

Index   *173*

ILLUSTRATIONS

Figures

3.1   Leadership for Learning and its principles   42
4.1   The PALLIC Leadership for Learning framework or blueprint   76
7.1   The theory of non-positional teacher leadership   143
8.1   A platform for challenges to policy, school, and classroom practice   157

Tables

4.1   A test of integrity for the PALLIC Program   78
5.1   Comparison of different practice perspectives of leadership   89

ACKNOWLEDGEMENTS

The ideas in this book owe much to the Cambridge University-led *Carpe Vitam* Leadership for Learning Project which ran from 2002 to 2006. Planning for the sharing of tasks to complete a co-authored work a decade later, with authors from Australia and the United Kingdom, required support from the Cambridge Leadership for Learning Network and the Griffith Institute for Educational Research (GIER). Both agencies provided tangible assistance for initial face-to-face and ongoing internet meetings to enable the project to proceed. Our appreciation of these efforts is warmly acknowledged. In addition, we are grateful to Elizabeth Stevens, a GIER Senior Research Assistant, for her editorial and proofing expertise in helping to finalise the manuscript for publication. Her work, as always, brings discipline to texts where multiple authors have been involved and for this we thank her sincerely.

John MacBeath
Neil Dempster
David Frost
Greer Johnson
Sue Swaffield

INTRODUCTION

This book is the result of more than a decade's work on trying to better understand the connections between leadership and learning. The starting point for the investment of a great amount of research time and effort in this task was the Cambridge University-led *Carpe Vitam* Leadership for Learning (LfL) Project about which more is said in the eight chapters which follow. What we found from the original project has been confirmed, complemented, extended, and applied through supplementary research and development activity in different international contexts. This has given us the confidence to locate our understanding of LfL as the centrepiece of a composite agenda which, as a combination, may help our profession to challenge positions taken in contemporary educational policy which we believe pose problems for leaders, teachers, and learners – hence, the subtitle of the book, *Challenges to policy, school, and classroom practice.*

We begin in **Chapter 1** ("The policy challenge") with a discussion of the direction and influence of education policy with a particular focus on the last decade. Referring to eight salient policy agendas which are international in their reach, we argue that these need to be subject to rigorous critique and challenge. Paradoxically, as competitive globalised policy continues to narrow the curriculum and diminish the discretion of teachers, policies on institutional autonomy increase the control and authority of the individual headteacher or principal. This has the effect of widening the "power distance" between senior leaders and their staff, intensifying accountability pressure so that conformity and compliance become the default positions for teachers. Quoting Michael Fullan, these are described as the "wrong policy drivers", creating conditions detrimental to learning and to student interests while innovation and change in pedagogy become increasingly constricted. The chapter concludes that such critiques should not be treated as reactive disagreement but rather acknowledged as an architecture built on the solid foundations of critical dissent.

In **Chapter 2** ("The backdrop to policy reform"), we follow on from the policy consequences and issues raised in the preceding chapter, to examine the nature of "dilemma space", contrasting a cooperative commitment to educational principles on the one hand, with competitive service provision, on the other. The impact of New Public Management, New Public Governance, and the politics of "earned autonomy" are examined with reference to Australia, Norway and Sweden, England, and New Zealand. The rationale for the adoption of school self-management is discussed with implications for the changing priorities of governments, local authorities, and schools in a competitive international policy environment. The themes at the heart of the book, running as a continuous thread through it, focus on the implications for "leadership", how to hold on to key principles while taking up the challenge to policymaking. The chapter shows that in a climate intolerant of dissent or opposition to authority, it becomes all the more imperative to foster a culture in which leadership at every level within a system is able to engage in constructive, civilised, but semi-permanent disagreement when learning is affected.

Chapter 3 ("Leadership for learning") gives us the opportunity to present a "practical theory", a "master key" which opens up a rich source of intelligence and a narrative with which to challenge policy, school, and classroom practice. When the term Leadership for Learning (LfL) was first coined in Cambridge in 2000, it brought a freshness and originality to the leadership discourse and prompted a number of international studies, exploring how we come to understand the connections between leadership and learning in different country contexts. In the two decades that have followed, the terminology has been widely employed but not always with the meanings and intent of its original conception. Adopting the LfL descriptor required, and still requires, a critical revisiting of what is widely understood as "leadership", what is commonly viewed as "learning", and how the connective "for" is critical in bringing these two big ideas together. That sometimes contentious preposition opens up a plethora of questions as to how learning is promoted, embedded, and reviewed in policy and practice. The five informing principles of the LfL framework are revisited, showing that they are integrally related and, when taken together, offer a practical theory which provides a platform for constructive challenges to policy.

The discussion in **Chapter 4** ("Professional integrity") picks up and expands on the framing values informing the Leadership for Learning (LfL) projects discussed in Chapter 3, examining what these imply for commitments to social justice, children's rights, breadth in student learning, and the democratic principle of parity of participation. These are identified as integrally important for everyone engaged in the educational enterprise and as essential components of a modern profession concerned to uphold its integrity. Case studies drawn from Australia and Ghana are described, helping to unpick the complex skein of economic, political, and cultural influences on the exercise of professional integrity. How school leaders and teachers, with a commitment to professional integrity, are able to "swim upstream" against the tide of prevailing policy is illustrated from a LfL stance. The chapter concludes with a series of questions which challenge the professional integrity of school leaders and teachers themselves, before suggesting how individuals, collectives, and the profession at large can take the challenge up to politicians and policymakers. This is of critical importance when reform mandates run counter to staunchly held professional positions.

Chapter 5 ("Leadership as practice") brings leadership as activity or practice into the foreground. It is reaffirmed as one of the five essential leadership for learning (LfL) principles. This is particularly relevant as a counter to the strength of the prevailing rhetoric on "heroic" leadership. In other words, the implementation of leadership as practice challenges individualistic positional approaches which occupy a pervasive presence in system and school hierarchies. The focus of the chapter is on an alternative view in which leadership is enacted in practice, bringing people together in collaborative dialogue. At the centre of leadership as practice is the spontaneous pursuit of professional learning and pedagogical activity, focused primarily on student needs. Drawing on Simpson's (2016) analysis of the work of Dewey and Bentley (1949) on self-action, inter-action, and trans-action, the discussion examines human agency using Simpson's three leadership perspectives – the *leader-practitioner, leadership as a set of practices* often distributed, and *leadership in the flow of practice*. While all three are evident in education systems, when a leadership for learning stance is apparent, the latter two categories come into prominence, encouraging open dialogue and increasingly frequent extemporaneous agency.

In **Chapter 6** ("Thinking differently about learning and teaching") we begin with the questions "Why do we need to think differently about learning and teaching? To what extent is it possible to think in new ways about leadership, about learning and about the interrelationship of the two?" Discussing the second *Carpe Vitam* principle – *creating favourable conditions for learning* – it is argued that the process of learning is hugely susceptible to the environment in which it takes place. From womb to classroom, evidence shows the powerful in-built capacity of human beings to adapt to the constraining forces that shape their mental models of the world. These include perceptions of relationships, of authority, of ourselves, our capacities and hopes. The necessary complement to David Perkins's characterisation of "learning in captivity" is "teaching in captivity" – teachers and taught bound together by convention, curriculum, and "deliverology". These insights carry far-reaching implications with regard to language, the "labels" and the categories we draw on to describe and differentiate students and the forms of assessment that we rely on to make categorical judgements. Case studies of innovative approaches to learning in the wild demonstrate a range of possibilities for thinking, and acting, differently. In Robert Mackenzie's (1965) *Escape from the Classroom*, the description of his pupils' physical release from the constraints of the timetable was more an escape from the conventions of the mind than from the rigours of routine. His was not a de-schooling agenda but a way of expanding physical and intellectual parameters so that return to the classroom was always invested with new insights and new ways of seeing (as we advocated in Chapter 3). Dialogue comes into its own here as an influential and authoritative strategy connecting people collegially across institutional boundaries and without deference to hierarchies.

In **Chapter 7** ("Enhancing professionality") we argue that nothing will provide a better basis for a challenge to policy than an informed, confident, and capable profession prepared to stand up for leadership for learning (LfL) values and the professional integrity so necessary in enabling them to be realised. What is the warrant for this claim? What does LfL research and practice tell us about the positive actions that enable the profession to reassert its integrity and commitment to learning for all? What does it take to enhance professionality? From a discussion of the early work of Eraut (1994) calling for professionals to extend their repertoires, self-monitor, and reflect on practice, we bring into sharper focus the contested relationship between personal agency and policy-led professional development. Given the dominance of policy restrictions on learning, what latitude remains for the expression of personal and professional agency, both individual and conjoint? The answers lie in teacher-led co-constructed professional knowledge, evidence-based "disciplined dialogue", networking, and exploring alternatives which challenge political orthodoxy. With reference to two case studies, this chapter explores and problematises the relationship between professional development and policy mandate, between individual and shared action for change as the route to enhanced professionality.

We commence **Chapter 8** ("Challenging policy, school, and classroom practice") with the notion of "repurposing", finding a new purpose for practices or ideas that have outlived their usefulness or relevance. The starting point is an understanding of the systemic constraints which bind school leaders and teachers to legislated and legitimated practice. This requires a close reading of any policy document with a definitive pause, to stop and consider the language, the choice of words, phrases and metaphors infused with cultural assumptions, views, values, and ideologies. Without a serious challenge to the rhetoric, it is argued, the ideologies that drive policy into practice soon become too commonplace, too invisible. This can be countered, however, by maintaining an unshakeable focus on professional integrity, seeing leadership as practice, thinking differently about learning and teaching, and continuing to work on the issues that enhance professionality. This is what we understand as "connoisseurship", a high-level and complex skill equipping us to challenge policy because it stems from a deep understanding of the way a student learns and the way that learning changes over time. A grasp of the complex, developmental nature of learning, leads inexorably to a revisiting and transforming of teachers' own practice. This is the basis for professional advocacy at its best but at the same time, it enables leaders and teachers to understand and embrace "critical dissent" and challenge counterproductive policies.

1

THE POLICY CHALLENGE

Where would we be without policy? We can, perhaps, recall a golden age when teachers didn't have to worry about policy. Teachers taught and children learnt; "It's as simple as that", as a previous chief inspector in England once wrote. Since that putative golden age, we have, fortunately, come to understand that this is a more complex and contested equation. We have benefited incalculably from social, psychological, and pedagogical research. It has, to both our benefit and cost, given us a deeper understanding of the complex and contradictory nature of what Perkins, Tishman, Ritchart, Donis, and Andrade (2000) term "learning in the wild" and "learning in captivity". We have come to understand learning as deeply "nested" within a policy environment in which the relationship between an individual and his or her learning is contained by the classroom context and constrained by the school context which is, in turn, nested within education authority and national policies.

It is all too easy to fall into the familiar language in which policies are couched and which refers almost reflexively to school *leaders* as the principal actors, and so the term *principal* is widely used in North America, Australasia, Singapore, and Hong Kong, for example. In countries where English is not the first language – in Europe for example – the French *proviseur* is the provider; *preside* in Italian, the one who presides. In the United Kingdom, the term *headteacher* carries different connotations again – the master pedagogue who, in many circumstances, still continues to teach. While *headmaster* and *headmistress* have travelled widely beyond the United Kingdom these terms tend to be found now mainly in private schools. These may be referred to in the United States as *administrators* but a visitor to the United Kingdom who asked to meet an administrator would be guided to one of the office staff.

From the 1970s onwards, the language of *management* and *managers* was becoming widely adopted, giving rise to a whole new literature and lexicon as illustrated by recent publications such as Keating and Moorcroft's *Managing the Business of Schools* (2007), the emphasis on managing giving rise to "performance management". Imported from the business sector, this idea has been defined as managing the relationship between the implementation of long-term strategic and short-term operational goals so that they are in keeping with requirements placed on employees' performance.

In Gerald Grace's classic 1995 text *Beyond Education Management*, he challenged the language and ideology of management and the rise and rise of management studies. He writes, "the language, assumptions and ideology of management has begun to dominate the language, consciousness and action of many of those working within the education sector" (p. 5). The issue at stake in this "Alice in Linguisticsland" is whether language is, or is not, worth making a fuss over. There are powerful arguments which illustrate the extent to which our perceptions, practices, and ways of understanding the world are shaped by the terminologies to which we have recourse. Recent developments in the appointment of school managers as a complement to headteachers may help to resolve some of the inherent tensions. Indeed, it is likely that language tensions were contested in a London school by the headteacher who changed the sign on her office door from headteacher to head learner.

If we are to suggest new ways of leading learning we have to recognise the power of language and an embedded discourse of leading, positional authority, and the nature of followership. We have to start with a more sophisticated understanding of the policy–practice relationship and the nature of the "force field" which may promote, but may also inhibit, a more radical agenda. In what follows, we describe eight salient consequences of policy agendas which have had, and continue to have, a powerful influence on schools and classrooms and, for that very reason, need to be subject to rigorous critique and challenge.

Eight policy consequences

1 The seductive power of managerialism

Managerialism may be described as seductive because it has an easy appeal with its endorsement of efficiency, effectiveness, and accountability. Who could argue against the need for a more stringent approach to an education system that has, for too many children, been ineffective, that has too often fallen short in its stewardship of public money, and failed in its accountability to parents and their children? This seductive argument has it that schools, and the organisations in which they are embedded, need to be more tightly managed, more transparent, and thus more easily held to account by their "stakeholders". Accountability is tied to indicators or measures of performance in the classroom, the board room, the senior management, and in the local education authority.

It is argued that the effectiveness of this approach is that it may be evaluated through a focus on outputs. A business that makes profits is self-evidently more efficient than one that does not, or one that persists despite continued and obstinate losses. So, with the requisite tools and measures, it becomes easier to identify those schools that succeed and those that fail, those that add value or fail to add value. Unarguably, with evidence of schools that are selling children short, it follows that there needs to be more stringent accountability, incentive, and performance affirmation.

While leaders and managers clearly need to be held to account, and as it may be the performance of their employees who are compromising the efficiency of the school, this magnifies the argument for a more stringent regime of target setting and benchmarking. Acknowledging that some of the blame may lie with parents, a tighter set of contractual arrangements and sanctions then needs to be put in place, including legal sanctions for absence and, in England for example, the prohibition on parents taking children for holidays during school time.

These measures may be described as seductive because they are hard to oppose. Who could argue against transparency and accountability? Who could dispute the need for measures or "indicators" of how well schools are performing? The questions that need to be asked, however, are:

- Accountability for what? And how is that accountability made transparent? How may it be contested and open to dialogue?
- What is measured, by whom, and in what way? And how do we guarantee the value of what is measured and the means by which practice is then affected?
- How do we disentangle the school effect from that of communities, social agencies, private tutoring, tuition centres and, most importantly, the social and educational capital residing in nuclear and extended families?
- How and where can we begin to undo or unravel the tightly woven skein of top-down strictures and accountabilities?

2 Control versus autonomy – successful and failing schools – reputational damage

The notion of "successful" and "failing" schools is now so embedded in common discourse that the rhetoric has become almost impossible to contest or reframe. The more the latitude for parental choice, the greater the patronage of successful schools and the less the attraction of so-called failing schools. The correlation between the social mix and parental choice is now so well established in so many different countries that policy initiatives have rarely been able to tackle the essential dilemma. Redrawing zoning and school catchment and other forms of social and demographic engineering have been attempted in order to mitigate the reputational effect. The policy of bussing in the United States (which has been in place since the 1960s), like so many other equalisation policies, is now widely regarded as a well-intentioned failure. While the adoption of community schools has enjoyed mixed success, the attendant problem is that as schools become microcosms of their local communities they are seen as bringing with them deprivations in language, motivation, learning difficulties, disaffection, violence, and challenges in home work and home study. Assisted places schemes which operate in some countries, giving some children entry to elite schools, further deprive low-status schools of social and educational capital. These are all compounding factors which are reflected in schools in which low attainment brings with it sanctions in different forms (e.g., in some countries such as New Zealand, report cards which urge schools and school leaders to "do better"; in England and Wales, schools categorised as in need of "special measures").

The issues are so historic, so systemic, and so international in character that it is difficult to conceive of solutions. Rather than seeing these issues as a counsel of despair, however, the educational community needs to engage strategically, with new partnerships and in new ways of thinking which do not simply re-tread familiar and tired programs.

3 The resilience of positional power and hierarchy in schools

Schools tend to be hierarchical places. That they could be otherwise seems unthinkable. The assumption tends to be that adults know more than children and some adults know more than others, while some professionals are not only better at teaching but also better at managing. It is further assumed that schools also need to be led and managed by those with high levels of expertise and insight. Position brings with it discretionary and institutional power so that on occasions when hard and uncomfortable decisions have to be made, teachers have to be reminded, as one headteacher put it, that "this is not a democracy". A common feature of schools across the globe is a three- or four-fold power structure with government, some form of local authority (perhaps regional plus district offices), and the front-end "delivery" system — schools. Each layer of the system is upwardly accountable and commonly held in place by some form of inspection or review.

The only escape from this policy and political hierarchy appears to be through private organisations, sanctioned in most countries by way of foundations, dissenting bodies, parental fees, and conditional government measures. At best, these privatised bodies loosen some of the hierarchical ties, allowing greater opportunity for teachers and young people to enjoy greater influence and decision-making power. The most radical alternatives, "free" schools, collectives (e.g., multi-academy trusts), and learning communities have almost everywhere enjoyed a brief life span. Places where democratic schools have been incorporated within the mainstream (Deans Centre and Wester Hailes in Scotland, Countesthorpe and Risinghill in England, for example) have all had to modify their ambitions and been progressively brought back into a more conforming mould by successive governments.

"Power distance" between highest and lowest levels of the educational hierarchy is one of the yardsticks used by Geert Hofstede (1983) in his comparative studies of schools internationally. While in some cultures the differential has been decreasing under the influence of international intelligence, in other historically more democratic countries such as Sweden, Norway, and Denmark (e.g., Abrahams &

Aas, 2016; Møller, 1999) the differential is now increasing as the decision-making independence of pupils, teachers, and heads has been curtailed.

Happily, there are headteachers and teachers resilient and professionally committed enough to work around the hierarchy, to diminish positional power, and to develop a strong internal accountability which increases individual and collective initiative. This requires an ability and willingness to "swim upstream" against the current which is constantly pushing for stronger individual leadership.

4 The pressure for stronger individual leadership

There is a common understanding of leadership as something practised by individuals, often heroic people. Historically, they have rescued their countries from tyranny, freed the oppressed, built new empires, and pioneered emergent democracies. There is a general acknowledgement that we owe a debt to those leaders because we couldn't have done it ourselves and without their heroism our lives would be very different.

Leaders are expected to be strong while weak leaders are deplored. We live virtually daily with that dichotomy in politics, business, and education. We rely on our elected, or self-elected, leaders to act fairly and in our interests, to tackle discrimination, inequality, and oppression, and to make our worlds better, more congenial places. At the same time under these conditions, we allow ourselves to be disempowered individually and collectively.

It is not only educational governance that favours strong heads and principals. Teachers have often suffered under weak headteachers and wished for tougher, less compromising leadership. Ambiguity, vacillation, and inconsistency simply make teachers' lives harder and the uncertain space is easily exploited by children and young people. There also may come a time, however, when teachers begin to regret what they wished for. They discover that the loss of leeway for pupils' behaviour has suddenly applied to them too.

At the root of this dilemma is what we understand as "strong". It is hard to see it as anything other than an individual quality and residing in a repertoire of individual behaviours. The problem is that when we settle for a quieter, less conflicted life, the very purpose of education itself becomes distorted. Where there is conflict we seek solutions in adult intervention, in appeal to hierarchy and institutional authority, rather than seeking more enduring approaches amongst ourselves.

To what extent do "successful schools" owe their apparent success to powerful headteachers who stamp their imprint on the school, in some cases perhaps reluctantly, driven by the external competitive climate by virtue of which their reputation is judged? In England, a research team led by Cambridge's Mary James published a case study of the most improved school in England. The success of the school was owed to its uncompromising headteacher who was not hesitant in claiming ownership of policy and strategy and confessed to his personal addiction – "control freakery". He is quoted as saying, "This policy has got a lot of me in it. It's largely me", and "that wasn't from the staff. That was from myself." Nor was the pressure disguised as collegiality or support: "It was quite brutal. It was tough. It was me." And the hand of steel in the velvet glove: "I think teachers have got to feel that they're making decisions but what I suppose I'm forcing them to do is make those decisions." Words like "tough", "brutal", and "forcing" are expressions of what is widely referred to as strong leadership, raising the stakes, creating followership, willing or otherwise. Peter Wilby, writing in *The Guardian* newspaper in 2008, captured the essence of a larger-than-life personality whose school was created in his image.

> You can imagine Sir Alan Steer, bearded, ample of figure, jolly in demeanour (what he says is frequently drowned out by gales of laughter), as an old-fashioned pub landlord, making convivial conversation over the bar as he pulls the pints. You can imagine, too, a flash of steel as he ejects from the premises an over-inebriated and troublesome customer. You could, I think, have a very good time in Steer's pub as long as you obeyed the rules.
>
> *(Wilby, 2008)*

A telling measure of this kind of uncompromising autocratic regime is for young people in their first year of university to return to the school to complain of the inhibiting legacy of unquestioning compliance with authority which had robbed them of initiative and ability to think for themselves.

5 Intolerance of dissent and challenge

What is it about our educational institutions from preschool to university that, in theory, encourages a liberal tradition of dialogue and dissent, yet sees these precepts rarely honoured in practice? The theory/practice divide has been stubborn and resilient. While there are liberal schools and universities which encourage independence of thought, more typically, children and young people experience an orthodoxy which is not open to question, reinforced by tests and exams and a commitment to right answers.

While universities, or university staff, are not always welcoming of dissenting options, when they do invite challenge from undergraduates they find that many young people lack the ability to inquire and critique, as described in the school mentioned above, lauded as the most improved secondary school in England. However, the ability to challenge what the great philosopher and educational thinker, Alfred North Whitehead (1929), termed "inert ideas" and to nurture a climate in which conflict is discussed, understood, and positively addressed, sees conflict itself become a subject of study.

> When young people are able to identify the elements of conflict, and with a developing self-awareness, gain both the competence and confidence to de-escalate, and so resolve conflicted situations, the liberal tradition referred to above will be actualised. These skills of critique and dissent progressively become valuable internal resources and capabilities which in turn enhance

young people's ability to manage conflict successfully in differing contexts. They then have access to a wider range of choices, which in turn leads to better decision-making and more positive outcomes in their lives.

(MacBeath, 2016, p. 50)

Described as "an asset-based approach", this not only provides a different and powerful set of principles for working with young people but can help to shape a different mindset among school staff.

6 The deprofessionalising effects of policy and practice on leaders and teachers

So powerful and so seductive are the accolades which fall to successful schools, and by association to successful leaders, that the essential purposes of what it means to lead are soon forgotten. Teachers may enjoy some of the prestige that comes with national and inspectorial recognition, yet cannot easily put aside the compromises that come with endorsement by authorities whose legitimacy teachers had previously questioned. At the heart of this issue is the extent to which the essential tenets of professional integrity may be bartered for what Willard Waller once described as "cheap praise" (1932).

Writing in *The Guardian* in 2010, Robin Alexander pointed out the extent to which the compliance culture in England had impacted on schools and on teachers' professional lives. He questioned the way governments, since the 1990s, had chosen to tackle the task of raising primary school standards by using high-stakes tests, league tables, prescriptive national teaching strategies, procedures for inspection, initial teacher training, continuous professional development, and "school improvement", all requiring strict compliance with official accounts of what primary education is about and how it should be undertaken. At the same time, teachers professed to being "fed up with interference, mindless paper work, lurches in policy, and daily announcements of gimmicky initiatives" (cited in MacBeath, 2010, p. 37).

Perhaps the most frequent and disturbing comment voiced by teachers at dissemination events, Alexander wrote, was this: "We're impressed by the Cambridge Review's evidence. We like the ideas. We want to take them forward. But we daren't do so without permission from our Ofsted inspectors and local authority school improvement partners" (Alexander, 2010, para 8).

Just as rewards and sanctions are used by teachers to "discipline" students, these same measures are writ large in the disciplining of teachers. The reprofessionalising of teachers would require, first, a reminder of the key elements of professionalism, together with a recognition of the force field that either inhibits or promotes disciplined inquiry together with liberated, and liberating, pedagogy.

Over three decades ago, Eric Hoyle (1974) described professionalism as lying on a spectrum from restricted to extended. At the more restricted end, the teacher is essentially reliant on experience and intuition, guided by a narrow, classroom-based perspective, valuing that which is related to the day-to-day practicalities of teaching. At the other end of the continuum, in the model of extended professionality, there is a much wider vision of what education involves, valuing the theory underpinning pedagogy and the adoption of a generally intellectual and rationally based approach to the job. Enhancing Hoyle's definition, Linda Evans (2008) casts this in the plural rather than the singular as an amalgam of multiple "professionalities".

If teachers and senior school leaders have allowed themselves to be deprofessionalised, what does it tell us about the potency of national and international agencies? What does it tell us about the power, focus, impact, and leadership of teacher unions and professional bodies? What have we learnt from resistance and strong principled practice that can offer a counterweight to sometimes ill-informed, but always powerful, orthodoxy? Can we possibly believe what is held to be orthodox? In other words, is it true what they say about Dixie?

7 The accountability imperative

To whom do schools owe their primary accountability? Each of the six preceding policy imperatives places schools within a hierarchical self-reinforcing set of pressures, in what has been described as a "vertical", and deprofessionalising, accountability. Teachers' primary accountability is owed to their departmental heads, measured by internal (subject or interdepartmental) competitiveness, and at school level, with other comparable (or very often non-comparable) institutions. There are no equivalent league tables for the quality of collaboration between home and school. There are no equivalent league tables for provision and impact on communities and community life. These would require a more sophisticated form of measurement, providing a gauge of horizontal accountability. The Organisation for Economic Co-operation and Development (OECD) (2017) suggests the following contrast:

> Vertical accountability is top-down and hierarchical. It enforces compliance with laws and regulation and/or holds schools accountable for the quality of education they provide. Horizontal accountability presupposes non-hierarchical relationships. It is directed at how schools and teachers conduct their profession and/or how schools and teachers provide multiple stakeholders with insight into their educational processes, decision making, implementation and results.
>
> *(p. 74)*

Taking the argument further, multiple horizontal school accountability widens the focus, "involving students, parents, communities and other stakeholders in formulating strategies, decision making and evaluation" (p. 74).

It raises the question as to whether, and how, school leaders and teachers, ensnared in the vertical accountability web, are able or enabled to step back from the tyranny of the urgent to embrace a collegial moral form of horizontal stewardship to those to whom they owe the most. But what is the likely consequence?

8 The "rocks" and "whirlpools" dilemma

"The winds of other people's demands have driven us on to a reef of frustration", wrote Charles Hummel in 1994 describing the "tyranny of the urgent". Steve Covey (1988) adapted this, devising a simple four-dimensional grid which senior leaders and teachers could use as a practical decision-making tool to categorise the important and urgent (critical), the important but not urgent (quality), the urgent but not important (deception), and the neither important nor urgent (waste). In their view, more than half of all demands on senior leaders fell into the deception category of urgent but not important.

Hampden-Turner and Trompenaars (1993) contrast what they term rock values and whirlpool values, the former placing emphasis on consistency, transparency, reliability, and comparison of performance, while the whirlpool values they describe as choice, diversity, dynamism, spontaneity, and autonomy. There are, they suggest, inevitable tensions between certainty and uncertainty, between individuality and collectivity. The easy compromise in a punitive policy climate is to take the line of least resistance, suppressing the tensions without addressing them.

Sustaining the whirlpool values requires a developmental approach, one which is not impatient for immediate answers, is not afraid of challenge, and treats "failures" as learning opportunities.

Productive failure

In Kapur's recent study in Singapore (2015), he draws attention to "productive failure", comparing this to "unproductive success", echoing Hampden-Turner and Trompenaars's (1993) findings that wrong answers stimulate greater cognitive activity than simply getting the answer right first time. In a 2017 paper, Zhao argues that since educational research tends to focus only on proving the effectiveness of practices and policies in pursuit of "what works", it has generally ignored the potential harms that can result. He writes, "damages caused by education may take a long time to be observed or felt. ... It is thus rather difficult to study or find out about education's side effects" (pp. 3–4). Comparing medical research in which adverse effects of intervention lead to withdrawal of the drug and then further trialling and development, Zhao remarks:

> It is extremely rare to find a study that evaluates both the effectiveness and adverse effects of a product, teaching method, or policy in education. I have not yet found an educational product that comes with a warning label carrying information such as "this program works in raising your students' test scores in reading, but may make them hate reading forever".
>
> *(p. 3)*

Zhao illustrates this claim with some of the difficulties accompanying the United States No Child Left Behind (NCLB) policy, such as widespread cheating before and during tests. Dishonest practices involved disturbing numbers of principals and teachers, for example, in manipulating test rolls, authorising unapproved test preparation, and misrepresenting results (p. 57). Clearly, these matters compromise the ethical behaviour of leaders and teachers.

Added to these practices, Zhao (2017, p. 12) argues, is the very serious and erosive effect of high-stakes testing on the health of the overall school curriculum. The narrowing of the general curriculum to a set of learning experiences dominated by test preparation is of grave concern. When it is known that a broad education leading to wide general knowledge is a critical factor in the learning of the young, any policy which consciously or unconsciously interferes with this provision must be challenged. This is particularly important in disadvantaged school communities where learning breadth adds immeasurably to student growth and the satisfactions both teachers and students feel as they teach and learn.

Yet, all "these damages" of a narrowing curriculum and high-stakes testing came during the NCLB policy period without much benefit, writes Zhao (2017). "The negative effects of educational products, when occasionally discovered, are not considered an inherent quality of the product or policy. Rather, they are often treated as unintended or unanticipated consequences or results of poor implementation" (p. 13). The fact that Campbell (1982) had much earlier highlighted difficulties attending the kind of quantitative indicators endemic in high-stakes testing remains instructive. Campbell's Law, as it is now referred to colloquially, states: "The more any quantitative social indicator is used for social decision-making, the more subject it will be to corruption pressures and the more apt it will be to distort and corrupt the social processes it is intended to monitor."

Zhao (2017) goes on to show that nowhere is the quantitative dominance of educational policy so evident than in international assessment programs such as Trends in International Mathematics and Science Study (TIMSS) and the Programme for International Student Assessment (PISA). He laments the influence that results from these tests have had on nation states' education policies and their debilitating effects on students' confidence and attitudes to learning. At the same time, he acknowledges that many countries participating in these tests (e.g., Korea, Chinese Taipei, Singapore, Viet Nam, Shanghai-China, and Hong Kong-China) have dramatically improved their test scores. In his own words: "It means that these systems have somehow made a large number of students lose confidence and interest in math, science, and reading, while helping them achieve excellence in testing" (Zhao, 2017, p. 10).

Therefore, it is not unreasonable to hypothesise that these educational systems may be effective in preparing students to achieve excellent scores AND effective in lowering their confidence and interest. They help with improving test scores but hinder the development of confidence and interest.

From dutiful compliance to rule breaking

Without a grasp of the eight deeply embedded and interlocking challenges described above, and without a willingness to confront them, teachers, teacher organisations, and senior leaders will continue to sell young people short. A study of school leadership in Scotland (MacBeath et al., 2009) identified five forms of response by senior leaders to external authority and policy mandate. These were characterised as:

- dutiful compliance;
- cautious pragmatism;
- quiet self-confidence;
- bullish self-assertion; and
- defiant risk-taking.

One third of all heads in the national sample claimed to have "very little" autonomy. In these circumstances and with that perception of one's role, being dutiful was perhaps the most judicious option. These were headteachers who saw very little or no leeway for their own initiative, who felt so oppressed by demands from government and local authorities that preservation of their "sanity", as one primary headteacher put it, required simply keeping up to date, being ready for the "hit" and getting a "star point" for simply achieving somewhat modest goals.

> We described these head teachers as "mortgaging their energy and time to their role demands". The tendency not to experience autonomy nor to exercise much personal discretion in decision-making left these heads "feeling good" only in respect of clearing the desk, moving paper from the in to the out box, being able to go home with a sense of job done although often at the expense of a work-life imbalance.
>
> *(MacBeath, O'Brien, & Gronn, 2012, p. 10)*

Yet, there were, at the opposite pole, the defiant risk takers, "flying below the radar", developing what Eric Hoyle called their "samizdat professionalism" (Hoyle, 2008). The opportunity for subversion depended to some extent on a weighing up of permission and sanction, and being "brave enough", as one headteacher put it, to navigate around the structures and bend, if not break, the rules. "I like to sail pretty close to the wind" said one highly experienced primary head who confessed to deploying a range of subversive strategies developed over a lifetime in headship. However skilled these heads might be, there was, nonetheless, a common plea for more "free space" and for a greater understanding of what it means to lead and manage a school.

The policy dilemma space

In Hampden-Turner and Trompenaars's "dilemma space" (1993), when faced with persistent and difficult problems (in policy or practice, for example), we tend to reach for compromise, what we might describe as a win–win outcome. But actually, this may result in a lose-lose situation as the essential challenge of addressing difficulty head on is lost. To achieve the synergy of a win–win requires a willingness to listen, to be open to evidence, to suspend preconception, to accept risk, but it also takes time and goodwill, commodities in short supply.

Bottery (2003) shares an equally pessimistic view of the latitude for reform in the face of powerful national and international pressures.

> Whilst it may be possible to conceptualise the leadership of a learning community, it may nevertheless be impossible to realise it because of a failure to see and counter an ecology of the forces which surround leadership and learning communities, forces global, national and local. These forces combine to create a low-trust culture of unhappiness, which in turn generates crises of teacher morale, recruitment, and retention.
>
> *(p. 187)*

Elmore (2008) refers to this as the "default culture" in which practice is "atomized", so that there are few opportunities for collective work on common problems, few opportunities to use any kind of external knowledge or skill to improve practice: "So the school lacks the basic organisational capacity to change" (Elmore, 2008, p. 47).

In this world of "detailed deliverology" (Hargreaves & Shirley, 2009, p. 110) there is no spare energy for teachers to contest the conditions and oppressive aspects of their work. In addition to (or as a concomitant of) pressure from above, writes Ann Lieberman (1992), strong teacher norms of egalitarianism can also be powerful inhibitors, dissuading anyone from presumptuous initiatives, from sticking their neck out too far, engendering a reluctance to exercise leadership without formal invitation or approval.

As Robinson (2011) commented in his book *Out of Our Minds: Learning to be Creative*, a combination of convention, timidity, and relentless pressure all too often stifle the unorthodox, the divergent thinker, the playful, witty departure from routine. Harnessing the creative energies that lie uninvited below the surface of classroom life assumes the ability to recognise it, to suspend the pursuit of incessant and unforgiving targets and to be surprised into new forms of interaction. In the ideas, insights, experience, and hope of the combined school community population, there is a creative energy to be released. A starting point, Robinson suggests, is with a radical recasting of language with its powerful effects on relationships and the static ideas which underpin them, adopting a new conception of human ecology which captures the richness of human capacity.

The two key ideas contained here refer to *ecology* and *capacity*. They also offer ideal parameters for a study of what inhibits a sense of human agency and how much of this may be attributed to the conditions in which heads and teachers find themselves. A dictionary definition of ecology describes it as "the study of interaction of people with their environment". As human beings, we create our environment and then in return it creates us, potentially increasing our capacity for action or, alternatively, reducing the space for individual or collective initiative (we expand on the positive side of this relationship in Chapter 4 in our discussion of leadership as practice). David Perkins (2003) argues that learning is generally invisible because "we are used to it being that way. As educators, our first task is perhaps to see the absence, to hear the silence, to notice what is not there" (p. 6).

The American academic Eisner (1991) has written extensively about connoisseurship, a high-level and complex skill which relies on knowing *where* to look and *how* to see. But this is, however skilled, a singular viewpoint. We observe from one perspective, constrained by where we sit, whom we observe, whom we talk to or listen to, when and in what conditions such a process may take place. In a paper entitled "How to Build Schools where Adults Learn", Fahey and Ippolito (2014) draw attention to the dynamic and complex nature of student learning:

> Student learning is developmental, and educators know that effectively supporting that learning should take into account the way a student learns, and the way that learning changes over time. The complex, developmental nature of learning is easily accepted when educators think about students, but this same idea is often overlooked when they consider the learning needed to improve their own practice. Adult learning is also developmental.
>
> A useful lens for helping learning leaders understand the complex nature of adult learning practice in schools is constructive-developmental theory (Kegan, 1998). Constructive-developmental theory makes two broad claims: Adults continually work to make sense of their experiences (constructive), and the ways that adults make sense of their world can change and grow more complex over time (developmental). One implication of these claims is that in any school, each teacher will have her own learning practice – just as she has her own teaching practice.
>
> *(p. 32)*

Conclusion

In this chapter, we have discussed eight policy consequences and themes, issues, and practices which emanate from governments intent on improved school performance. In combination, they create a policy challenge for school leaders, teachers, and others who have their sights set on furthering the interests of children and young people through learning. Where are the chinks in this apparently impenetrable policy armour? And why do we argue that there is a challenge waiting to be taken up to politicians and school policymakers?

Like Michael Fullan (2011, p. 6), we believe that there is enough evidence to show that the overall effect of educational policy is, at best, the protection of a status quo unable to lead to long-term improvement, and at worst, the creation of conditions detrimental to learning and student interests. Fullan attributes harmful policy effects to what he calls the "wrong policy drivers". He goes on to list and explain four of these: (a) accountability: using test results, and teacher appraisal, to reward or punish teachers and schools; (b) individual teacher and leadership quality: promoting individual capacity; (c) technology: investing in and assuming that the wonders of the digital world will carry the day; and (d) fragmented strategies: unaligned between schools and systems. Two of these have been firmly lodged in our analysis – accountability and individualism – though we have discussed both in the light of policies which purport to enhance autonomy and accountability. So, what are the policy challenges we have distilled? There are at least four.

First, the reduction of a considerable proportion of primary school learning to the requirements of a narrow measurable curriculum has been exposed. But more than this, what exacerbates the negativity is the deception that making schools and nation states the units of performance comparisons will improve learning. This is misleading and far from helpful. Diagnostic assessment is essential and it is most influential when it applies to individual learners and their particular needs, rather than in comparisons among institutions and countries. Why these aggregated units of analysis and comparison persist may be found in the commercial world with companies competing for big-dollar government test design and administration contracts. If and when governments want reassurance on the outcomes being achieved by a nation's children and young people, whole population testing is not necessary. Reliable and valid results can be obtained from representative samples at a much reduced cost and with fewer effects than those accompanying the high-stakes testing now dominant in schooling.

Second, policies on institutional autonomy have increased the control and authority of individual headteachers and principals, adding to the power distance which already exists between themselves and their staff. This effectively reinforces the resilience of positional power, status, and hierarchy, but also intensifies the accountability pressure felt by individuals in leadership positions. What loses out is the non-positional power of collectives, motivated by professional interest in the issues arising in the workaday world. Compliance with the power invested in authority figures continues uncontested so that conformity becomes the default position for members, while thinking about innovation and change in pedagogy becomes increasingly challenging.

Third, the deprofessionalisation of the teaching service persists. The reduction in professional discretion already evident in a narrowing curriculum is further promoted through government testing, performance standards, appraisal, and continuing registration processes. None of these are automatically in the hands of professionals themselves or their associations. Professional development is largely under the control of policymakers and system authorities with the personal agency of the school leader or teacher taking a back seat. Value is placed on what the employer wants, not what teachers, parents, or children themselves might value.

Fourth, we have argued that there is an intolerance of dissent and challenge alive and well in the present-day policy environment. Words such as compliance, conformity, and docility and phrases such as "keeping your head down", "not making waves", and "maintaining a low profile" have entered the professional discourse and have become commonplace. The perception that sycophancy is expected by system policymakers reduces disagreement, debate, difference, and innovation. Novelty in practice is something neither welcomed nor encouraged without one eye on "what the leadership hierarchy expects".

The chinks in the policy armour referred to above are implicit in the issues we have highlighted as indicative of a possible challenge to policy. Advocating and adopting the principles and practices of leadership for learning can provide a powerful counterpoint to much of what is disempowering in the modern educational policy environment. Added to this is the need to push forward the key elements of professional integrity with pride and purpose; to adopt and implement leadership as a collaborative practice in the everyday life of schools and their communities; to engage in the divergent thinking about learning and teaching that is the constant companion of those concerned with improving children's educational experience in schools, in the community, and in society at large; and *to enhance professionalism* so that the great majority of those employed as teachers continue to learn individually and collectively from research, practice, and their interrelationship. For politicians and policymakers well fed on a diet of compliance, this should not be dismissed as mere reactive disagreement but rather acknowledged as an architecture built on the solid foundations of critical dissent.

In Chapter 2, we provide a description of the general backdrop to policy reform in the education sector with added detail related to the school policy environment in the countries which participated in the original *Carpe Vitam* Leadership for Learning Project.

References

Abrahams, H., & Aas, M. (2016). School leadership for the future: Heroic or distributed? Translating international discourses in Norwegian policy documents. *Journal of Educational Administration and History, 48*(1), 68–88.

Alexander, R. (2010, April 27). Post-election priorities from the Cambridge review. *The Guardian*. Retrieved from https://www.theguardian.com/education/2010/apr/27/primary-education-cambridge-review-election

Bottery, M. (2003). The leadership of learning communities in a culture of unhappiness. *School Leadership and Management, 23*(2), 187–207.

Campbell, C. (1982). A dubious distinction? An inquiry into the value and use of Merton's concepts of manifest and latent function. *American Sociological Review, 47*(1), 29–44.

Covey, S. R. (1988). *The 7 habits of highly effective people: Powerful lessons in personal change*. New York: Simon & Schuster.

Eisner, E. (1991). *The enlightened eye: Qualitative inquiry and the enhancement of educational practice*. Toronto: Merril.

Elmore, R. (2008). Leadership as the practice of improvement. In B. Pont, D. Nusche, & D. Hopkins (Eds.), *Improving school leadership, Volume 2: Case studies on system leadership* (pp. 37–67). Paris: OECD.

Evans, L. (2008). Professionalism, professionality and the development of education professionals. *British Journal of Educational Studies, 56*(1), 20–38.

Fahey, K., & Ippolito, J. (2014). How to build schools where adults learn. *Journal of Staff Development, 35*(2), 31–39.

Fullan, M. (2011). *Choosing the wrong drivers for whole system reform*. Melbourne, Victoria: Centre for Strategic Education.

Grace, G. (1995). *Beyond education management.* London: Routledge.

Hampden-Turner, C., & Trompenaars, L. (1993). *The seven cultures of capitalism.* New York: Doubleday.

Hargreaves, A., & Shirley, D. (2009). *The fourth way.* Thousand Oaks, CA: Corwin.

Hofstede, G. (1983). Culture's consequences: International differences in work-related values. *Administrative Science Quarterly, 28*(4), 625–629.

Hoyle, E. (1974). Professionality, professionalism and control in teaching. *London Education Review, 3*(2), 13–19.

Hoyle, E. (2008). Changing conceptions of teaching as a profession: Personal reflections. In D. Johnson & R. Maclean (Eds.), *Teaching: Professionalization, development and leadership* (pp. 285–304). London: Springer.

Hummel, C. E. (1994). *Tyranny of the urgent.* Downers Grove, IL: InterVarsity Press.

Kapur, M. (2015). Learning from productive failure. *Learning: Research and Practice, 1*(1), 51–65.

Keating, I., & Moorcroft, R. (2007). *Managing the business of schools.* London: Sage.

Lieberman, A. (1992). Teacher leadership: What are we learning? In C. Livingston (Ed.), *Teachers as leaders: Evolving roles* (pp. 159–165). Washington DC: National Education Association.

MacBeath, J. (2010). *Education and schooling: Myth, heresy and misconception.* London: Routledge.

MacBeath, J. (2016). *Understanding conflict.* Cambridge: University of Cambridge.

MacBeath, J., Gronn, P., Forde, C., Howie, C., Lowden, K., & O'Brien, J. (2009). *Recruitment and retention of headteachers in Scotland.* Edinburgh: Scottish Government.

MacBeath, J., O'Brien, J., & Gronn, P. (2012). Drowning or waving? Coping strategies among Scottish head teachers. *School Leadership and Management, 32*(5), 421–438.

Møller, J. (1999). Re-culturing educational leadership in Norwegian schools: A trade-off between accountability and autonomy. *Journal of In-Service Education, 25*(3), 497–517.

Organisation for Economic Co-operation and Development (OECD). (2017). *Schools at the crossroads of innovation in cities and regions.* Paris: OECD.

Perkins, D. (2003). Making thinking visible. *New Horizons for Learning.* Retrieved from http://www.newhorizons.org/strategies/thinking/perkins.htm

Perkins, D., Tishman, S., Ritchart, R., Donis, K., & Andrade, A. (2000). Intelligence in the wild: A dispositional view of intellectual traits. *Educational Psychology Review, 12*(3), 269–293.

Robinson, K. (2011). *Out of our minds: Learning to be creative.* West Sussex: Capstone Publishing.

Waller, W. (1932). *Sociology of teaching.* New York: Wiley and Sons.

Whitehead, A. N. (1929). *The aims of education and other essays.* New York: The Free Press.

Wilby, P. (2008, September 23). Ain't misbehavin'. *The Guardian.* Retrieved from https://www.theguardian.com/education/2008/sep/23/pupilbehaviour.alansteer

Zhao, Y. (2017). What works may hurt: Side effects in education. *Journal of Educational Change, 18*(1), 1–19.

2

THE BACKDROP TO POLICY REFORM

Why has the present policy mix in education occurred and with such seeming global reach and consistency? In the previous chapter, we described eight broad consequences of policy reform and their impact on schooling. We also considered some of the difficulties created by the "policy dilemma space" over the last few decades. These have a history in global politics and global policy trends. Bringing the sources of the dilemma space and the consequences of reform to light requires a brief account of the backdrop to policy in contemporary democratic economies.

Global policy trends and the policy dilemma space

The following account of global policy change draws attention to some of the powerful influences which create a dilemma space for school principals and teachers. Changes in the public administration of government educational services over time have led to a continuing debate. This contrasts a cooperative commitment to educational principles on the one hand with the competitive service provision notions embedded in modern nation states on the other.

In Western democracies, inexorable global trends have been accompanied by a general retreat from Keynesian economics which, after the Great Depression, carried the argument that intervention by the state is necessary to moderate the booms and busts so apparent in free-marketplace economic activity. Consistent with this principle, after World War Two, government intervention extended to the development and implementation of services across a plethora of policy fields affecting many post-war economies.

What has now overtaken Keynes's interventionist view in policy formulation is a greater reliance on the marketplace and therefore the non-government sector for the management and implementation of the services which taxpayers expect. Osborne's (2006) analysis describes three overlapping modes in the way democratic governments have gone about the public administration and management of their policies over the last 100 years.

> Public Administration and Management has actually passed through three dominant modes – a longer, pre-eminent one of Public Administration (PA), from the late nineteenth century through to the late 1970s/early 1980s; a second mode, of New Public Management (NPM), through to the start of the twenty-first century; and an emergent third one since then, of New Public Governance (NPG).
>
> *(p. 377)*

The Public Administration (PA) mode, Osborne argues, was characterised by a focus on policymaking as the prerogative of governments, as were the processes of policy implementation. These processes were managed by a hierarchical public service working in accordance with an established public sector ethos. Towards the end of last century, New Public Management (NPM) advocates argued for service delivery organisations to be at arm's length from governments so as to distance policy implementation from policymakers. Government control was retained through an emphasis on inputs and outputs, performance management, and audits. Competition in the marketplace was seen as a central value to encourage entrepreneurial leadership. These changes were often accompanied by the disaggregation of public services to basic units responsible for outsourcing contracts in a competitive marketplace, allocating resources and demanding evidence of efficient and effective service delivery by successful agencies. Osborne (2006) puts it this way. NPM is apparent when "policy making and implementation are at least partially articulated and disengaged, and where implementation is through a collection of independent service units, ideally in competition with each other" (p. 379).

New Public Governance (NPG) shifts the focus towards an interrelationship between government and private sector agencies so that interorganisational governance is acknowledged and enabled. NPG emphasises service processes and outcomes with interrelationships cemented through partnership-oriented contracts or agreements. While competition in the service delivery marketplace still plays a role in NPG, the emphasis shifts towards neo-corporatist values and responsibilities. Governments retain an indisputable measure of control through the reporting of outcomes, often against accountability standards (Osborne, 2006, p. 383). The charter school movement in the United States is one high profile example of NPG in the education sector. In other sectors, for example aged care, employment/unemployment, and healthcare, agencies are "trusted" but required to comply with government standards and, more often than not, governed and managed by de facto private sector entities in competition with one another.

There is increasing evidence in many parts of the world that government policies are coincidental with the competitive outsourcing ethic of NPM and the aspirational trusting interrelationships of NPG. In education, this is most apparent in policies which use "loaded" words to highlight nuances in the incremental steps towards NPM and NPG. Terms such as *school-based management* and *school self-management* (Caldwell & Spinks, 1988; Gammage, Sipple, & Partridge, 1996), *decentralisation* and *devolution* (Ainley & McKenzie, 2000), and *local autonomy* (OECD, 2008) illustrate the influence of public administration and management thinking on the centre-periphery movement of decisions about education service provision.

The reach of global policy influences has been evident since the NPM of the 1980s, rapidly extending to governments in the farthest corners of the world. No field of government, however remote, is immune from their effects. Education and schooling in particular command a large share of government budgets, with attendant legislative and policy pressures for those seeking improvement in school systems. Reforming school systems so as to show observable improvement in student attainment has become a high priority for governments internationally (Caldwell & Harris, 2008).

There are several reasons why particular policy positions in education have been pursued in Western democracies. First, the OECD (2008) has influenced the reformist zeal of many of its member countries, especially with its analysis of the relationship between high-performing systems and the extent of the autonomy exercised by principals with respect to decisions about local needs. Some nations have responded to the suggestion that greater autonomy is linked to enhanced student performance by making changes to the processes of school governance, leadership, and management. There are many examples of the extension of so-called autonomy to schools with developments such as Independent Public Schools in Western Australia and Queensland and some "earned autonomy" in New South Wales as illustrative cases. Other cases exist in countries where it may have been least expected, such as Norway and Sweden. England's and New Zealand's turn towards local school self-management, however, preceded any suggestion of links between greater school autonomy and high system performance reported by the OECD in 2008. In New Zealand, other reasons drawn from the claimed benefits of NPM (Dunleavy & Hood, 1994; Ferlie, Ashburner, & Pettigrew, 1996) were used as the initial motivators for the tectonic policy shift which created local community governing boards of trustees and principals as local managers in every school in "The Shaky Isles" in one fell legislative swoop in 1989, almost three decades ago.

Second, there is no doubt that the arrival of international testing regimes and the analysis of student results has put politicians "on edge" over national performance comparisons. These widely publicised data push politicians to seek out explanations for the high performance of some countries and reasons for the poor performance of others, including their own.

Third, the concept of autonomy is somewhat masked by the tenacious use of common terms such as *school-based management, school self-management*, and *local management*. All of these hide different structural relationships between system administrators, school leaders, and their management responsibilities – relationships which mark out quite distinctive powers in the various forms of management adopted in different country contexts. Different versions of management have been and are being overtaken by the variable use of the term *autonomy*, now almost a global reform mantra, although methodological difficulties remain in drawing causal links between autonomy and improved performance. School autonomy, as used by the OECD, refers to extending school self-management to include some or all aspects of funding, decision-making regarding the curriculum, hiring staff, professional development, and educational service "delivery". In some cases, power has been handed to school governing entities; in others, the power of the principal or head-teacher has been enhanced. It seems to us, though, that discussions of autonomy by policymakers fail to emphasise the central purpose of schools.

The global policy backdrop and flirtation with managerialism

The flirtation with different versions of managerialism, whatever their forms, over the decades of the eighties and nineties and into a new millennium has, in our view, left a baleful legacy. With its emphasis on legal-rational authority, efficiency, and effectiveness, it introduced us to objectives (sometimes behavioural), outcomes, measurement of achievement, indicators of comparative performance, competition, incentives, and "incentivisation". Managerialism came as a total package, neatly tied and presented.

In Erving Goffman's 1961 study of total institutions he contrasted them with the spontaneous activity of human beings moving among multiple sites:

> A basic social arrangement in modern society is that we tend to sleep, play and work in different places, in each case with a different set of co-participants, under a different authority, and without an overall rational plan. The central feature of total institutions can be described as a breakdown of the kinds of barriers ordinarily separating these three spheres of life.
>
> First, all aspects of life are conducted in the same place and under the same single authority. Second, each phase of the member's daily activity will be carried out in the immediate company of a large batch of others, all of whom are treated alike and required to do the same thing together. Third, all phases of the day's activities are tightly scheduled, with one activity leading at a prearranged time into the next, the whole circle of activities being imposed from above through a system of explicit formal rulings and a body of officials. Finally, the contents of the various enforced activities are brought together as parts of a single overall rational plan purportedly designed to fulfil the official aims of the institution.
>
> *(p. 6)*

Such a description may seem a crude caricature of schools as we know them, yet to what extent has policy, nationally and internationally, fitted us progressively more snugly into that very mould? To what extent have we failed to realise "the richness of human capacity" by too ready a compliance with convention and external authority? In the *Carpe Vitam* Project (which we describe in the following chapter), we undertook research in seven countries where global policy trends were interpreted and applied in different ways. All of these countries were members of the

OECD which has had, and continues to have, a very strong influence on education reform agendas worldwide. As Peter Wilby (2015) has written in his critique of government's addiction to slick journalism:

> Like the "red menace" of the Cold War era, the "progressives" were always lurking, never idle in their mission to subvert decent, common-sense, traditional values. ...
>
> "Trendy" teaching methods, the narrative argued, were imposed for ideological reasons by an "educational establishment" comprising some prominent heads and teachers, professors of education, teacher-trainers, local authority officers and advisers, and even Her Majesty's Inspectors of Schools whose pronouncements were once treated as the Holy Grail.
>
> ... the growth in the number of columnists – nearly every newspaper has two or three of them each day – who express opinions on a large range of issues, and are employed for their ability to write provocatively and entertainingly, rather than for their understanding of a particular subject, further marginalises the role of expertise and informed critical scrutiny. Professors of education and other specialist academics are almost wholly excluded both from policy making and from newspaper coverage of education.
>
> These policies, they say, have been too numerous, short-term, incoherent and partisan; governments have been indifferent to professional opinion and serious research, and have relied excessively on measurable outcomes and simplistic Ofsted judgments. Our current system is narrower and less democratic than it was, but evidence is hard to find that English pupils are doing any better in international comparisons.
>
> *(p. 200)*

An alternative to this dismal caricature of educational policy influence would include at least some of the following common-sense actions:

- trust teachers more;
- reinstate a reliance on leaders' and teachers' professional judgement;
- make the accountability of leaders and teachers supportive rather than punitive;
- base policy on compelling educational research findings;
- seek parents' and students' perspectives on issues for publication; and
- open schools to the policy influence of students' voices.

Global policy effects in *Carpe Vitam* Project countries

Most of the countries involved in the OECD experienced economic recession as a result of the global financial crisis first felt in 2007–08. In simple terms, the financial crisis was the result of overly ambitious and excessive risk-taking by banks. At its worst, it threatened the collapse of the world's financial and banking systems. In reality, it pushed many economies into debilitating recessions, resulting in what is termed a debt-deflation spiral with wages and prices falling but debts increasing. This inevitably had an impact on schools, teachers' salaries, and capital costs.

In 2009, Education International reported that almost half of the countries in Europe (10 out of a total of 21 countries) had experienced new cuts as a result of the global economic crisis. These countries included Austria, Norway, and the United Kingdom, where there was a reduction in overall government expenditure on education. While in some countries public spending on education did not initially seem to suffer from the crisis, the picture since 2010 has been less positive, stated an OECD report in December 2014. Fiscal consolidation led half of the OECD countries to cut or freeze teachers' salaries. "OECD countries will not be able to mobilise additional public resources in the coming years, so investment in education will need to become more efficient and be motivated by considerations to improve the quality of teaching" (OECD, 2013, p. 4).

Despite GDP rising in most OECD countries between 2009 and 2010, public expenditure on educational institutions fell in one third of them. Teachers' salaries were either frozen or cut between 2009 and 2011 in 12 out of the 25 OECD countries with data available, a phenomenon that was seen as potentially discouraging the highest performing students from joining the teaching profession. A European Commission report, *Key Data on Education in Europe 2012*, predicted that several member states including Germany, the United Kingdom, Italy, the Netherlands, Austria, and Belgium would face serious teacher shortages in the future. It found that the number of graduates specialising in education was falling at a time when a rising number of teachers were approaching retirement age. In March 2015, a poll for the *Daily Mail* in England reported that 73% of local authorities said that their schools were struggling to find suitably qualified staff, while in Scotland in 2017 teachers were being recruited after a 5-week period of induction.

In the United States, many school districts have seen layoffs, larger class sizes, and cuts in professional development and assistive technology. In Philadelphia, one of the worst hit school districts by virtue of state-level cuts, the reasons offered were as follows:

> This is arising because the basic cost of education has been rising and the funding has not. You can't continue to try to bring those in line by cutting your way out of the problem, because you've reached the point where you can no longer provide the services that are required, and because it's a prescription for disaster for students.
>
> *(M. Churchill, quoted in Superville, 2014, para 11)*

With a $304 million budget deficit, two dozen schools were forced to close.

The downward spiral affected all seven of the *Carpe Vitam* countries, some much more than others. For example, it hit hardest in Greece where by 2014, teachers had witnessed between 30–70% reductions in their salaries and deep cuts to staffing levels, with up to 2,000 teachers suspended.

Michael Barber, close attendant on policymaking in the UK Blair government, interpreted four decades of the policy/practice interface in these terms. He characterised the 1970s as the era of "uninformed professionalism", the 1980s as the era of "uninformed prescription", the 1990s as "informed prescription", with the 2000s as "informed professionalism" (Barber, 2005). Two decades later, we might argue that uninformed prescription is, in many countries, alive and well. The evidence is compelling. Prescription has, in many schools and classrooms, undermined professionalism, with a significant impact on virtually all schools in the *Carpe Vitam* Project orbit. In the section which follows, we confirm this in an account of some of the policy effects we have observed in the *Carpe Vitam* countries in the 10 years since the project ended.

A question of leadership

How to compare leadership in different *Carpe Vitam* countries was to prove problematic due not only to language and differing structures of school systems but also by cultural conventions and in what ways that "leading" might be described and categorised. The concept of agency was to become a central theme running through the project, and it is revisited throughout this book, as it provides a differentiating test of a system's commitment to learning and to leadership. To what extent do different actors – teachers, children, and parents – experience a sense of their own agency so as to effect change, to express their voice, to be heard?

In Austria, a centrepiece of reform has been directed towards enabling disparate voices to be expressed so that leading and learning are open, collegial, and inseparable. An ongoing intervention, led by Michael Schratz and Wilfred Schley, starting in 2004, was an attempt to tackle a highly bureaucratic system, hierarchically organised, light on outcomes with too many actors, numerous parallel structures and too little congruence in task orientation, responsibility, and partisan politics (Schmid, Hafner, & Pirolt, 2007). As Schmid and others have written, the focus of leadership has by tradition been on one person with restricted autonomy (finance, curriculum, personnel), inhibiting the ability of colleagues to engage in collective action. The fragmented policy context, it was argued, has made it very difficult to introduce coherent approaches to developing a less hierarchical school system while eclectic government interventions compound an overload problem, "piling disconnected policies one upon another".

There are parallels to be found with the Greek education system which, by tradition, has been highly centralised and with a top-down decision-making structure. The division of labour in the field of decision-making is still seen as lying between those who make the decisions and those who carry them out, so that leadership is firmly in the hands of the principal and senior staff. School heads serve as the administrative and educational leaders of their schools, co-ordinating and guiding teachers in their work and making provision for in-service training. Under a recent reforming act (Act:3848/2010), headship competencies, roles, and responsibilities were redefined. These included selection criteria and procedures designed to adapt to the emerging new model in governance, emphasising autonomy but also accountability in relation to state-specified goals and outcomes.

In Australia, the focus on achievement measures in literacy, numeracy, and science continues to demand the attention of school principals who are held to account by their system authorities for school performance. Needless to say, wherever time can be devoted to the preparation for tests, it is. Indeed, because the NAPLAN tests are scheduled for May each year, they dominate first semester timetables in many Australian schools. Parallels in other countries are not hard to find.

No more primus inter pares

Looking across six national cultures which, in many respects, could hardly be more diverse, there are some surprisingly common features. Despite the deeply embedded democratic traditions in Nordic countries and an inherent resistance to hierarchy, there has been an inexorable tide of uncompromising policy diktat.

In 2013, Christiansen and Tronsmo characterised Norwegian culture in these terms:

> High ethical standards; proximity to employees, team orientation, and preference for good working relations; striving for consensus; high gender equality, strong focus on process; conflict avoidance; low results-orientation; slow decision-making; fuzzy control mechanisms; and lack of "warrior attitudes".
>
> *(Christiansen & Tronsmo, 2013, p. 122)*

Matching trends in most other of our *Carpe Vitam* countries, for over a decade or two there has been a political will to make school leaders strong decision-makers and visible leaders in the everyday life of the school as well as in relation to its vision and strategic work. The tradition in Nordic countries of collegial relationships among staff in a flat, democratic school structure has given way to more hierarchical relationships, with "stronger" individual, positional leadership.

As Moos and Møller (2003) write, while there is a strong traditional belief in equality, comprehensive schools, and education for democratic participation, the focus is shifting to detailed national performance standards and competitive advantage. The democratic approach which left many curriculum decisions to professional leaders and teachers, in collaboration with students and parents, has been superseded by mandated standards, decentralisation, consumer choice, competition, outcomes, effectiveness, efficiency, inter-school and inter-country comparisons.

Core democratic values, it is argued, are being eroded by free choice of services and maximising of personal gains. The Danish comprehensive education system has been hugely influenced by transnational reviews (for example, the OECD annual *Education at a Glance*) and national comparative data (such as PISA and TIMMS). The Danish Government, in common with many other regimes, has consequently embraced a "back to basics" stance.

These shifts in discourse and governance have in both Denmark and Norway deeply affected new forms of relationship between schools and local and national authorities. At both ministry and local authority level, schools are required to adopt a more stringent accountability approach with greater upward competition so that, in the process, key terms such as *leadership, professional,* and *learning* acquire new meanings.

The commitment is to a learning organisation, making use of the expertise of educational leaders at all levels of the system. Nonetheless, in common with other *Carpe Vitam* Project countries it has to contend with transnational reviews and OECD comparative data which exert their own pressures on policymaking and on the impact of policy priorities. So, however distributed the leadership, there are always individuals to be held accountable.

The deep commitment in Nordic countries to a comprehensive system is no longer matched in the United Kingdom or the United States where, in both countries, there has been a proliferation of school types emerging over the last decade. "Academies", carrying a cachet of traditional values, have been embraced in both those countries, in England sitting uncomfortably alongside comprehensive schools, grammar schools, church schools, free schools, secondary modern schools, and "public" schools. This serves a policy of parental choice, widening both the attainment and the socioeconomic gap.

> The wholehearted embrace of parental, and pupil choice, while unarguably a matter of first principle, has, with changing political ideology, proved hugely divisive in respect of favoured and disfavoured schools. The increasing pressure on senior leaders to maintain their competitive status by not taking in pupils who will harm their academic credibility was referred to in one school as "reputational damage".
>
> *(Galton & MacBeath, 2015, p. 5)*

Or by any other means

Is school a "right" or a responsibility? In most countries, and in all seven of the *Carpe Vitam* jurisdictions, both of these principles are enshrined in law, although there is an inevitable tension between them. Children have a right to an education while their parents have a duty to ensure that their children attend school, delegating that obligation to teachers who act *in loco parentis*. This is a concept not without contention as there is very little latitude for parents to object to, or ask for, a different teacher or class. Most countries include an "otherwise" clause which permits home education or education "by other means". These are not laissez-faire caveats but come with a corresponding duty on parents to demonstrate that the chosen environment and forms of tuition meet minimal standards, in some cases accompanied by municipal or national testing. These testing requirements appear to be particularly stringent in Austria where children must submit to testing along with their schooled counterparts, requiring them to attend school if standards are not met. English-speaking parents have complained that these tests are impossible for their children to pass as they are in German while children's home education is conducted in English.

In all these countries, the number of parents opting out are, however, small, often stemming from religious reasons or to protect children from adverse peer influence or from bullying. As the curriculum in many places becomes increasingly narrow and sanctions for non-attendance become increasingly punitive, the rationale for education otherwise may become more compelling. In England in 2017 parents who took their child on an educational holiday for a week were fined £360, which soon doubled to £720 because they did not pay up quickly enough. It was a sum which they refused to pay, taking their case to the Royal Courts of Justice where the sanctions against them were upheld and they were threatened with imprisonment, saying in a press interview, "We had no choice but to plead guilty otherwise me and my wife could have been behind bars."

Risking reputational damage

School "reputation" is so deeply entrenched a concept that in Australia, the United Kingdom, and the United States among our *Carpe Vitam* countries, parental choice is exercised primarily in terms of with whom your child goes to school. As the OECD commented in 2011:

> While the performance of private schools does not tend to be superior once socio-economic factors have been accounted for, in many countries these schools may still appear as an attractive alternative for parents looking to maximise the benefits for their children, including those that are conferred to students through the socio-economic level of the schools' intake.
>
> *(OECD, 2011, p. 301)*

In further work published by the OECD on this very matter, Musset (2012) comments:

> Critics worry that even though autonomous and government-dependent private schools perform no better than public schools, they exacerbate stratification by ethnic origin and ability. Indeed, in most of the OECD countries (for example, in the United States, Hungary, Austria, Poland, Czech Republic), autonomous and specialized schools are often competitive and selective, and they tend to attract the privileged parents. There are also concerns and that this harms the students left in public schools, as financial resources and motivated families are skimmed away.

What is observed, for example, in Australia, is repeated in virtually every other *Carpe Vitam* country. Schools in lower socioeconomic communities, or communities with high proportions of migrants or refugees, or communities in geographically remote locations, or schools with significant proportions of Indigenous students, do not perform as well as schools in well-off areas, particularly metropolitan areas. So, after a decade of comprehensive testing, the pattern of Australian school performance is so well known that it becomes something of a self-confirming pattern. While there is nothing new in this systemic discrimination, governments of both political persuasions in Australia have claimed that they want to "close the gap", echoing all-too-familiar aspirational rhetoric in other countries.

Practice in Denmark offers a challenging exception to this pattern. Researchers, for example Rangvid (2008), suggest that the limited parental interest is explained by the fact that public schools are not generally regarded as being inferior to private schools. Public schools are, in fact, quite similar to each other because of decades spent on equalising the school system, which, since 1903, has been developed on egalitarian lines, that is, integrated, non-selective primary and lower secondary comprehensive schools (Wiborg, 2009). As a consequence, parents are not strongly motivated to choose schools for their children. In a study of the voucher system in Denmark, Rangvid has written that parents will only select an alternative school if children of immigrant families exceed 30% of the intake in the school assigned to them by the municipality. Another reason is that parents want a small school or a school with a particular pedagogical practice that is not usually available in a public school, such as a Rudolf Steiner school.

Interestingly, write Wiborg and Larsen (2017), exam results have little or no influence on parents when selecting a school for their children. The main drivers are qualitative issues, such as the school's ethos, quality, and values. The exception to prove this general rule is the expectation of immigrant parents who place a heavy emphasis on exam results. A final reason, which is not investigated in the research literature, is the observation that children enrolled in day care centres tend to transfer to the same schools. A likely reason for this is that parents wish to maintain and nurture their children's formative social relations with their peers. Given the fact that the vast majority of Danish women work, the day care centres may determine, to some extent, the school to which to send their children.

In Norway, concern has been expressed about choice of schools, citing the "segregation effect" in neighbouring Sweden and in other countries where, it has been argued, schools have become segregated on grounds of ethnicity, student performance, parental educational background, and income. Also, the logistics problems for Norwegian students have tended to increase after free choice, leading students to travel longer distances in order to get to their schools. Typically, centrally located schools have been seen as the most attractive, with the following effect that disadvantaged students living in urban areas have been forced to attend schools in the suburbs, while resourceful students from the suburbs attend the city centre schools. As in Denmark, there is the historic alternative of home schooling, the law stating that there is an "obligation to education", not an "obligation to schooling".

Policy discontinuity

School leaders and teachers in all schools of our seven *Carpe Vitam* countries understand and live with policy discontinuity. It is obviously felt more acutely in some countries than in others. In the United Kingdom and Australia, policy, and ensuing practice, are highly susceptible to political caprice; in the United States, where education is a bipartisan issue, this does not, however, prevent discontinuity in and distraction from the essential purposes of school. Even in Denmark and Norway schools have to respond to changes in political intervention while in Greece, "overhaul" of the curriculum, with changes to assessment and class size (no more than 15 per class), is a recent and quite radical reform.

A common question among our *Carpe Vitam* countries has been whether curriculum policy is genuinely "uninformed" or simply a disingenuous appeal to the lowest common denominator of public opinion. In England, for example, despite decimalisation, a commitment to the 12 times table remains, in spite of one government minister's embarrassed inability to answer 12 × 11 when challenged on television. This is, however, symbolic of a backward-facing nostalgia to a time when dates of battles, kings, and queens, and drawing rivers and mountains on blank maps, were the unquestioned staples of a pre-technological age.

The silencing of dissent

A market system in which the client calls the tune is claimed by its supporters to be more efficient because the use of available funding is determined by the clients' expressed needs and is subject to competitive tendering, thus leading to substantial savings, and so allowing a greater range of services to be provided. The expression of needs does, however, depend on having a voice, having a voice heard, and in a register which is seen as fitting with policy preconceptions. The silencing of teachers' voices in Australia is paralleled in the United Kingdom where many headteachers and teachers have learnt not to air dissenting opinions for fear of a punitive response. Having the temerity to speak out in opposition at public meetings is unlikely to be a good career move.

In the United States, the federal policy, *No Child Left Behind* (NCLB), while replete with good intentions, say its critics, has left school leaders and their schools behind due to its narrowing agenda and punitive sanctions. NCLB uses "motivational methods" (threats, punishments, and insidious comparisons) and an overreliance on high-stakes tests that have been shown to have highly demoralising effects, and even corrupting influences on administrators, teachers, and students (Ravitch, 2000).

The standards enigma

The quality of entrants to the profession has been a continuing issue among *Carpe Vitam* countries, and was pursued relentlessly in Australian government rhetoric during 2016. Concern with the ability of students being enrolled by universities in teacher education programs has been a continuing issue, in part owing to the consequence of university funding protocols and the chase for student numbers and their dollars. One of the motivations is the need for universities to be fully enrolled each semester if they are to receive the full recompense to which they are entitled from the government. Thus, padding out enrolments by taking in less able students has been commonplace for many years. Politicians' mantra that "the most important influence on a child's achievement is the teacher" allows the decline in standards to be blamed on those who have entered the profession with less than desirable school and academic results, both considered by politicians as measures of teacher quality.

So, how is the Australian Government addressing this much publicised problem? First, a set of standards for entry to the profession has been agreed; second, tests in literacy and numeracy must be passed after graduation by teachers seeking registration and employment; and third, a Teach for Australia program to attract high-performing graduates into teaching for a few years has been announced. Nothing has been said about the most important influence on a child's life and the role of those people in improving children's chances, namely, parents and family members. There has been little attention given to engagement with parents in policy debate, the preference being to "blame the teachers" for the achievement downturn.

What is interesting in descriptions of some of the policy movements in Australia is the silence on learning – testing has a strident voice and its volume continues unmodulated, but there is silence on the kind of policy shifts necessary to advance Australian education fairly for children from all walks of life. While "Closing the Gap" has been the policy mantra for decades in Australian education, the improvement terrain has been pockmarked with short-term projects with little evidence of government commitment to selecting those which have shown outstanding effects on learning. For example, in 2008–2010, the then Labor government called for projects in literacy and numeracy aimed at improving the learning outcomes for disadvantaged students and over 40 were funded (DEEWR, 2009). After a change of government, none continued to attract funding. This short-termism in governments' dedication to improve learning continues to characterise Australian education policy implementation.

In the United States, a major study in 2006 (Guarino, Santibanez, & Daley) lent support to the theory that the recruitment and retention of teachers depends on the attractiveness of the teaching profession relative to the alternative available opportunities, its relative attractiveness determined by the notion of relative "total compensation" – a comparison of all rewards stemming from teaching, extrinsic and intrinsic, as against the rewards of other possible activities. A key, and perhaps unsurprising finding, is that urban schools and schools with high percentages of minority students proved difficult to staff and that teachers tended to leave these schools when more attractive opportunities presented themselves. What was also evident, however, was that factors that can be altered through policy can have an impact on the decisions of individuals to enter teaching and on the decisions of teachers to stay, to migrate to other schools, or to leave teaching. The research findings support the notion that individual schools and districts can affect their attractiveness to current and prospective teachers relative to other opportunities available to these individuals.

In England where there is a large measure of devolution to individual schools and to headteachers, the same pattern of retention and recruitment has had a significant impact on schools' capacity building. In one of the most deprived areas in London (Hammersmith and Fulham), the headteacher was able to promise high salaries in return for at least a 3-year commitment, and a substantial bonus on leaving. As he writes himself (in MacBeath, 2016):

As the situation became totally untenable I came up with a bonus system to pay teachers up to three thousand pounds a year on the condition that they remained in post for that period and, at end of the three year contract, that bonus would be paid. With agreement from the governing body it gave us, for the first time, continuity and the possibility of extending and enriching professional development. With children seeing the same teachers term after term, it affected their perception of the school and their reaction to what they were being asked to do. This set up a virtuous circle, as teachers began to internalize a common set of expectations and values.

A further bonus was the Neighbourhood Regeneration Project which enabled us to bring in a number of adults other than teachers – a specialist in speech and language, a parent advocate, a social worker, a youth worker, a specialist in reading – taking some of the workload off teachers, freeing them to do what they were paid to do. As we raised our expectations of what we expected, parents began to see their children coming back from school with homework, and then getting class work and homework marked. When they came to parent evenings these parents had something to talk about instead of simply moaning about some grievance they might be nurturing.

(p. 66)

Change without improvement

As can be seen from developments in policy and practice over the last decade, the *Carpe Vitam* Project countries have been on differing trajectories in response to economic, social, and political change. The resistance to what is described as NPM has been most marked in the two Nordic countries steeped in democratic values, and among countries internationally with the shortest "power distance" (between those with most and least power).

While some of the resistance has been overt, as in Denmark's 4-week lockout of teachers in 2013 in response to lack of consultation over the extension of the school day, resistance has, in other places, taken a more quietly subversive approach. That said, in UK countries "defiant risk taking" has been one response, where teachers and school leaders have continually reported that longer working hours and increased and unrelenting pressure have left school staff with too little energy to invest in opposition. As one teacher put it in a recent study: "Wearing teachers down so that they have no residual energy, has drained off any challenge to the government mandate which appears to be a cynical policy ploy" (Galton & MacBeath, 2008, p. 20).

At a time when international leadership research and scholarship were defining and illustrating the benefits of distributive leadership practice, as was the *Carpe Vitam* Project, the power distance between teachers and headteachers increased in some of the participating countries. In England, for example, some heads now earn more than double the salary of a Member of Parliament, three times the salary of the average teacher, and up to 20 times that of a teaching assistant ("State Schools Heads Paid More Than £150,000", n.d.).

The strengthening of leadership with those at the apex of the hierarchy appears to be a developing trend in all countries, perhaps with the exception of Austria, although comparative performance data and accountability pressures push systemically against more collaborative or "distributive" models. There also appears to be a growing intolerance of dissent or challenge to authority.

> Many contemporary democratic theorists argue that the most essential element of democratic communities today is their ability to engage in civilized but semi-permanent disagreement. Articulating a humanist voice that calls for respecting and listening to all positions – but then being able to move forward in the absence of consensus – will be the critical skill that school leaders need to develop when the environment makes consensus impossible.
>
> *(Louis, 2003, p. 105)*

This counsel from Karen Seashore Louis lies at the very heart of the *Carpe Vitam* Project discourse and defines one of the essential qualities of leadership for learning.

Conclusion

The policy terrain we have discussed in this chapter is complex, and so too is the challenge. The transitions from the old-fashioned public administration of government services to an amalgam of NPM and NPG are ongoing and evident in a variety of forms in different country contexts. However, the overall thrust of these shifts is powerfully similar in the democratic economies to which we have referred. None of the accompanying public–private policy momentum is likely to diminish over the next decade, deeply embedding standards, competition, efficiency, choice, accountability, and value for money in the concrete pillars of education policy.

In the next chapter, we tell the story of the *Carpe Vitam* Leadership for Learning Project and its principles, which we believe can act as the centrepiece of a narrative presenting a challenge aimed at reframing education policy.

References

Ainley, J., & McKenzie, P. (2000). School governance: Research on educational and management issues. *International Education Journal, 1*(3), 139–151.

Barber, M. (2005, June). *Informed professionalism: Realising the potential.* Presentation to a conference of the Association of Teachers and Lecturers, London, June 11.

Caldwell, B. J., & Harris, J. M. (2008). *Why not the best schools?* Camberwell, Victoria: ACER Press.

Caldwell, B. J., & Spinks, J. M. (1988). *The self-managing school.* London: Routledge.

Christiansen, L. L., & Tronsmo, P. (2013). Developing learning leadership in Norway. In *The innovative learning environments: Learning leadership* (OECD report circulated to the Governing Board in September 2013). OECD.

Dunleavy, P., & Hood, C. (1994). From old public administration to new public management. *Public Money and Management, Jul–Sep,* 9–16.

European Commission. (2012). *Key Data on Education in Europe 2012*. Brussels: EACEA P9 Eurydice.

Ferlie, E., Ashburner, L., & Pettigrew, A. (1996). *The New Public Management in action*. Oxford: Oxford University Press.

Galton, M., & MacBeath, J. (2008). *Teachers under pressure*. London: Sage.

Galton, M., & MacBeath, J. (2015). *Inclusion: Statements of intent: Schools' and authorities response to the new education, health and care plan*. London: National Union of Teachers.

Gammage, D. T., Sipple, P., & Partridge, P. (1996). Research on school-based management in Victoria. *Journal of Educational Administration, 34*(1), 24–40.

Goffman, E. (1961). *Asylums: Essays on the social situation of mental patients and other inmates*. New York: Anchor Books.

Guarino, C. M., Santibañez, L., & Daley, G. A. (2006). Teacher recruitment and retention: A review of the recent empirical literature. *Review of Educational Research, 76*(2), 173–208.

Louis, K. S. (2003). Democratic schools, democratic communities. *Leadership and Policies in Schools, 2*(2), 93–108.

MacBeath, J. (2016). *Understanding conflict: Changing mindsets*. Cambridge: National Union of Teachers.

Moos, L., & Møller, J. (2003). Schools and leadership in transition: The case of Scandinavia. *Cambridge Journal of Education, 33*(3), 353–371.

Musset, P. (2012). *School choice and equity: Current policies in OECD countries and a literature review*. OECD Education Working Papers, No. 66, OECD Publishing.

Organisation for Economic Co-operation and Development (OECD). (2008). *Improving school leadership. Volume 1: Policy and practice*. Paris: OECD Publishing.

Organisation for Economic Co-operation and Development (OECD). (2011). *Education at a glance 2011: OECD indicators*. Paris: OECD Publishing.

Organisation for Economic Co-operation and Development (OECD). (2013). What is the impact of the economic crisis on public education spending? *Education Indicators in Focus, December*, 1–4.

Osborne, P. (2006). The new public governance? *Public Management Review, 8*(3), 377–387.

Rangvid, B. S. (2008). Private school diversity in Denmark's national voucher system. *Scandinavian Journal of Educational Research, 52*(4), 331–354.

Ravitch, D. (2000). *The death and life of the great American school system*. New York: Basic Books.

Schmid, K., Hafner, L., & Pirolt, T. (2007). Reform Schulgovernance Systemen, *Vergelichende Analayse der Reform Prozess Osterreich and bei enigen PISA-Teilnehmerinlander Forschungsbericht* (Vol 135) IBW Vienna, IBW.

State schools heads paid more than £150,000. (n.d.). *Teaching Times*. Retrieved from https://www.teachingtimes.com/articles/heads-salaries.htm

Superville, D. R. (2014, May 6). School budget problems have deep roots in Philadelphia. *Education Week*.

Wiborg, S. (2009). *Education and social integration: Comprehensive schooling in Europe*. London: Palgrave Macmillan.

Wiborg, S., & Larsen, K. R. (2017). Why school reforms in Denmark fail: The blocking power of the teaching unions. *European Journal of Education, 52*(1), 92–103.

Wilby, P. (2015). Media and Education in the UK. In R. Pring & M. Roberts (Eds.), *A generation of radical educational change: Stories from the field*. London: Routledge.

3

LEADERSHIP FOR LEARNING

An essential narrative in a challenge to policy

How can school leaders and teachers, held to account by layers and overlays of policy, challenge those very controls? In search of an answer to that question this chapter leads us into an informing narrative, leadership for learning (LfL), and into what we have called elsewhere "a practical theory" (Dempster & MacBeath, 2009, p. 178). As such, it provides us with a master key, one which opens up a rich source of intelligence and a challenge to policy. We describe this as a key because it gives access to what the Delors Report (UNESCO, 1996) describes as the "treasure within", in this case, four treasures of the profession: (a) the reaffirmation of professional integrity, (b) the significance of thinking differently about learning and teaching, (c) the dedication to enhancing professionalism, and (d) the impetus for the redefinition of leadership as activity. These four keys to practice are of little value in isolation. They are integrally related and draw strength from the conception of LfL – the pedagogical "home" of school leaders and teachers ready to stand up for what is important to them and to their students. Here we turn the key to revisit our approach to LfL and its principles for practice, leaving each of the other treasures for the following four chapters.

Millennium change

The catalyst for LfL as a narrative with which to challenge policy – the nucleus of this book – and its predecessor, *Connecting Leadership and Learning*, followed the creation of a Chair in Educational Leadership in the Faculty of Education at Cambridge University in 2000. In the following year, Leadership for Learning: The Cambridge Network was created, with a new professorial post in recognition of the increasing significance of leadership in a global policy context. This coincided with the establishment in England of the National College for School Leadership. While the creation of such an agency was designed to put the spotlight on leadership in an arm's length "quango" (a quasi-autonomous non-governmental agency), it was required to tread a delicate line between challenging inert connotations of leadership on the one hand, and following the government's managerialist "party line" on the other.

Through both formal and informal dialogue over time with local, regional, national, and international educators in a variety of roles, key decisions were made that shaped what was to become the work of the LfL: The Cambridge Network. Some of these decisions sought conceptual clarity where this was possible, while others produced a "testable" consensus. For example, we agreed initially on a view of leadership as broader and more encompassing than management and managerialism. Leadership, we agreed, was not simply to be found at the apex of an organisation but at different levels and in different places. It includes teachers and students, and should be seen as a shared and collaborative exercise. It should be centred on a learning climate at school and the conditions for learning at classroom and school-community levels (MacBeath, 2001).

We also agreed on the basis of a number of values-based precepts:

- Learning, leadership, and their interrelationship should be our central concern.
- Learning and leadership are a shared, as much as an individual, enterprise.
- Collaborative modes of working build and strengthen teams.
- It is vital to adopt a critical perspective, informed by research.
- There should be a persistent questioning of the status quo and of received wisdom.
- A permeating commitment to equality should underpin all our work.
- Trust, honesty, openness, and interdependence should characterise our relationships.

To put our consensus positions to the test and to try to realise our developing values base, revisiting our assumptions and values, we turned to field research. The international *Carpe Vitam* Leadership for Learning Project was conceived as an action-based initiative in which research teams would facilitate change in schools and collect data to inform a series of four international seminars, each offering an occasion to review what we had learnt and where to go next. The first of these took place in 2002.

The *Carpe Vitam* Leadership for Learning Project

We found support for a radical reappraisal of learning and learning-centred leadership from the Swedish philanthropist Peder Wallenberg who provided funds from his *Carpe Vitam* Foundation. This allowed us to embark on a seven-country study in which, over a 3-year period, we could forge a new practical theory of LfL. The challenge was not simply to create a theoretical framework, but to develop a theory of action which would be seen as useful in seven countries and eight localities (two in the United States). While each was culturally distinct with their own cultures and traditions, they were, nonetheless, subject to the same globalising imperatives of comparative performativity. The choice of Austria, Australia, Denmark, England, Greece, Norway, and the United States (Washington State and New Jersey) was a consequence of links already established through prior work with the Cambridge team rather than by virtue of random or stratified international sampling.

National clusters comprising researchers, critical friends, and three schools from each country (24 schools in total) agreed to undertake a learning journey together, a longitudinal study which would stretch over a period of 3 years. Each school would benefit from the support of a critical friend, who would, as far as possible, combine that role with research tasks, becoming at times an "insider". This would imply getting to know each school in its own country context, offering what we described as "supportive challenge". The researcher would then take a more distanced stance in the documentation process.

Across our "sample", however culturally disparate, all schools held in common a set of educational ideals, while experiencing a sense of frustration at the distance between where these schools were at that time and where they would have liked to be. Yet it may have been too easily assumed that we had a common view of learning. It may have been easily assumed that we shared an understanding of leadership and that there was consensus as to the relationship between these two foundational concepts. A whole continent of geographical, political, and cultural difference stood between the Nordic countries and Greece; and what could Australian and Austrian teachers have in common? The two countries are separated not only by language but also by uneasy underlying histories and, in the case of Austria, unhappy connotations as to the one who leads – der Fuhrer.

It proved to be a long and sometimes conflicted journey to arrive at a shared understanding and an eventual agreement on a set of common principles of LfL among the 80 or so participants. It is significant that it took until the third year of the study for a genuine common understanding to emerge, as teams of teachers, researchers, and critical friends followed the well-trodden path of storming (often impatient, fraught, emotional), norming (forging alliances, seeking out some common ground), performing, and, finally, reforming – small cycles or eddies of dissonance and resolution, disequilibrium and stability (Tuckman, 1965). There were peaks of enthusiasm and the embrace of new ideas when school principals and teachers came together for extended conferencing and workshops to exchange stories and theories of practice. There were troughs when they returned to their schools to be met with other pressing priorities and impatient government mandates.

Each stage in the journey was marked by the location of the country meetings. The initial gathering in Cambridge, bringing together teachers, researchers, and other participants for the first time, however convivial, was also challenging. The unfamiliarity with social conventions, the ambiguities of language, and untested cultural assumptions required a suspension of our ambition to move on and agree on a working timetable. While frustrating for the leadership team it was a salutary lesson in intercultural understanding and what "research" implied for different participants. A continuing restlessness was evident at the second international workshop, in Innsbruck, where the direction of travel was still not clear to all.

At the third meeting in Copenhagen there was not only a dawning conceptual clarity but a grasp of practical applications, in no small measure facilitated by visits to Danish classrooms and dialogue with young people. It prepared the ground for a final encounter with concept and practice in Athens, inspired by the interventions and additional insights brought by Harvard's David Perkins, a critical friend to the project as a whole.

In between these annual conferences, national and local meetings continued to develop and these provided feedback on progress. In Athens, for example, English schools were invited to join with Greek schools in a 3-day workshop, while teachers from Oslo and London visited each other's classrooms. In Princeton, schools came together for a series of workshops led by members of the Cambridge team, and on the other side of the United States a 3-day retreat brought together Seattle school staff and community members with a member of the research team. Each face-to-face encounter added to our collective and growing understanding of leadership, learning, and their connections.

Conducting the study across very different contexts created methodological challenges and opportunities. One common instrument was a questionnaire, with staff and student versions. Arriving at the final version required pragmatism in identifying student year groups that could be considered comparable across all of the settings, involving the research team in many hours of discussion as to the wording of each item, seeking contextually sensitive equivalence in five languages. In implementing the study, it was important to find common instruments while still respecting the different research traditions which each site brought with it. In Austria, photo evaluation; in the United States, portraiture; and from other contributors, spot checks, critical incident analysis, shadowing – all contributing to the toolbox of strategies. In Norway, the framing paradigm was "action learning", in New Jersey it was "appreciative inquiry", in Denmark, "collaborative inquiry", and in Seattle it was described as "co-construction" (see the 2006 special issue of *Leading and Managing*, volume 26, issue 2).

These differing stances on the nature of research and the form of school-based inquiry, although sharing some essential features, led us to characterise the project methodology as "eclectic and emergent" (MacBeath, Frost, & Swaffield, 2005). Understandings and project outcomes were developed through ongoing discourse, engaging with a range of data, theories, and perspectives on practice. The five LfL principles (described later in the chapter) which provide the inspiration and resources for this book were derived through an iterative process with the team of international researchers identifying key learning emerging from the project, expressing this in a list of statements, working with them and getting feedback from project participants through workshops in conferences, revising and trying out successive versions.

Significant dimensions of this international dialogic process included a debate about how best to characterise *leadership* as enabling everyone within or around the school community to exercise it. While the managerialist idea of "delegation" was easily set aside, terms such as *distributed leadership*, *dispersed leadership*, and *parallel leadership*, all in common usage in various contexts, had to be considered. Eventually consensus was achieved around the idea of *shared leadership*, encompassing teacher leadership and student leadership but broad enough to include the exercise of leadership by parents, community stakeholders, auxiliary staff, and other key stakeholders. Our American colleagues contributed the idea that we should be seeking to cultivate leaderful communities (Raelin, 2003). At the time, the issue of accountability provoked protracted debate given that it was experienced very differently in participating countries. For instance, accountability was yet to become an equally immediate concern in the Nordic states; the contrast with New Jersey, where the input of federal funding was tied to outcome measures, was not only illuminating but a portent for the future. Ten years on, the impact of fiscal and professional accountability is now more widely experienced. The fifth principle in the LfL framework addresses the language and assumptions of the all too pervasive concept of accountability.

While the project ended in 2007, the *Carpe Vitam* LfL principles forged in its short lifetime have not only survived and spread among the seven *Carpe Vitam* countries, but have also travelled and been applied internationally in countries as disparate as Malaysia, The Netherlands, Hong Kong, New Zealand, Pakistan, Poland, and many others in eastern Europe (Swaffield et al., 2014). In Ghana, the principles have been incorporated into government policy with attendant guidelines for headteachers/principals and for classroom practice (Ghana Education Service [GES], 2010, 2014). These have been complemented by training materials for use in the Colleges of Education with the next generation of teachers (MacBeath & Swaffield with Oduro & Hassler, 2016a, b, c).

Most of the countries from the original *Carpe Vitam* study have experienced an economic recession since 2007. The effects of this crisis on education internationally, described in Chapter 1, are witness to a decade of "belt tightening". In many countries, this has been allied with continuing pressures on school principals to raise "standards", yet with diminishing resources. In this policy environment, it may prove increasingly challenging to prioritise the important over the expedient, but with LfL principles as a guide there is a much clearer path through the political thickets.

Leadership for Learning: Principles for practice

Revisiting five sets of principles for practice some 10 years after their first exposure might seem somewhat superfluous, but such has been the influence of the LfL framework that each of its principles has been applied and confirmed in subsequent international research. In reviewing 40 years of empirical leadership research, Hallinger (2011, p. 126) went as far as to say that the term "leadership for learning" was overtaking the common usage of "instructional leadership" in the United States and more widely. While this may be an optimistic assumption, 6 years on from Hallinger's paper, where the terminology has been adopted, it is not always with the same meaning or resting on the same cardinal principles depicted in Figure 3.1.

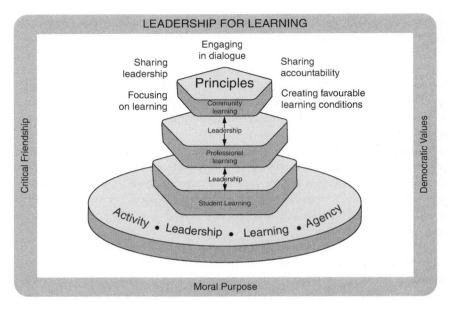

FIGURE 3.1 Leadership for Learning and its principles

As illustrated in Figure 3.1, LfL principles provide a set of common framing values we observed in, and drew from, the seven participating democracies. These are depicted on the outer rim or frame of the diagram. Moral Purpose forms the base of the frame, with Democratic Values and Critical Friendship on the two sides. Inside the frame, and on the base, Agency and Activity are depicted as encompassing Leadership and Learning, emphasising that leading and learning are necessary forms of activity, enacted by those with a strong sense of their own human agency.

What was referred to in the Seattle *Carpe Vitam* workshop as the "wedding cake" is depicted as three interconnecting tiers, a visual reminder that learning and leadership are present at every level of the educational community, flowing in every direction – the shared province of students, teachers, senior managers, and communities of learners. All are guided by the five principles (headlined at the top of the figure) and their expression in day-to-day practice. It is to an explanation of these principles that we now turn.

Principle No. 1. Leadership for learning practice involves maintaining a focus on learning as an activity

When this principle is recognised in practice there is a renewed appreciation of the interplay among social, emotional, and cognitive processes and to the differing ways in which individuals learn. In other words, learning is individual, social, and cultural, and almost always influenced powerfully by these three perspectives acting in concert (Berryman & Bishop, 2011). A corollary of Principle 1 is the capacity for leadership to arise out of the learning experiences in which students and teachers engage (Hunzicher, 2012; Lizzio, Dempster, & Newmann, 2011).

While the notion that students, teachers, and headteachers should focus on learning may seem obvious, cultural circumstances can too easily frustrate that intention, and indeed build conflicting habits. Pressures for good exam results, for example, may lead to a focus on ways of enhancing marks and grades rather than focusing on the learning that tests are supposed to assess. School principals, teachers, and students can all too easily be locked into a performativity culture. As Stobart (2008) illustrates, pressures such as these may profoundly affect the learner's outlook, identity, and sense of self-worth in ways that are detrimental for even the highest attaining student. When school leaders have had very little professional development which is challenging of insistent political premises, it may not be surprising to find that everyday priorities are subject to immediate pressures. In Ghana, for example, Oduro and Bosu (2010) reported that 75% of headteachers had received less than a week's training in the preceding 5 years, and that a headteacher might, typically, be more concerned with keeping books safe than having them put to use (Oduro, 2008).

How easy or difficult is it for principals, teachers, and students to maintain a focus on learning in the busy-ness of school life? Unanticipated interruptions occur, some trivial, some very serious. For example, in Australia, the 2008 global financial crisis turned school principals into construction overseers as the government implemented a much-championed Building Education Revolution (BER) for every school in the country. This was intended to stimulate the economy and save Australians from the effects of a deep recession. Such was the speed in expenditure required that, for a 2-year period, many principals claimed they were able to do little else than attend to architectural plans, building approvals, inspections, payment schedules, and endless paperwork, all of which stole time and energy from them, removing the chance or the drive to maintain a focus on learning. Yet, we met principals who were able to keep their sights on learning in schools where the BER was characterised as a necessary evil but not one which should override leadership work in the interest of students. The leaders of these schools were able, at a stretch, to accommodate immediate and urgent demands but equally, they were able to "snap back" to their essential purpose, LfL.

We have seen this process of snapping back to a focus on learning in other challenging situations. An illustration of this is the extremely troubling times confronting principals and teachers when a child dies. In one of our Australian schools, a branch from a gum tree standing in the playground fell on a young girl, killing her. The gum tree, a eucalypt known colloquially as "The Widow Maker" because of the frequency with which it "self-taps" or "self-prunes", is still found in schoolyards. Imagine how stretched the school principals and teachers would have been in dealing sensitively with this appalling incident. They would have been strained to the limit and, for quite some time, dealing with shock, grief, care, recrimination, reports, and possible litigation. Nevertheless, hard as it may be and without diminishing the trauma and dismay which attends accidents such as this, school leaders and teachers must spring back with renewed purpose to their pedagogical home, a focus on learning, as soon as it is practicable to do so.

The first sub-principle here is that "everyone is a learner". "Everyone" is a totally inclusive term emphasising that while we readily accept that students are the formal learners in focus, it is easy to overlook the equally important commitment that applies to every member of a school community. If this is not observed, student learning is impoverished, making it more difficult for schools to cope with persisting challenges and ever-changing contexts. One of the 30 statements in the student version of the LfL questionnaire is *teachers talk to us about their own learning*. This requires two responses, one in relation to perceived importance, the other in relation to its frequency in practice. It is consistently rated as one of the lowest items, most particularly in terms of practice. This same result has been found in every country where this tool has been used, perhaps not so surprising given pupils' long-ingrained habits of seeing the teacher as all powerful and all knowledgeable.

Principle No. 2. Leadership for learning practice involves creating conditions favourable to learning as an activity

What are these conditions and how are they created by headteachers and teachers? Our *Carpe Vitam* Project discussions produced a series of five prompts to action. Taken together, these point to the development of a learning culture, one able to nurture the learning of everyone. This is achieved by creating opportunities for all to reflect on the nature, skills, and processes of learning, using tools and strategies to stimulate thinking and discussion. This can only take place when the physical and social spaces are convivial for learning, where the environment is safe, when risks are encouraged and taken, and where the frustration of failure and the satisfaction of success are equally valued and celebrated. These five prompts have an acute bearing on the understanding of leaders, teachers, and students in a school where the learning culture embraces everyone.

In Australian research stimulated by the LfL principles (Dempster et al., 2012; Johnson et al., 2014; Townsend, Dempster, Johnson, Bayetto, & Stevens, 2015), the importance of attending to the conditions for learning is exemplified. That said, however, it may not come as a surprise that school principals reported that they gave greater attention to physical spaces for student learning and learning resources than they did in the case of teachers. There was, in addition, far less attention in these Australian findings to the social and emotional conditions for learning, perhaps because these are frequently accepted as "taken for granted". Notwithstanding these comments, there were cases observed where the joy of achievement was so obvious and so sincerely celebrated that the effects – moral and motivational – were palpable. And sustained in practice.

One example from the Principals as Literacy Leaders with Indigenous Communities (PALLIC) Project underlines the sociality and emotionality of adults genuinely engaged in learning. In a remote Indigenous township, a young aboriginal man of some 18 years was approached by the school principal and invited to become a Leadership Partner, to take the lead in reading improvement in the school and the community. He accepted. At a later gathering in a project workshop on the Australian coast more than 2,000 kilometres from his home, he stood up in front of 48 white principals and some 90 Indigenous Leadership Partners to say:

> When I was at school, I gave my principal lotsa trouble. But I can read and now I can lead. I'm doin' something for him and for the kids at our place. I'm a leader of reading and I'm glad I'm learnin' and helpin'. And that's gotta be good.

As one, the audience applauded this young man for his pride in bringing leadership and learning together for the benefit of his community. His bashful smile set the audience off again and he was applauded back to his seat. The message in this brief account is that acknowledgement and celebration are necessary companions of the social and emotional conditions for learning.

Principle No. 3. Leadership for learning practice involves creating dialogue about learning and teaching

As already mentioned in discussion of Principle No. 2, it is the use of tools and strategies that helps to stimulate dialogue. This third principle emphasises the importance and nature of dialogue itself as an essential and challenging strategy. More is said about this for shared and collaborative leadership practice in Chapter 4, and for professional enhancement in Chapter 6. Dialogue is, by its very nature, interactive – but what are the motivations which inform this principle in practice?

Dialogue, especially among people from different contexts, opens up new perspectives, often generating challenges to established patterns of thought. However, this does require active listening and openness to challenging existing ways of thinking. In the *Carpe Vitam* Project, this took time to develop, reliant on an ethos in which participants felt safe to venture, to listen unconditionally. This sequential development of dialogue among school participants from different countries mirrored, to some extent, Tuckman's (1965) stages. Initially, learning about practice in other countries tended to be focused on comparison with one's own familiar practices, followed by beginning to see one's own practice in a new light. This paved the way for comparisons among practices and principles which followed at a later stage (Portin, 2009).

Dialogue was particularly productive when different points of view sowed the seeds for new ways of thinking (Portin, 2009), often as a precursor to action. This lent further weight to Knapp and colleagues' depiction of teachers "interacting with other professionals who offer ideas, critique, inspiration and moral support. … Through such interactions teachers begin to look at their own practice differently and to enhance students' learning opportunities in the classroom" (Knapp, Copland, & Talbert, 2003, p. 10).

However, productive dialogue does not simply take place as a result of people coming into contact with one another or through cross-boundary networking. Rather, it is fostered through collegial inquiry, the deliberative sharing of values, new understandings, and a focus on breakthrough practices. Specific tools and strategies to support dialogue were gathered, further developed, and used in the *Carpe Vitam* Project (Swaffield, 2006) and, over following years, these have continued to be refined to develop this repertoire across many LfL activities and projects. Recently the Cambridge Schools Leadership for Learning Community (CSLfLC) Project used portraiture, narratives, and the LfL questionnaire (among other tools) to support schools' improvement. For several of the schools their individual improvement focus explicitly included "dialogue". Many participants reported an enhancement of dialogue among teachers, students, school leaders, and parents and more widely. The planned inter-school dialogue did not, however, fully materialise given the challenges that this border crossing has continually presented. After an initial face-to-face 2-day conference that brought all participants together, a virtual learning environment was used quite successfully for regular webinars. This is not the place for a detailed discussion of the role of technology in supporting educational dialogue, but it is one of the aspects being researched by the Cambridge Educational Dialogue Research Group (CEDiR[1]). This newly established centre builds on a long tradition of related research at Cambridge by colleagues including Robin Alexander, John MacBeath, Neil Mercer, and Jean Rudduck, who have all written extensively about dialogue in schools.

As a foundational principle, learning should be made the explicit focus for dialogue, whether amongst teachers or with students. Secondly, through collegial inquiry there should be an active exploration of the links between learning and leadership. Third, this assumes a sharing of values, understandings, and practices leading to greater clarity and coherence. Fourth, it requires that factors which inhibit and promote learning and leadership should be examined and addressed. As a fifth imperative, the link between leadership and learning should be a shared concern for everyone. Finally, differing perspectives should be explored through networking with researchers and practitioners across national and cultural boundaries wherever possible.

From the *Carpe Vitam* Project work, we coined the term "disciplined dialogue" (Swaffield & Dempster, 2009). Since then, much has been written on the importance of dialogue internationally. While other terms are common in the literature, such as "peer conversations" (Timperley, 2015), "problem encounters" (Robinson & Timperley, 2007), "constructive problem talk" (Robinson & Timperley, 2007), and "professional learning conversations" (Danielson, 2009; Earl & Timperley, 2009), the term disciplined dialogue has travelled well and been found useful by principals and teachers alike. For a detailed account of the strategy and evidence on its use and effects see Dempster et al. (2017). In brief, disciplined dialogue is an approach to the professional discussion of qualitative or quantitative data on matters affecting learning, stimulated by three generic questions:

i.   What do we see in these data?
ii.   Why are we seeing what we are?
iii. What, if anything, should we be doing about it?

In the words of a principal who had participated in a professional development program on literacy leadership in Australia:

The three disciplined dialogue questions are powerful, very simple and able to be kept in your head. I am now applying this knowledge.

A second participant said:

I've become much more confident in this area and have put much more energy into gathering evidence. I've used this to back up opinions, help clarify our philosophy and help us set directions. I use the disciplined dialogue questions regularly. The staff are beginning to use them when we are discussing data at staff meetings.

A third reported:

We saw a third or more of the principals not really confident about reading their own data who walked out (of the workshop) with a notion of "I can do this with my staff." I couldn't wait to get back to school because I knew I could do this with my staff. Powerful simple questions that remained the same each time so people knew what they were asked.

(Dempster et al., 2012, pp. 20, 21)

From Australian research (Townsend et al., 2015) it is encouraging to find that structured professional discussions employing the disciplined dialogue sequence of questions are commonplace amongst teachers in many antipodean schools. Sometimes they are led by principals; sometimes by teachers. What the sequence does is to value teacher judgement, especially when reasons are sought for what has been occurring locally, and in determining what might be done in the future. The last question in the set brings principals and teachers back to the moral purpose which frames LfL – what can and should be done to improve learning and ultimately the lives and life chances of learners?

In Pakistan, pioneering research into the practicality and use of LfL in schools (Javed, 2013) has highlighted the importance of dialogue among all stakeholders (principals, teachers, students, and parents) in order to establish a shared vision for effective learning. Dialogue emerged very strongly as "the missing link" in bringing about and embedding change, linking different people, levels, and aspects (for example curriculum, assessment, and accountability) of a school community. Javed adapted the LfL model and wording of the principles, explaining, "When working with people in the more remote areas of Pakistan for whom English is their fourth or fifth language, I have to modify the terminology and I am more focused on the meaning that I want to convey" (in Swaffield et al., 2014, p. 5).

Principle No. 4. Leadership for learning practice involves the sharing of leadership

This is an appealing principle but one difficult to translate into day-to-day practice. We are so inured to the notion of leadership as an individual quality or activity that it is challenging to think of how this may be enacted in the day-by-day business of schools. School principals/headteachers are too well aware that in a high-stakes accountability context the "buck" stops with them. They may delegate, they may take their turns with day-to-day tasks, they may work collaboratively on planning, supervision, and evaluation – but any risk they may take with their colleagues carries with it an upward accountability. At the same time, there is a growing recognition that within an increasingly demanding and complex environment, no single leader will have all of the skills to effectively perform the range of leadership tasks and that, therefore, he or she has little option but to trust colleagues and create an environment in which that trust is reciprocated. Nearly two decades ago Elmore (2000, p. 15) argued that "leadership of schools is beyond the capacity of any one person" and that a principal alone can no longer reasonably be responsible for leadership and all outcomes in a school. The growing size, complexity, uncertainty, and diversity in schools, allied with societal changes, it was argued, all conspired to make a new leadership paradigm necessary. Carson and colleagues (2007) have suggested that such an environment may be created when there is a sense of shared purpose, social or reciprocal support, and a sensitivity to "voice". It is the interconnectivity of these three concepts that allows a genuine sharing to take place. It rests on an honest, even generous, recognition of other team members' contributions, a willingness to suspend judgement and exercise followership; or, in Carson's words, "interrelated and mutually reinforcing", and "representing a high order construct".

The ability and willingness of a school principal to exercise followership is illustrated in the following incident which took place in Hong Kong in 2011. Following a keynote, the speaker was approached by a 16-year-old student who introduced him to his school principal whom he had encouraged to attend the conference. She recounted how this young man had offered to lead a self-evaluation program in the school including questions on the effectiveness of the principal and the senior leadership team. This was followed by focus groups and development planning sessions led by young people. The point so evident here is the reciprocal trust between leader and student.

Principle No. 5. Leadership for learning practice involves a shared sense of accountability

This fifth principle reiterates what has been said in relation to shared leadership, the commitment to joint initiative, and the mutual responsibilities that attend it. There is a sharp distinction to be made with much of what is understood and mandated in government policies. The very structural hierarchies of the school system require teachers to be answerable to their heads of department who in turn report to senior managers and ultimately to the principal/headteacher. Referred to in Chapter 1, the following from the most improved school in England and its much-lauded headteacher is a reminder of just how deeply hierarchy, heroic leadership, and upward accountability are embedded in policy and practice: "This policy has got a lot of me in it. It's largely me"; "that wasn't from the staff. That was from myself"; "It was quite brutal. It was tough. It was me." And next, the deception that speaks volumes about the reality of accountability: "I think teachers have got to feel that they're making decisions but what I suppose, I'm forcing them to do is make those decisions." The actions in this brief tale clearly show the absence of reciprocal trust.

A challenge to policy

Why should LfL be elevated to the centrepiece of a challenge to policy? More than a decade's research has convinced us of the broad applicability of the principles for practice which we have restated in this chapter. Each of them carries a message for policymakers concerned about students' learning and the learning of headteachers, teachers, and others who influence young lives. We expressed this opinion in a series of policy implications for each principle in 2009. We now use five short extracts to anchor our present views in that earlier work.

On Principle No. 1, A Focus on Learning, in 2009 we said:

> Our first principle, a focus on learning, implies a shift in the balance of policy towards a stronger emphasis on learning as life wide and lifelong, developing criteria and indicators which give greater weight to achievements other than exam performance. If imaginative pedagogy is to be encouraged and teaching to the test discouraged, it means releasing the pressures on teachers and engaging professionals in finding new and creative ways to assess the quality of learning. Policy needs to build from the ground up as well as top down, attuned more sensitively to professional experience.
>
> *(MacBeath & Dempster, 2009, p. 181)*

What we now say is predicated on the almost universal acceptance of a test-driven improvement agenda for schools in OECD countries, but elsewhere in the world as well, despite considerable criticism of the Programme for International Student Assessment (PISA). In Australia for example, participation in international comparative testing programs and national tests of the whole student population yearly has produced repetitive results. Internationally, as we have shown earlier, Australia is slipping down the rankings while nationally, it is well known where performance is less than desirable. These outcomes beg the question, "Why is this repetitive pattern of performance occurring?" Could educational policies which are now into their second decade of influence be part of the problem? Answering these two questions is pertinent not only for the countries where national testing is established, but perhaps even more so for those many developing countries that are following the same path.

When we examine research into literacy we find salient messages with broader applicability. For example, preparing citizens for literate lives requires wide exposure to oral language exchanges, an extensive vocabulary, and a wide general knowledge. While the importance of student literacy is unquestioned, these three conditions are essential ingredients in enabling them to confidently comprehend both what they read and what they write (Bayetto, 2014). Without this breadth, particularly in the primary school years, reading to learn in depth in later school life is restricted. Extrapolating this view tells us that narrowing the curriculum will be counterproductive to improving outcomes over time.

As we have consistently maintained, a focus on breadth in learning should be unassailable as long as policies which erode this position are challenged. Business and industry leaders in the United Kingdom repeatedly call for schools to focus more on "soft skills" such as teamwork and communication, and in a globalised interdependent technological world, cultural understanding, innovation, and creativity assume huge importance. Yet many of the subjects most likely to promote those skills tend to be marginalised or removed entirely from the curriculum.

The fact that Australia performed especially well in the first round of PISA tests (Thomson, De Bortoli, & Underwood, 2017) in the absence of mandatory annual and quadrennial tests, suggests that a return to a more open and flexible curriculum will be beneficial to students and their learning. Such a curriculum is also potentially liberating for teachers. When freed from the limiting practices of test preparation, they are more likely to embrace experimentalism and innovation in the search for engaging learning experiences. The focus on learning is thus a focus for everyone in the school, teachers and students alike. But we now argue for more than this. The focus on learning breadth has to be realised at classroom, school, and system levels, each layer supporting the other, with top-down and bottom-up exchanges directed at improving the very nature of learning at each of those levels. Added to this is the centrality of parents' position in their children's learning so they, too, need to maintain a focus on learning. Generally, the capacity of parents to deal with content depth declines as their children grow through adolescence in secondary school, but their ability to deal with breadth increases, because of their knowledge of life and the growing independence of their offspring. There is little policy noise on a commitment to the essential place of parents in learning right up to the final years of schooling.

On Principle No. 2, Creating the Conditions for Learning, in 2009 we said:

> Yet we are reminded of the famous quote at the beginning of the 1963 Newsom report, "It could be all glass and marble Sir, but it's still a bloody school!" The conditions for learning are greater than the sum of the physical parts. They are the social, emotional and psychological conditions which provide the breathing space, the reflection time and above all the trust that distinguishes the intelligent school from the 'bloody' school.
>
> *(p. 182)*

The "intelligent" school nowadays puts processes in place which show, unambiguously, that the principal and teachers are there to nurture the learning of everyone. This requires continuous attention to the physical, technical, social, and emotional conditions for learning. What we now say is that these five prompts to action define a compelling set of practices which, when present, encourage a strong sense of belonging in students, and affiliation with, and trust in, their teachers. Students who are nurtured in a culture of learning find that their personal motivation is valued, they share joy with their teachers in the satisfaction which accompanies success in learning, and they welcome support to improve when they encounter failure. When supportive conditions for learning are absent, it leads to anxiety, mistrust, misbehaviour, disaffection, and alienation. Having a safe, supportive, and trusted environment is a precursor to the establishment of a learning culture for children and young people. Such a claim has reached axiomatic status as a consequence of the findings of multiple school climate and environment studies since the 1970s.

The mix of children we find in the schools of today sometimes makes the warm positive tone conveyed by the five prompts to action difficult to achieve. But doing so is non-negotiable because a learning culture must embrace everyone, no matter their backgrounds, aspirations, or abilities. Holding firmly to the pursuit of the best possible conditions for learning is as much a local school policy matter as it is a system's policy responsibility.

On Principle No. 3, Creating Dialogue about Learning and Teaching, we said in 2009:

> Our third principle asserts the importance of dialogue, the lifeblood of professional learning. The quality of dialogue is enhanced when teachers have the opportunity to research their practice, to travel physically and virtually beyond their schools.
>
> *(p. 182)*

What we say now is that it is encouraging to see how this particular principle has been acknowledged in a wide range of professional activities over the last 10 years. Dialogue is the major strategy employed in mentoring, coaching, critical friendship, and professional inquiry. All of these processes require time and opportunity, both with resource costs attached. Yet there is more to do, because the application of, and commitment to, these dialogical activities is often sporadic and causal connections with improved outcomes difficult to verify. Likewise, funding from system authorities is variable and rarely guaranteed for the long term. Qualitative differences in teachers and leaders' practices frequently cited in professional development research reports are not regarded by politicians and policymakers with the same conviction as increases in student test scores. As a consequence, it is school leaders and teachers themselves who need to take the initiative to press on with the reflective and developmental capacity enhanced through dialogue about their pedagogy.

While we acknowledged the usefulness of virtual and real-time travel to enable teachers to discuss their practice with others, we understand the costs associated with the latter. That said, professional bodies and informal networks of teachers now provide many opportunities for synchronous and asynchronous dialogue amongst like-minded teachers. There is no doubt that this will continue. Dialogue at school level though remains the most significant way in which ideas about learning and teaching may be tested amongst peers. Principle No. 2 indicates that a learning culture is the most important of the five conditions for learning – and this applies to the professional learning culture as much as it does to the culture children experience.

On Principle No. 4, Shared Leadership, in 2009, we said:

> Parents and pupils, along with teaching and support staff need to feel that they
> have a vital leading and learning role to play within the school community as
> well as beyond its immediate physical boundaries. Parents need to have access
> to the kind of information which steers them away from simplistic judgments
> about quality and encourages them to engage in dialogue with teachers and
> with children about the purposes of education in a changing world.

We now say:

There has been a slow but growing recognition of the hidden capital of students and the surprising insights that they can, and often do, bring when their
voice is encouraged and genuinely heard. Five years ago, we were aware of UK
schools which involved students in the appointment of new staff, sometimes offering their opinions on applicants, often involved in the interviewing of candidates.
This became increasingly commonplace in both primary and secondary schools
with testimony from staff that they unfailingly selected the best candidate.

In many countries, school improvement teams were progressively more likely
to include students and they were also likely to be included on governing bodies.
An external evaluation of school improvement in Hong Kong (MacBeath, 2014)
concluded that pedagogy is becoming more engaging, more student-centred,
more open and receptive to student voice (p. 26). It had assumed a higher priority among schools in the embedding of self-evaluation and at classroom level
the report concluded: "There are many examples of individual teachers who
are comfortable with critical reflection on their practice through peer lesson
observation or student feedback on classroom learning and teaching" (p. 5). So
common has this become that a number of websites offer advice to prospective
candidates and suggest some of the questions they may ask and qualities they
might be looking for.

For example, a teacher who:

- Is fair (particularly in terms of being even-handed)
- Runs a classroom in such a way that everyone can learn
- Is enthusiastic about her/his subject/teaching
- Likes young people
- Will challenge them
- Will challenge bullying
- Has a sense of humour
- Is a problem-solver
- Is an expert
- Is a professional
- Is caring
- Is "strict in a polite way" (i.e. doesn't scream and shout to create discipline)
- Is fun (i.e. likes to have fun and help others have fun)
- Can make learning fun

- Acts the same with pupils and teachers

(https://www.smartschoolcouncils.org.uk/resources/school-council-interview-questions/)

On Principle No. 5, A Shared Sense of Accountability, in 2009, we said:

> Our fifth principle addresses the accountability issue. It posits a recasting of responsibility and accountability, promoting an internal accountability which rests on mutual trust and a strong sense of collegiality. External accountability is acceptable and motivating when it moves beyond duty or compliance to external demands, and builds on a school's own intrinsic commitment to essential educational values.

What we say now …

In the previous chapter, we referred to developments in Austrian schools where there was a system-wide commitment to forge future-orientated school cultures rather than a retrospective one, always with one eye on external accountability. "Building on a school's own intrinsic commitment to essential educational values" is as relevant now as it was when those words were written but acquires an even greater emphasis as accountability acquires an even harder edge. International competition is no less unforgiving 5 years on but it has, in the intervening years, "benefitted" from the growing emphasis on, and sophistication of, quantitative comparative measures. With every annual OECD report, a worldwide sharing of intelligence among leading statisticians gives great weight and validity to measures which are then put to the service of governmental drives for accountability.

At the same time, successive OECD reports acknowledge the weaknesses within accountability measures and express concern as to the leverage on the individual school as a unit of change, and the nature of the accountability which this brings with it. "Education's powerful role does not mean that it can work alone. Reducing inequality also requires policies for housing, criminal justice, taxation and health care to work hand in hand with education to make a lasting difference" (OECD, 2016, p. 10). In Scotland, the government argues that "while schools have an important role in closing the attainment gap, what they contribute is only one aspect of the multi-dimensional efforts across various organisations, policies and practices" (Marcus, 2016, in Mowat, 2017, p. 17).

A range of other commentators concerned about the failure in OECD documentation to relate educational equity to equity more broadly in society argue that schools cannot be expected to be accountable and address inequities in educational outcome without addressing structural inequalities (Bøyum, 2014). This does raise hope for a more sophisticated form of "intelligent accountability" in the future.

Conclusion

In this chapter, we have revisited the five informing principles of our LfL framework, arguing that together, they provide the centre of a platform for challenges to school policy. We add to that platform in the following chapter where we examine the nature of the challenges to democratic values and what it means to assert and maintain professional integrity. We suggest five essential principles, each of which contributes to creating a strong foundation – a "blueprint" for professional behaviours. These are moral purpose, curriculum breadth, the rights of the child, social justice, and inclusivity. These values find strong support in statements made by the United Nations about democracies, their processes, and the importance of overarching and all-embracing democratic values. What these mean, and how they may be observed in practice, we argue, needs not only to be addressed but also to be problematised with recognition of the challenging contexts in which teaching and learning must pursue the vital support needed to maintain clear moral purpose.

This requires what we refer to in Chapter 5 as "social capital", the progressive accumulation of professional assets which lay the groundwork for a shared "common wealth" of values-in-action. While these imply agency, choice, and initiative, how to maintain these in competition with strong cultural and political commitment to hierarchy may seem a long way off. When we see this less as resting on the individual, a more radical form of "conjoint agency" offers scope for leadership that is collective, collaborative, and participative.

In Chapter 6, we are brought back to the essential need to think differently. Each of the five principles described in this chapter requires a process of reframing, an "escape" from the conventions of classroom-bound learning, from the "steady drizzle of helplessness and hopelessness that can wear teachers down" (Weissbourd, 2003, p. 10) and constrain and narrow horizons for their students. In the words of the OECD, *school* and *classroom* do not offer a satisfactory architecture for framing learning environments, as these "construction sites" are essentially institutional and partial and too much time is given to documenting their intelligence or talents instead of developing them. We offer a counterpoint in the seven key evaluation criteria used in the out-of-school initiative of the Children's University – attitudes, ambition, aspiration, adventure, adaptability, advocacy, and agency. How well, we ask, do school and classroom practice measure up to these?

Enhancing teacher professionality, the theme of the seventh chapter, proposes an alternative to a training model. Rather than concentrating on outcomes and objectives, the focus is redirected to the nature of the processes through which teachers, both singly and collectively, develop their professional expertise. It is argued that an essentially technical approach to professional development fails to acknowledge the need to build teachers' capacity to lead and manage innovation and to have an active voice in change. It fails to understand or celebrate the nature and significance of "tacit professional knowledge" and the ways in which it is made explicit, shared, and developed in leading-edge schools, as international case studies illustrate.

The final chapter revisits the key issues that run through the previous seven chapters and the challenges they present to our thinking. It begins with the concept of "repurposing", an idea that goes beyond the continuous recycling of inert ideas and equally inert practices. It argues for a more discriminating reading of policy documents, the nature of the language, the choice of words, phrases, metaphors, and tacit ideologies that by their very nature advantage some and disadvantage others. As education becomes more widely accepted as a marketable commodity, the language of "service delivery" becomes worryingly commonplace. We argue for reasoned dissent, for the ability and capacity to challenge national, local, and school rhetoric and to consider ways in which teachers are able to create an alternative to the performativity agenda, and embrace principled pedagogy.

Note

1 http://www.educ.cam.ac.uk/centres/networks/cedir/

References

Bayetto, A. (2014). *Oral language.* Australian Primary Principals Association. Retrieved from https://www.appa.asn.au/wp-content/uploads/2015/08/Oral-Language-article.pdf

Berryman, M., & Bishop, R. (2011). Societal and cultural perspectives through a Te Kotahitanga lens. In C. M. Rubie-Davies (Ed.), *Educational psychology: Concepts, research and challenges* (pp. 249–267). London: Routledge.

Bøyum, S. (2014). Fairness in education – A normative analysis of OECD policy documents. *Journal of Education Policy, 29*(6), 856–870.

Carson, J. B, Tesluk, P. E., & Marrone, J. A. (2007). Shared leadership in team: An investigation of antecedent conditions and performance. *Academy of Management Journal, 50*(5), 1217–1234.

Danielson, C. (2009). *Talk about teaching: Leading professional conversations.* Thousand Oaks, CA: Corwin Press.

Dempster, N., Konza, D., Robson, G., Gaffney, M., Lock, G., & McKennariey, K. (2012). *Principals as literacy leaders: Confident, credible and connected.* Kingston, ACT: Australian Primary Principals Association.

Dempster, N., Townsend, T., Johnson, G., Bayetto, A., Lovett, S., & Stevens, E. (2017). *Leadership and literacy: Principals, partnerships and pathways to improvement.* Cham, Switzerland: Springer.

Dempster, N., & MacBeath, J. (Eds.) (2009). *Connecting leadership and learning: Principles for practice.* London: Routledge.

Earl, L., & Timperley, H. (Eds.) (2009). *Professional learning conversations. Challenges in using evidence for improvement.* New York: Springer.

Elmore, R. (2000). *Building a new structure for school leadership.* Washington DC: Albert Shanker Institute.

Ghana Education Service (GES). (2010). *Headteachers' handbook.* Accra: GES.

Ghana Education Service (GES). (2014). *Leadership for learning: A manual/handbook for headteachers and circuit supervisors.* Accra: GES, Teacher Education Division.

Hallinger, P. (2011). Leadership for learning: Lessons from 40 years of empirical research. *Journal of Educational Administration, 49*(2), 125–142.

Hunzicher, J. (2012). Professional development and job-embedded collaboration: How teachers learn to exercise leadership. *Professional Development in Education, 38*(2), 267–289.

Javed, U. (2013). *Leadership for learning: A case study in six public and private schools of Pakistan.* Unpublished PhD Thesis, Birmingham: University of Birmingham.

Johnson, G., Dempster, N., McKenzie, L., Klieve, H., Flückiger, B., Lovett, S., Riley, T., & Webster, A. (2014). *Principals as literacy leaders with Indigenous communities: Leadership for learning to read – "Both ways".* Canberra: The Australian Primary Principals Association.

Knapp, M., Copland, M. A., & Talbert, J. E. (2003). *Leading for learning: Reflective tools for school and district leaders*. Seattle, WA: Center for the Study of Teaching & Policy, University of Washington.

Lizzio, A., Dempster, N., & Neumann, R. (2011). Pathways to formal and informal student leadership: The influence of peer and teacher-student relationships and level of school identification on students' motivations. *International Journal of Leadership in Education*, *14*(1), 85–102.

MacBeath, J. (2001). Letter to academic staff in the School of Education and Homerton College, 6 July.

MacBeath, J. (2014). *Report of the impact study on the implementation of the 2nd cycle of the School Development and Accountability Framework on Enhancing School Development in Hong Kong*. Hong Kong: Education Bureau, Quality Assurance and School-based Support Division.

MacBeath, J., & Dempster, N. (Eds.) (2009). *Connecting leadership and learning: Principles for Practice*. London: Routledge.

MacBeath, J., Frost, D., & Swaffield, S. (2005). Researching leadership for learning in seven countries (The Carpe Vitam Project). *Education Research & Perspectives*, *32*(2), 24–42.

MacBeath, J., & Swaffield, S., with Oduro, G., & Hassler, B. (2016a). *Leadership for learning: Handbook for facilitators*. T-TEL Professional Development Programme. Theme 6: Leadership for Learning (Handbook for Facilitators). Published by the Ministry of Education (Ghana), under Creative Commons Attribution- ShareAlike 4.0 International. Available online at http://oer.t-tel.org. Version 1, December 2016.

MacBeath, J., & Swaffield, S., with Oduro, G., & Hassler, B. (2016b). *Leadership for learning: Handbook for PD coordinators*. T-TEL Professional Development Programme. Theme 6: Leadership for Learning (Handbook for PD Coordinators). Published by the Ministry of Education (Ghana), under Creative Commons Attribution- ShareAlike 4.0 International. Available online at http://oer.t-tel.org. Version 1, November 2016.

MacBeath, J., & Swaffield, S., with Oduro, G., & Hassler, B. (2016c). *Leadership for learning: Professional development guide for tutors*. T-TEL Professional Development Programme. Theme 6: Leadership for Learning (Professional Development Guide for Tutors). Published by the Ministry of Education (Ghana), under Creative Commons Attribution- ShareAlike 4.0 International. Available online at http://oer.t-tel.org. Version 1, December 2016.

Mowat, J. G. (2017). Closing the attainment gap – A realistic proposition or an elusive pipe-dream? *Journal of Education Policy*, *33*(2), 299–321.

Oduro, G. (2008). Promoting learning in Ghanaian primary schools: The context of leadership and gender role stereotypes. In J. MacBeath & Y. C. Cheng (Eds.), *Leadership for learning: International perspectives* (pp. 137–152). Rotterdam: Sense.

Oduro, G. K. T., & Bosu, R. (2010). Leadership and management of change for quality improvement. *EdQual Policy Briefs, September*. Retrieved from www.edqual.org/publications/policy.briefs/p65.pdf

OECD (Organisation for Economic Co-operation and Development). (2016). *Trends shaping education spotlight 8: Mind the gap: Inequity in education*. Paris: OECD Centre for Educational Research and Innovation.

Portin, B. S. (2009). Cross-national professional learning for school leaders. *International Journal of Leadership in Education: Theory and Practice*, *12*(3), 239–252.

Raelin, J. A. (2003). *Creating leaderful organizations: How to bring out leadership in everyone*. San Francisco, CA: Berrett-Koehler.

Robinson, V., & Timperley, H. (2007). The leadership of the improvement of teaching and learning: Lessons from initiatives with positive outcomes for students. *Australian Journal of Education*, *51*(3), 247–262.

Stobart, G. (2008). *Testing times: The uses and abuses of assessment*. London: Routledge.

Swaffield, S. (2006). Scaffolding discourse in multi-national collaborative enquiry: The Carpe Vitam Leadership for Learning Project. *Leading and Managing, 12(2)*, 10–18.

Swaffield, S., & Dempster, N. (2009). A learning dialogue (principle 3). In J. MacBeath & N. Dempster (Eds.), *Connecting leadership and learning: Principles for practice* (pp. 106–120). London: Routledge.

Swaffield, S., Dempster, N., Frost, D., & MacBeath, J. (Eds.) (2014). Leadership for learning travels. *Inform No. 17.* Cambridge: University of Cambridge, Faculty of Education.

Thomson, S., De Bortoli, L., & Underwood, C. (2017). PISA 2015: Reporting Australia's results. Retrieved from http://research.acer.edu.au/ozpisa/22

Timperley, H. (2015). *Professional conversations and improvement focused feedback: A review of the research literature and the impact on practice and student outcomes.* Prepared for the Australian Institute for Teaching and School Leadership, AITSL, Melbourne.

Townsend, T, Dempster, N., Johnson, G., Bayetto, A. & Stevens, E. (2015). *Leadership with a purpose: A report on five case studies of Principals as Literacy Leaders (PALL) schools (Tasmania).* Unpublished report, Griffith Institute for Educational Research, Griffith University, Brisbane, Queensland.

Tuckman, B. W. (1965). Developmental sequences in small groups. *Psychological Bulletin, 63*, 384–399.

UNESCO, (1996). *The treasure within* (The Delors Report). Report to UNESCO of the International Commission on Education for the Twenty-First Century. Paris: UNESCO Publishing.

Weissbourd, R. (2003). Moral teachers, moral students. *Creating Caring Schools, 60*(6), 6–11.

4

PROFESSIONAL INTEGRITY

In the previous chapter, we explored three framing values which inform leadership for learning – moral purpose, professional integrity, and critical friendship. These three values are consistent with those held by many professions in democratic countries. Indeed, they find strong support in statements made by the United Nations about democracies, their processes, and the importance of overarching and all-embracing democratic values. What these mean, how they are interpreted, and how they are observed by educators within a constantly evolving global context needs to be both addressed and problematised. The multi-country *Carpe Vitam* Project (MacBeath & Dempster, 2009) gave us a starting point for exploring widely differing cultural and political contexts from Austria to Australia, and the confidence to assert a bedrock of educational values which we hold to be sacrosanct. At the core of our common commitment is a sense of moral purpose which can neither be advocated nor observed without a strong sense of professional integrity. In a highly demanding and competitive policy climate, it is challenging for teachers and senior leaders to hold to these without the third member of the triad – critical friendship. With the benefit of a critical friend we may be continuously reminded that as education professionals we work in an accountability context, at the root of which are the rights of the child. As such we are constantly drawn back to essential educational processes – teaching, learning, and leadership as activities suffused with, and exemplified by, a clear moral purpose.

In this chapter, we draw attention to five essential elements of professional integrity which lie at the core of teaching in contemporary education systems so often subject to testing pressures in the present political and policy environment. The five elements are interrelated by their commitment to leadership for learning (LfL), each firmly grounded in essential principles – moral purpose and professional integrity, curriculum breadth, the rights of the child, and social justice. In the following discussion, we suggest that these elements provide the blueprint for professional behaviours which are worth advocating vigorously, implementing courageously, and defending tirelessly, no matter the shifting policy sands.

Moral purpose

To what extent is moral purpose in the foreground of government policies? Exemplified in teaching or learning objectives? In curriculum, lesson planning, assessment, and evaluation? In professional development activities? In targets and in accountability measures? Perhaps the conspicuous absence of moral purpose in school, local authority, and government documents is because it is taken as implicit in day-to-day practice, or left to ritual school assemblies, or in Cinderella "subjects" which deal explicitly with religious and moral education.

Although not always recognised as such, and too easily forgotten, education is essentially about the moral development of children and young people. So says Gerald Grace in his classic text *Beyond Education Management* (1995). In his critique of "value-added" language he argues that such terminology has little to do with a values discourse, and more to do with attainment. The educator's moral purpose has a broader reach. In a nutshell: "For school leaders and the profession as a whole, the moral purpose is to enhance the lives and life chances of children and young people through learning" (p. 5).

In his discussion of moral leadership, Michael Fullan (2001) has argued that exhortation in the classroom as to a school's moral purpose is virtually futile without approaches at wider systemic levels. He identifies five interrelated levels at which issues need to be conceived and addressed: individual, classroom, school, regional, and societal levels. In each of these instances, moral purpose relies on mutual respect, integrity, and trust, and is difficult to achieve (but potentially achievable) within asymmetric power relationships. When it comes to the discussion of professional integrity we gain a deeper insight into the unbreakable nexus among them.

Professional integrity

Professional integrity and moral leadership are inseparable and embedded in the second *Carpe Vitam* LfL framing value. As with moral leadership, this can be taken as implicit; nonetheless, it is essential to emphasise because (a) in our view there has been an insidious undermining of professional integrity since the move to New Public Management, with competitive measures coming to dominate educational policy and practice from the late 1980s on; (b) the broader purposes of education have been narrowing as a result of national and international competition, placing ever-increasing pressure on practices which, in the view of most in the profession, are essential; and (c) the "scripting" and delineation of curriculum has been reducing the capacity of principals and teachers to make professional judgements about the best course of action in particular circumstances which are relevant to a diverse student body.

As it is with lawyers, doctors, and social workers amongst others, professional integrity is manifested and tested through the exercise of professional discretion in decisions taken by teachers. Decision-making is guided primarily by what is to the benefit of clients. When integrity prevails, self-interest is relegated to a back seat, replaced by the interests of those being served. Integrity is upheld when personal interest is put aside so that the interests of those to whom we are accountable occupy centre stage. Professional discretion is evident when no obvious course of action is apparent and decisions about specific actions are taken from among a range of possible alternatives. Given these potential options, acting "in the best interests of clients" is open to interpretation and subject to close scrutiny and contention. The touchstone must, however, be the moral purpose served.

A key test of professional integrity internationally is in relation to the increasing prevalence of high-stakes testing. There is a substantial body of professional opinion internationally that a reliance on compulsory testing has contributed to a narrowing of the curriculum, constraining learning opportunities, reducing ambition, and creating greater institutional dependence. This is an argument made in the 2009 Australian Primary Principals' Association Report on nationally comparable school performance data.

> Schools tend to narrow their curriculum around the focus of the tests, the importance of areas of the curriculum that are not assessed is diminished, higher order skills that are not able to be tested decline, large amounts of valuable instructional time are consumed by coaching and practising tests, a testing industry grows which is driven by its own commercial interests and authorities and schools are encouraged to participate in various forms of "gaming" designed to improve performance.
>
> *(p. 2)*

In England, the National Union of Teachers 2015 survey of its members (Galton & MacBeath, 2015) reached very similar conclusions:

- 85% of teachers think that accountability measures are harming the self-esteem, confidence and mental health of pupils;
- 92% agree that accountability measures are reducing the time and quality of teacher-pupil interaction;
- 88% agree that they have less flexibility to respond to young people as individuals; and
- 71% considered that government policies were making it more difficult to include students with special education needs.

What stance can school leaders or teachers adopt when they believe testing and the accountability that accompanies it are de-motivating and inimical to learning? While unequivocal as to their accountability to students and parents for test results, teachers speak candidly of the challenge of adopting more authentic and all-embracing forms of accountability. In the face of these demanding issues, the onus is on senior leaders together with teachers to find ways which both lead and manage a learning agenda, one that will meet that challenge. It is this task, so apparently simple yet so complex to address, that underpins our discussion of professional integrity and its links with a clear moral purpose.

We suggest that in the current political climate, the educator's moral purpose must be the locus for decisions and actions and that these should be guided by a robust sense of professional integrity. We refer again to the inherent professional dilemma raised by Karen Seashore Louis (2003):

> Many contemporary democratic theorists argue that the most essential element of democratic communities today is their ability to engage in civilized but semi-permanent disagreement. Articulating a humanist voice that calls for respecting and listening to all positions – but then being able to move forward in the absence of consensus – will be the critical skill that school leaders need to develop when the environment makes consensus impossible.
>
> *(Louis, 2003, p. 105)*

That educators should understand the need for "semi-permanent disagreement" with government policies they find limiting, puts professional decision-making under the harsh light of populist politics, sensationalist media, and often ill-informed public opinion. It implies a need to "move forward" with principled and defensible arguments in the face of contested views. It helps when the moral purpose of the decision-maker's profession is explicit, unambiguous, enduring, widely understood, and universally held. The moral purpose of a profession should make clear whose interests it serves and why this is so. By extension, decisions for moving forward should also make visible the costs and benefits to all involved in the education enterprise, raising challenging questions as to the failure to serve with integrity. What does it mean, and for whom, if we fail to challenge the policy status quo? Rising to this challenge requires a bringing together of the educator's moral purpose and what we understand by the concept of integrity.

In conceptualising a "practical theory" of LfL, the team explicated the long-held view that leadership work should be driven by a moral purpose affecting all children and adults in their care (MacBeath, Frost, Swaffield, & Waterhouse, 2006). However, to a large extent, that moral purpose has become lost in the strictures placed on schools by contemporary test-driven policies.

Test-driven narrowness versus a broad education

In relation to testing and accountability protocols, school and local authority personnel could be forgiven for taking a negative stance with regard to the international educational policy environment and much of the body of research it has generated. The reality is that schools today seem certain to face a hard-edged, competitive, test-driven environment well beyond the present decade. As education is, on the one hand, a personal commitment, it is also a political process and for those who lead and those who are led, these two realities have to be understood and addressed. The personal aspect is revealed in the words of a "Grumpy Old Grandfather", writing to an Australian Senate inquiry into the effects of the National Assessment Program in Literacy and Numeracy (NAPLAN). He comments on the constraining impact of testing and the demeaning effects of school results reported on the Australian *MySchool* website in the open public domain. His lament is palpable:

> My grandchildren will be denied the chance to explore newer and broader ways of developing idiosyncratic processes of learning. If they were encouraged to develop their natural love for learning and taught the beauty behind mathematics, language and science with vigour but without threat, as part of the obvious essentials of schooling, I would have more faith in the system. I had hoped – but now pray – to see them develop as happy, contented human beings.
>
> *(Cullen, 2010)*

The views of this grumpy old grandfather find support in the Cambridge review of primary education in the United Kingdom, probably the most influential review of this stage of education for a generation.

> As children move through the primary phase, their statutory entitlement to a broad education is increasingly but needlessly compromised by a "standards" agenda which combines high-stakes testing and the national strategies' exclusive focus on literacy and numeracy.
>
> *(Alexander et al., 2009, p. 22)*

The aspiration of the statutory entitlement referred to above from England and Wales is repeated in the words of the Australian Government's Melbourne Declaration (Ministerial Council for Education, Early Childhood Development and Youth Affairs [MCEECDYA], 2008) on Educational Goals for Young Australians, a national statement agreed by state and territory governments and confirmed by the Australian Federal Government – all pointing to the need for breadth in children's and young people's education:

> As a nation, Australia values the central role of education in building a democratic, equitable and just society – a society that is prosperous, cohesive and culturally diverse, and that values Australia's Indigenous cultures as a key part of the nation's history, present and future.

Likewise, in Scotland, the breadth considered essential for an educated society is spelt out in its Curriculum for Excellence as four capacities:

> The purpose of the curriculum is encapsulated in the four capacities – to enable each child or young person to be a successful learner, a confident individual, a responsible citizen and an effective contributor.

> The curriculum aims to ensure that all children and young people in Scotland develop the knowledge, skills and attributes they will need if they are to flourish in life, learning and work, now and in the future.
>
> *(The Scottish Education Office, 2016)*

When he takes his granddaughter to school, the "grumpy" grandparent referred to earlier will naturally hope that the principal and teachers will attend to the breadth of her learning needs. He may, perhaps with unwarranted optimism, hope that teachers will take her side as the priority and not the side dictated by a constricting state agenda. However, given that headteachers/principals and teachers are, for the most part, employees of education systems funded by governments, they are, to quote a colloquial phrase, "caught between a rock and a hard place". In an era when compliance appears to trump resistance, it is impossible for principals, held accountable for school performance, to ignore the measures by which they and their schools are judged. Their professional integrity is constantly under pressure in this environment. They know that society depends on a broadly well-educated citizenry and that they are amongst the primary guardians of this understanding. Hence the importance we attach to professional integrity in defence of the moral purpose of education.

To this point in the chapter, we have suggested that two related matters of principle are tied together as underpinnings to the professional integrity of educators. First, advocating that the moral purpose of education (improving the life chances of children through learning) is the default position to which all decisions about professional practice should be referenced; and second, advocating that a broad education for all must be the "staple diet" of schools. Moral purpose and professional integrity are also closely tied to the inalienable rights of the child – the most relevant expression of human rights applicable to schooling and individual school experience.

The rights of the child, moral purpose, and professional integrity

The moral purpose of educators is enshrined in the UN Convention on the Rights of the Child (Human Rights, Office of the High Commissioner, 1990) which carries a series of implications for professional practice. Its 54 articles raise contentious notions for some, especially in a context where teachers complain that they themselves have few "rights". Take the second article of the convention for example:

> Article 2
> Parties shall take all appropriate measures to ensure that the child is protected against all forms of discrimination or punishment on the basis of the status, activities, expressed opinions, or beliefs of the child's parents, legal guardians, or family members.

This article sets out a challenging set of behavioural standards, most especially in countries with long-established traditions of corporal punishment and intolerance of difference. So embedded are these in some places that children themselves regard it as a part of their implicit "contract with the teacher".

> Sir, if they don't punish us we will not behave.
>
> *(12-year-old, Ghana)*

Children's rights and freedoms are further developed in the 13th Article which extends the right of self-expression within a broad curriculum with an emphasis on the right to choose. And the 29th Article, paying attention to and encouraging diversity of personalities and talents, is for many teachers a tall order in highly challenging circumstances.

> Article 13
> The child shall have the right to freedom of expression; this right shall include freedom to seek, receive and impart information and ideas of all kinds, regardless of frontiers, either orally, in writing or in print, in the form of art, or through any other media of the child's choice.

> Article 29
> Parties agree that the education of the child shall be directed to: (a) The development of the child's personality, talents and mental and physical abilities to their fullest potential ...

The rights of children with special needs defined in Article 23 not only raise the bar extremely high in disadvantaged communities but even in so-called "developed" countries such as the United Kingdom where this article is observed frequently in the breach (Galton & MacBeath, 2015).

> Article 23
> Parties recognize that a mentally or physically disabled child should enjoy a full and decent life, in conditions which ensure dignity, promote self-reliance and facilitate the child's active participation in the community.

However challenging these rights are, very often, and perhaps in the majority of circumstances, they are aspirational. They help to define what we may understand as an informing ethos for professional integrity and how it may be expressed. When involved in professional development dialogue with colleagues and critical friends, Ghanaian teachers and headteachers commented:

> I met them and told them and they said, "Master, look at how these children are behaving". I told them you have to sit down with them and talk with them. It's a matter of dialoguing with them because they actually don't know what they are doing.
> If we are trying to create a conducive environment for the children, the environment should not be a threatening one. Some of them are so afraid that

when the teacher lifts it [the cane] their minds go away and whatever you teach, they are looking at the cane and will not try to contribute to anything just because if perchance the answer is wrong, they will be caned.

Deeply embedded in discussions around punishment and rights are words such as "justice" and "fairness". Justice may be seen to be administered in retribution for perceived wrongdoing, of for restoring order and stability. This does not necessarily imply that retributive behaviour is fair or just. Among the many meanings of *just* commonly offered are "ethical" and "moral", which may require what David Hargreaves described in a talk to Cambridge students as "swimming upstream", against convention and conventional wisdom, against the current of policy priorities.

Rawls (1971) defines the "social" imperative as assuring the protection of equal access to liberties, rights, and opportunities, as well as taking care of the least advantaged members of society. Thus, whether something is just or unjust depends on whether it promotes or hinders equality of access to civil liberties, human rights, or opportunities for healthy and fulfilling lives, as well as whether it allocates a fair share of benefits to the least advantaged members of society. To this we might add, in an educational or school context, access to what is sometimes described as the school "offer", an ironic counterpoint to "prescription". This is a moral as well as a logistical issue, making access to, and the allocation of, a fair share of benefits, a procedural imperative – challenging leaders' own priorities in a highly politicised climate.

In practical terms, what might this imply for school leaders? It involves:

- creating and sustaining a professional dialogue around values and priorities;
- embedding an ongoing self-evaluation which is "testing" of practice on a daily basis and how it aligns with professional and moral imperatives;
- revisiting the nature and impact of rewards and sanctions, created through conversations and negotiated protocols with teachers and young people; and
- a commitment to learning the meanings and impact of "disability" and "inclusion" and what this implies in ensuring access to learning for all.

Conditions such as these are reinforced for children in Articles 3, 28, and 29 of the UN Convention on the Rights of the Child (Human Rights, Office of the High Commissioner, 1990) reiterating the primacy of the educator's moral purpose, going to the root of what we understand by professional integrity.

Article 3
In all actions concerning children, whether undertaken by public or private social welfare institutions, courts of law, administrative authorities or legislative bodies, the best interests of the child shall be a primary consideration.

These rights speak not only to teachers, but to children as well, as demonstrated clearly in the following three "child-friendly" versions (UNICEF, 1990):

> All adults should do what is best for you. When adults make decisions, they should think about how their decisions will affect children.

Making decisions in the best interests of children means adults putting aside their own interests, requiring them to exercise professional discretion in response to the diversity of children's situations, as reiterated in Article 28:

> You have the right to a good quality education. You should be encouraged to go to school to the highest level you can.

The words "a good quality education" have been watchwords for philosophers, politicians, and parents from different countries and cultures over the centuries; however, what may have been a good quality education at one point in time is unlikely to be considered so at another. The Australian Government's (2008) Melbourne Declaration referred to earlier is a contemporary example of the intent of these words, a nation's public position on the kind of education it wants for its children and young people. In an age where there is more global movement of people than at any other time in history, when nation states are dealing with an unprecedented influx of migrants and refugees, providing a good quality education for increasingly diverse populations tests the resolve of those in positions of power. Providing breadth and embracing all will be two of the issues at the heart of a good quality education. In this kind of demographic environment, the social justice underpinnings of professional integrity come starkly into the spotlight.

Article 29 addresses the student's rights but also responsibilities:

> Your education should help you use and develop your talents and abilities. It should also help you learn to live peacefully, protect the environment and respect other people.

While we acknowledge that literacy and numeracy skills are essential for the citizens of today's world, they are not the only skills. So-called "hard" and "soft" skills are required, again pointing to the need for a broad education if the development of individual talents and abilities is to prevail. Article 29 indicates that there are cultural understandings, social skills, and environmental sensitivities to be learnt and applied if peaceful and respectful coexistence is to be realised wherever people make their home in the world.

Taken together, the articles highlighted from the Rights of the Child direct our attention to matters of social justice and their impact in shaping the nature of professional integrity for school leaders and teachers. In a very real sense, the professionalism of educators relies on altruistic practices focused on students and the learning they need in the certainty of an uncertain future. It is worth noting an underlying principle, voiced in Article 18, that as far as is possible, states should recognise that "Parents or ... legal guardians, have the primary responsibility for the upbringing and development of the child". The significance of this statement lies in the assertion that professional integrity must ensure that parents and carers are afforded opportunities to contribute to the education of their children throughout their developmental years.

Our concentration on human rights and the Rights of the Child is consistent with a strong belief in the power of democratic values as the informing source for professional integrity. As defined by the United Nations declaration, democratic practices come to life and are exemplified in dignity, responsibility, respect, justice, and care – values intrinsic to human rights in general, and, in relation to which, teachers are expected to take a determined stand. The right to life, liberty, freedom from slavery and torture, freedom of expression, and the right to education and work are the categorical imperatives in all just human societies, regardless of race, gender, nationality, ethnicity, language, religion, or status. In short, as the UN states: "Everyone is entitled to these rights, without discrimination". The professional integrity of educators provides the agency through which these rights, and the particular rights of the child to which we have referred, can be achieved.

These categorical imperatives and the entitlement of students, teachers, and parents to human rights *without discrimination* "test" our view of, and commitment to, social justice as a further cornerstone of professional integrity.

Social justice dimensions as a further test for professional integrity in education

Two well-known theorists concerned with issues of social justice in modern economies, Nancy Fraser and Amartya Sen, suggest a framework against which professional integrity may be assessed. In her 2007 work, Fraser outlines three dimensions and a number of associated processes addressing injustice, while Sen (1992) writes about the importance of the "capability to function" in an individual's life experience. It is an arresting phrase as it draws attention to something that we would be very unlikely to question but that can be all too real when children, or adults, feel disempowered and are prone to question their own capabilities.

Fraser's (2007) three dimensions of injustice are socioeconomic, cultural, and political, all of which may be evident in a country's social structures and practices. She argues that each needs to be addressed directly if social justice is to be achieved. To do so, she attaches a series of operational processes to each dimension as follows:

Socioeconomic injustice requires *redistribution* processes. Operationally, redistribution processes focus on access to aspects of the human condition such as material welfare (e.g., housing quality, health care, community environment, education, sport, recreation, and cultural pursuits), standard of living, wealth and income, and employment/career opportunities. Cultural justice requires *recognition* processes which draw attention to the ways in which the cultures of people and their communities (their lifeworlds) are valued, in common with others in the larger community. Addressing political injustice requires *representative* processes which emphasise power and decision-making, and open up wider opportunities for participation in policy-making procedures.

For Fraser (2007), these three operational processes signal the need for an overarching principle. This she calls the *parity of participation* principle. In her own words: "Justice requires social arrangements that permit all to participate as peers in social life" (p. 60). Gilbert, Keddie, Lindgard, Mills, and Renshaw (2013) underscore the importance of this principle, arguing that the three processes – redistribution, recognition, and representation – are the means by which access to equitable processes and outcomes may be realised, but only if and when parity of participation prevails. This principle lies at the core of democratic values, the starting point for the *Carpe Vitam* Project. The power of participation for all those engaged in the learning enterprise brings us back to the ancient maxim, *nihil de nobis, sine nobis* (nothing about us without us). With this as pre-eminent and explicit, democratic participation and partnerships enable all voices to be heard and action to be forged through negotiated agreement.

Fraser's (2007) dimensions and processes echo Sen's work (1992) on social justice. Of particular importance to Sen is the balance between an individual's right to make decisions about his or her own life and the social arrangements which enable people to have real choices irrespective of the particular culture or social grouping into which they may have been born (Gilbert et al., 2013), what has been referred to as the capability to function in the social setting in which people live out their lives (Sen, 1992). Gilbert et al. (2013) argue that the relevance of this for social justice in education is quite clear. If it were possible to identify the essential capabilities which would give people the widest repertoire of abilities to function effectively and maximise their well-being, then it follows that a key role for education is to create opportunities which develop these capabilities. The questions posed below may act as a test for professional integrity as they pinpoint social justice issues which arise during curriculum project and program design and implementation.

Testing integrity questions for school leaders implementing projects and programs

Processes of redistribution, recognition, and representation, and the parity of participation principle as described by Fraser (2007), together with Sen's (1992) concept of the capability to function, suggest a list of questions. These may be used to "test" the professional integrity of educators responsible for the design, development, and implementation of projects and programs for schools and the students within them, together with parents, carers, and other advocates of children's rights.

Redistribution

- Do health and welfare concerns figure in the program's responses to student needs?
- Is the program inclusive of all?
- Are learning resources clearly directed towards students with identified needs?
- Does the program address and include minority cultural knowledge?
- Does the program privilege only mainstream cultural knowledge?

Recognition

- Is the student's cultural lifeworld visibly valued within the program?
- Is the lifeworld incorporated in the program's curriculum?
- Are the necessary capabilities to function in the social setting included in the curriculum?
- Does the approach to pedagogy acknowledge students' paths to learning, their cultural and community backgrounds?
- Is assessment attuned to students' cultural and community experience and future needs?

Representation

- Does the program involve teachers in decision-making about policy, procedures, and resource allocation?
- Are parents involved in decision-making about policy, procedures, and resource allocation?
- Does the program involve students in decision-making about curriculum, pedagogy, and assessment?

Parity of participation

- To what extent does the program seek out the voices of minorities?
- To what extent does the program give these voices equal weight with those of majorities?
- Are equal representative processes in place in the program's implementation?
- Is leadership shared amongst participants, beyond formal leadership positions?
- Does the program make (infra)structural arrangements for the equal participation of all groups?

Assuming that there is an uncompromising allegiance to the moral purpose centred on the student and a commitment to pedagogical and curriculum breadth, the above questions go a long way towards shaping an agenda which may test the professional integrity of principals and teachers. The questions come sharply into focus as teachers and senior leaders (re)design and implement school programs in a variety of settings. To what extent then, have some or all of these questions been addressed in the LfL projects in which we have been involved over the past two decades? The following cross-examination of two cases tests their allegiance to the key issues of professional integrity discussed above.

Two illustrative international Leadership for Learning cases

In order to provide sufficient information to make sense of our testing questions, we have drawn on cases describing leadership development programs in Ghana and

Australia. Each account is followed by judgements of the nature of the responses made by educators to the issues the questions raise.

The Leadership for Learning Ghana program

Background

Present-day Ghana gained independence in 1957 following five centuries of European rule and influence principally by Portugal, Denmark, the Netherlands, and latterly, Britain. The right to schooling was a priority immediately following independence, but many years of political instability hindered progress and free compulsory primary education was not introduced until 2005. The intertwined legacies of traditional Indigenous community values and practices, colonisation, post-independence political changes and development, global commercial and social influences, and international aid create a highly complex situation for current education provision (see MacBeath & Swaffield, 2013; Swaffield, 2017 for fuller discussion).

As with other developing countries in sub-Saharan Africa, it has been the norm in Ghana for headteachers to be appointed on the basis of seniority and teaching service. Research conducted in the first decade of the 21st century showed preparation for taking up the post to be very limited (Zame, Hope, & Respress, 2008), and typically heads had less than a week's training for their role (Oduro, 2010). The Ministry of Education published a *Headteachers' Handbook* in 1994 setting out both management and leadership proficiencies necessary for the smooth running of the school and for improving the quality of learning, yet in practice Zame and colleagues found that "Head teachers of basic schools are involved in management and administrative behaviors to the exclusion of leadership behaviors" (2008, p. 126). This echos Oduro's findings 5 years earlier.

This then was the context and rationale for the LfL Ghana program, a collaboration among the Institute for Educational Planning and Administration (IEPA) at the University of Cape Coast in Ghana, the Ghana Education Service (GES), and the University of Cambridge. It was instigated in 2008 by the Ghanaian Director of the IEPA, George Oduro, who proposed using the LfL framework and principles (MacBeath & Dempster, 2009) as the basis for building headteachers' leadership capacity to enhance quality teaching and learning in Ghanaian basic schools (more fully described in MacBeath & Swaffield with Oduro & Hassler, 2016a, b, c; Swaffield, 2017).

The program

A group of 15 Ghanaian professional development leaders (PDLs) – university and college lecturers, GES training officers, and a headteacher – were initially introduced to the LfL framework, working with the Cambridge team to contextualise the LfL principles. They then helped plan and lead a residential course for the initial cohort of 124 headteachers, introducing them to the program. These heads had been selected in pairs, a male and female from the same local area, and from all 10 regions across the country. They came together for 3 weeks in August 2009, then returning to their schools to begin putting the LfL principles into practice, reassembling for 2 weeks in April 2010 to share and review developments. Meantime, the PDLs and Cambridge team also ran workshops for the GES circuit supervisors (the heads' immediate supervisors) and for district training officers, as well as for district, divisional, regional, and national directors of education. There was another opportunity for the initial cohort of headteachers and their circuit supervisors to come together again and work with the PDLs and the Cambridge team in November 2011; by this time a significant number had been promoted or moved school or circuit, often explicitly to extend the take-up of LfL.

A real groundswell of enthusiasm and activity developed, with PDLs, headteachers, GES officials, and a full-time coordinator promoting the LfL principles through both formal and informal means. It was estimated that by 2013 over 3,000 headteachers had been introduced to LfL. The GES adopted the LfL five principles as official policy for all its 18,000 plus kindergarten, primary, and junior-high schools, revising their headteachers' handbook to include LfL (Ministry of Education, 2010), and subsequently producing a separate 100-page guidance manual demonstrating how each of the principles could be put into practice in Ghanaian classrooms (GES, 2014). Whenever the Cambridge team has been able to secure funding they have also provided or facilitated additional forms of support, for example newsletters, weekly text messages (Swaffield, Jull, & Ampah-Mensah, 2013), a handheld LfL aide memoire ("the fan"), a MOOC, and most recently, a suite of handbooks for use in colleges of education with trainee teachers and their tutors. These examples of additional assistance are evidence of Cambridge's continued interest in and support of the work in Ghana, but LfL and its future in Ghana is, and always has been, in the hands of the Ghanaian partners.

Outcomes

The LfL Ghana program is best described as collaborative development and research. Research has always been integral to activities led by the Cambridge team, with ongoing findings used to shape and feed into workshops. Data, gathered predominantly through questionnaires, interviews, and documentation, provided the stimuli for these professional learning activities. An orthodox intervention study with pre- and post-measurement was inappropriate as the "intervention" itself evolved iteratively, shaped by partners and participants through their formative input. The process was aligned with the LfL values and framework and encouraged participants to take the initiative, devising context-specific approaches to putting the principles into practice. It was important that headteachers in particular felt able to try things out and to act in new ways without fear of professional sanctions. Risk taking in learning and teaching were encouraged by the open-ended, collegial nature of the program, and in the absence of predetermined measures or standards to be met.

The first two aims of the program were to strengthen the leadership capacity of headteachers of basic schools in Ghana, and to improve the quality of learning through school/classroom leadership. Research findings (Jull, Swaffield, & MacBeath, 2014; MacBeath & Swaffield, 2011; Malakolunthu, MacBeath, & Swaffield, 2014) point to impact in both of these areas, particularly in terms of:

- headteachers' knowledge, attitudes, and behaviour;
- teachers' professionalism;
- pedagogical practices;
- pupil attendance and engagement;
- pupil attainment, especially in reading;
- parental and community involvement; and
- school environment and learning opportunities.

Selected specific examples concerning leadership and learning from the research data are described in the following section.

The third and final aim of the program was to influence policymakers to make leadership development a condition for appointing headteachers of basic schools. This policy aim has not been realised, at least not as yet, but the early adoption of LfL as national policy as demonstrated through the two handbooks produced by the Ministry of Education (2010) and GES (2014) was very encouraging and a significant indicator of impact.

Redistribution, recognition, representation, parity of participation

Reflecting on the LfL Ghana program with reference to the issues and questions based on the work of Sen (1992), Fraser (2007), and Gilbert et al. (2013), the overall general impression is of some positive points and others that would benefit from greater attention, with considerable room for further improvement overall.

In relation to redistribution, health and welfare concerns align with the second LfL principle – conditions for learning, of immediate relevance to a school's physical environment. Program participants reported securing the water supply so essential for hygiene, tree planting to provide shelter from sun and rain, and scrub clearance to reduce the likely presence of dangerous snakes. Some headteachers helped particularly needy pupils in very practical ways such as by giving them a bar of soap. Heads and teachers also made allowances for, and gave extra help to, children who arrived at school late and tired after walking many miles to school, or having been fishing early in the morning to earn extra money for the family. One headteacher went to extraordinary lengths on behalf of a young teenage girl, persuading her father not to marry her off in exchange for some cattle but to let her continue her education.

Ghanaian schools are typically very poorly resourced indeed, a situation quite a number of LfL headteachers attempted to remedy, to some extent, making considerable efforts to procure additional resources. There were examples of creative approaches such as hanging sheets of text from trees for children to read and discuss outside the classroom. The inclusive aspect of redistribution was clearly visible in a number of ways: unlike many aid-related projects that focus their efforts on the capital, Accra, and the south of the country, the LfL Ghana program was spread equally throughout the whole country, with the leading-edge headteachers selected from all 10 regions. Nevertheless, minority cultural knowledge was not explicitly addressed.

Curriculum, pedagogy, and assessment were addressed in general terms through the application of LfL principles, and more specifically with reference to the GES LfL handbook of guidance for headteachers and circuit supervisors. This resource locates the LfL principles in specific cultural contexts and exemplifies them in classroom teaching and learning in Ghanaian basic schools. Some teachers acknowledged that their own behaviour towards students had changed from autocratic and punitive to caring, rewarding, and encouraging. The recognition of students' lifeworlds was not explicitly highlighted, although it came about as teachers and headteachers placed more emphasis on creating dialogue with pupils (LfL Principle 3) and gave consideration to the social, emotional, cognitive, and contextual aspects of learning (LfL Principle 1).

Representation was encouraged particularly through the fourth and fifth LfL principles – shared leadership and a shared sense of accountability. There was clear evidence that the LfL Project had brought about greater involvement and participation by teachers, students, parents, guardians, and other community members, although the nature and level of involvement could still be much improved. While some teachers assumed budgetary responsibility, for example, parental involvement could still be regarded as limited, despite evidence of significant progress. One headteacher commented,

> Every PTA meeting we talk about the measures, how they can help their kids. Parents may not be educated; at least, they can ask "What did you learn today at school?" This will show the kids that parents care for their education. This will promote learning. I also ensure that parents provide their kids with learning materials, pens, books, etc.
>
> *(Malakolunthu et al., 2014, p. 710)*

Parity of participation has already been mentioned in relation to the geographical representativeness of the initial group of headteachers. The 124 were also very deliberately selected to ensure gender parity through pairing of men of women, ensuring equal numbers and facilitating cross-gender dialogue. Similarly, the PDLs came from the far north and centre of the country as well as the south, and included women as well as men. The enactment of LfL Principles 4 and 5 relate to parity of participation as well as representation, so the sharing of leadership – for example with teachers, pupils, Parent Teacher Associations, and School Management Committees – was a major area of development.

While redistribution, recognition, representation, and the parity of participation frameworks are major achievements, less apparent is the huge influence of the values base of LfL and its critical emphasis on moral purpose. The dedication of individual headteachers was evident from the first residential workshop for which many had travelled long distances, leaving family and subsistence farming unattended. The discussions of moral purpose appeared to change attitudes, such that heads subsequently went to extraordinary lengths on behalf of their pupils and schools. One head has now for many years been keeping guard over his school at night in order to protect its meagre resources. Another, a woman headteacher who was battling to secure a water supply for her school in the face of threats and intimidation from a powerful village chief, finished relaying the situation by drawing herself up and defiantly declaring, "I am not a boot licker".

We now turn to the second of our cases to examine a leadership for literacy program in remote Indigenous school communities in Australia.

The Principals as Literacy Leaders with Indigenous Communities (PALLIC) Project

Background

Over the past two decades, Australian governments have invested in programs to strengthen the abilities of Indigenous children to speak and write Standard Australian English (SAE). The rationale is that literacy ability will have a positive influence on the well-being and life chances of Australia's current and future Indigenous generations. In political terms, this action points towards a state-based social justice agenda. Consistent with Sen's view (1992), improved literacy will strengthen Indigenous children's capability to function in contemporary society. It is well recognised that in Australia and elsewhere there is a parallel need for what Fraser (2007) has called redistribution of social capital. Many of Australia's Indigenous children live in substandard housing conditions, especially in remote and very remote areas, within large transient family groupings that have survived on welfare payments over multiple generations. Healthcare is sporadic. Neglect and abuse are facts of life for many and school attendance is often irregular for a variety of reasons. Most Indigenous elders and families are keen to support children's learning but economic, health, social, and financial realities are just some of the constraints they face. Current work in Australia is addressing this concern in partnership with government services and not-for-profit organisations through interventions based on a collective impact approach (Homel et al., 2016).

In terms of literacy education needs, many Australian Indigenous children come to school not speaking SAE and, when they begin to learn English, its use is confined to the classroom. Many Indigenous families speak various forms of English including creole, Aboriginal English, and pidgin. At the same time, many of Australia's Indigenous languages have been eroded, leaving many family groups without a sense of belonging to an ancestral tribal language or to the English language. There are many reasons for this, all connected in some form to hotly debated political decisions of the past. So, questions of moral purpose and professional integrity loom large when determining the actions to be taken by systems' personnel, university academics, and school leaders involved in planning new literacy programs for Indigenous children.

The program

The PALLIC Program involved 46 government administered schools across two Australian states (Queensland and South Australia) and the Northern Territory. More than half of the schools enrolled only Indigenous children. These schools were located in remote, and very remote, areas of Australia. The schools were selected by the respective education systems on the basis that the children enrolled were overly represented as performing below benchmarks on the NAPLAN tests administered to all children in Years 3, 5, 7, and 9. The PALLIC Program was driven by three overarching research questions designed to progress the conceptualisation and implementation of a practical leadership for learning theory, linking leadership actions in specific settings to student literacy learning outcomes:

- What are the necessary leadership capabilities and practices that link the work of leadership teams to Indigenous student literacy learning and achievement? What works and why?
- What actions do principals and leadership teams need to take to form productive leadership partnerships with Indigenous school community members, parents, and families over the teaching of reading? What works and why?
- What are the overall effects of the actions of leadership teams, parent and family partnerships on Indigenous children's learning and achievement in reading?

A key feature of this program was its attempt to ensure, from the outset, parity of participation by Indigenous and non-Indigenous people. In material terms, this meant that each school was asked to invite an Indigenous person to work alongside the principal, in the role of Indigenous Leadership Partner and as an integral member of the school leadership team. Some schools chose two people for the role. This trio was augmented by the support of a Leadership Mentor, an experienced principal acting as a critical friend to the school. The team's remit extended to professional learning, informing the design, implementation, and evaluation of a site-based learning program to teach Indigenous children to read SAE. The Indigenous Leadership Partners who took up the invitation were mostly familiar with the workings of the school. Many were local teaching support staff who had been connected to the school for some time – much longer than the often very brief tenure of the principals and staff. Others were relatives of children who had established close links to the school.

Over the 18-month program there was some degree of turnover in the Indigenous Leadership Partner position, yet in the main, most schools sustained a form of shared leadership, working together with their Leadership Mentor on aspects of a framework called the Leadership for Learning Blueprint (LfLB)

(Dempster, 2009). The central dimension of the framework, developing a shared moral purpose, is illustrated in Figure 4.1, surrounded by dimensions influenced by the *Carpe Vitam* research and other compelling studies (OECD, 2008; Robinson, 2007, 2009).

Using the LfLB as a guide, the program design sought, right from the outset, to engage the principal and Indigenous Leadership Partners together in five face-to-face professional learning modules. In these partnerships, they completed inter-module follow-up tasks, including the development and implementation of a Reading Action Plan with the support of their Leadership Mentor (as critical friend).

Shared professional learning afforded frequent opportunities for all voices to be heard in designing the Reading Action Plan. Across the schools there was general agreement from Indigenous community members that they wanted their young people to learn English, yet at the same time they insisted that children be encouraged to keep their Indigenous cultural capital at school and at home. It was the role of the Indigenous Leadership Partners to seek out the voices of community members and bring them to the school leadership table.

The overall intent of the program was for the principal and the Indigenous Leadership Partners to share in decision-making about policies, procedures, and processes involved in LfL in order to promote reading across the school and eventually throughout the community. Ideally, this meant that reading pedagogy would take a "both ways" approach in which Indigenous knowledge and "Western" knowledge would be blended, allowing children to retain their linguistic and cultural identities at school and in the world outside school. The inclusion of Indigenous Leadership Partners in the school leadership team brought Fraser's (2007) parity of participation

FIGURE 4.1 The PALLIC Leadership for Learning framework or blueprint

principle to life as well as her call for equal representation. The leadership role drew out the potential for Indigenous people to lead as "institutional agents" enabling parents, family, and community members, who were less familiar with the workings of the school, to be welcomed, and their voices sought in the attempt to construct a trusting partnership.

The PALLIC Program applied Fraser's concept of recognition by openly valuing the lifeworlds of Indigenous people and their communities. This was evident, for example, in the engagement of Indigenous Leadership Partners, Leaders of Reading from the community and Indigenous family members in the construction of a home literacy practices guide. The process involved in the production of this guide promoted an Indigenous call for a two-ways learning-to-read pedagogy. A familiar complaint in school programs for Indigenous children in Australia is that they fail to start with the rich knowledge (in this case linguistic knowledge) that many children elsewhere have learnt at home. Engaging families in sharing with teachers what they were teaching their children at home, was a means through which this literacy program sought to enhance the value that parents attached to children's learning at school. At the same time, it acknowledged children as future biliterate citizens needing particular capabilities to function in both of their contemporary worlds.

Social justice issues were to the fore in the PALLIC Program design. One of the complaints about Indigenous education is that it fails to recognise the views of those on whom the immediate most salient problems have the greatest impact. Only one of the 46 principals in the program was an Indigenous person. A consequence of this was the lack of comprehensive cultural knowledge held by principals as they took up their appointments. There was, therefore, a clear need to engage with local knowledge holders to gain cultural understandings essential to the shaping of teaching and learning. The model of shared leadership went a long way to ensuring both *cultural recognition* and *representation* as choices were made about culturally appropriate Reading Action Plans. The fact that most principals testified to productive relationships with their Indigenous Leadership Partners speaks well of the concern for professional integrity in the pursuit of the moral purpose to teach Indigenous children to read both ways. As Ryan has written:

> [T]he task to be accomplished is not to revise and amend, and repair deficient children, but to alter and transform the atmosphere and operations of the schools to which we commit these children. Only by changing the nature of the educational experience can we change the product. To continue to define the difficulty as inherent in the raw material, the children, is plainly to blame the victim and to acquiesce in the continuation of educational inequality.
>
> *(1976, pp. 61–62)*

With this brief account of the intent of the PALLIC Program, to what extent would this program meet the integrity test foreshadowed earlier in the chapter, using the series of questions against which the design and implementation of programs may be checked?

Putting the PALLIC Program through a test of its professional integrity

What responses can we make to the questions which offer a test of professional integrity? In Table 4.1, the left-hand side reproduces the questions, while the right contains our considered responses, both positive and negative.

What can we learn about the application of professional integrity principles through our assessment of the PALLIC Program? It is clear that there was much

TABLE 4.1 A test of integrity for the PALLIC Program

Questions testing professional integrity	Responses from the PALLIC Program
Redistribution:	
Did health and welfare concerns figure in the program's responses to student needs?	Health and welfare needs were not explicit in the PALLIC design and implementation though concern for student emotional health through literacy achievement was evident in attention to this in the school's moral purpose.
Was the program inclusive of all in the community?	No, although a start was made in this direction through plans to involve members of local communities as Leaders of Reading. This was only partially successful.
Were learning resources clearly directed towards students with identified needs?	Yes, this is a redistributive process for which there is ample evidence in the PALLIC Program Report (Johnson et al., 2014).
Did the program include and address minority cultural knowledge?	Yes, but through the eyes of Indigenous Leadership Partners in the main. Wider involvement of community members was somewhat limited.
Did the program privilege only mainstream cultural knowledge?	Mainstream cultural knowledge was privileged because of the program's focus on reading in SAE but a commitment to balance this with local Indigenous language stories and vocabulary was apparent.
Recognition:	
Was the student's cultural lifeworld visibly valued within the program?	The inclusion of Indigenous Leadership Partners who acted as cultural brokers in explanations of the children's backgrounds was a visible design feature of the PALLIC Program.
Was the lifeworld incorporated in the program's literacy curriculum?	This occurred to some extent through local oral and written Indigenous children's stories included in the program.
Were the necessary *capabilities to function* in the social setting included in the curriculum?	Yes, but with respect to literacy only. While improvement in students' literacy was the primary purpose of the program, leadership development was its funding focus.

(Continued)

TABLE 4.1 (Continued)

Questions testing professional integrity	*Responses from the PALLIC Program*
Did the approach to pedagogy acknowledge students' paths to learning: their cultural and community backgrounds?	No known Indigenous approaches to pedagogy were captured in the PALLIC design. The essential elements of learning to read were taken from Western research-informed improvement action.
Was assessment attuned to students' cultural and community experience and future needs?	Not particularly – diagnostic assessment was used to identify what students could do, but this was related to the essential elements referred to above.

Representation:

Did the program involve <u>teachers</u> in decision-making about policy, procedures, and resource allocation?	Yes, this followed the program's advocacy for shared leadership within the school.
Were <u>parents</u> involved in decision-making about policy, procedures, and resource allocation?	While this was a design feature, parent involvement in decision-making was sporadic. The best examples involved parents in the preparation of Home Reading Practices Guides but there was variability there too.
Did the program involve <u>students</u> in decision-making about curriculum, pedagogy, and assessment?	Student involvement in decisions about curriculum, pedagogy, and assessment was not specifically addressed in the PALLIC Program's design or its implementation.

Parity of participation:

To what extent did the program seek out the voices of minorities?	The inclusion of local Indigenous peoples as Leadership Partners and Leaders of Reading was integral to the program.
To what extent did the program give these voices equal weight with those of majorities?	The voices of Indigenous Leadership Partners were critical to the nature of the PALLIC Program. Equal weight was considered axiomatic to the implementation of both-ways leadership.
Were equal representative processes in place in the program's implementation?	This question is partially answered again through the engagement of Indigenous Leadership Partners and in the search for local Leaders of Reading. Beyond this, there was variable evidence of more widespread representation.
Was leadership shared amongst participants; beyond formal leadership positions?	Sharing leadership occurred within the school amongst teachers taking responsibility for implementing the school's agreed Reading Action Plan. Externally, shared leadership was seen in the development of a Home Reading Practices Guide in a minority of communities.
Did the program make (infra)structural arrangements for the equal participation of all groups?	No. There was nothing evident in the PALLIC Program design about creating organisational structures based on equal representation.

"good intent" in the program's design, but the evidence we have assembled shows that there is still a long way to go before the program can claim to meet all of the integrity demands implied in our set of testing questions. For example, much more attention needs to be given to understanding and incorporating the cultural backgrounds and lifeworlds of Indigenous people and their children in approaches to teaching and learning. The pedagogy of cultural relations about which Bishop, Berryman, Cavanagh, and Teddy (2009) have written so eloquently should be adopted as the standard. While leadership both ways was brought well into the foreground and attempts were made to spread the leadership of reading into the community, no forums or structural arrangements for local decision-making were apparent. If both-ways leadership is to become a practical reality, then a greater commitment to authentic decision-making roles is required. Overall, it is obvious to us that meeting the intent of this set of integrity questions is no easy task. It requires strength of character on the part of professional educators, principals, and teachers alike, particularly where communities have suffered poor recognition and representation for decades, and where redistributive processes still fail to address entrenched need. That said, a program in literacy, while necessary, is insufficient to enable Indigenous children to develop the necessary capability to function in the twin worlds they inhabit. A much wider and richer curriculum is essential if the breadth of learning required for effective citizenship is to be achieved.

A final word on critical friendship

Critical friendship, briefly described in the introduction to this chapter, was the third *Carpe Vitam* LfL framing value. It refers to a concept that has been much discussed and widely adopted but not always with a grasp of its deeper meanings and implications. Few people welcome critics and none less so than beleaguered teachers who spend their lives on the front line of criticism. They do, of course, welcome and reach out to friends. The problem is, however, that friends do not always risk confronting hard truths, and in a highly sensitive policy climate it may seem wiser to play safe, to support and sympathise. Doing so in the disadvantaged environments encountered during the PALLIC Program does nothing to assist people to break the shackles of that disadvantage. A much more assertive and informed friendship is imperative.

The role of critical friends, writes Hedges (2010), is to "create dissonance and confront practice" (p. 306) but this can only occur when the friend in the role takes sufficient time to understand the context of teachers' work, to walk in their shoes, to see it from the inside, to generate the trust that opens the door to critique. This is what Costa and Kallik (1993) emphasise in their depiction of the critical friend.

> [A] trusted person who asks provocative questions, provides data to be examined through another lens, and offers critique of a person's work as a friend. A critical friend takes the time to fully understand the context of the work

presented and the outcomes that the person or group is working toward. The friend is an advocate for the success of that work.

(p. 49)

To enable a school principal or teacher to have his or her work viewed through another lens is not always welcome and sometimes virtually impossible, such may be the subject individual's backlog of resentment and frustration. An assistant head-teacher who described being "caught between challenging students, confrontational parents and wholly unreasonable policy dictates" may have little investment in seeing it from others' points of view.

In Guskey's (2002) model of professional change, he argues that external opinion is not always likely to carry great weight. Teachers need not only for the problems they face to be understood, but also to see actual evidence of benefits that may come with a change of practice or a change of mind. Describing her own work as a critical friend, Hedges (2010) writes, "[As] I established a climate and relationships ... I came to genuinely appreciate teachers' expert knowledge in deeper ways" (p. 309). This enabled her to confront her own captive viewpoint and see things through "another lens". In other words, a precondition for helping a teacher, school leader, or parent to see things from a different viewpoint is to demonstrate the ability to do the same.

Valuing critical friendship is the pragmatic expression of one of Eraut's (1994) tenets of professionalism, namely, to accept the obligation to contribute to the quality of practice in an individual's organisation and to the changing role of the profession in society at large. We argue that critical friendship is tied to professional integrity with a Gordian knot because, as Eraut writes, professionals who accept their obligations reflect on their practice, self-monitor, and review their work. Doing so enables them to improve personally, allows them to extend their practice repertoires, and enhances the standing of the profession as a whole. All of these processes are enriched by critical friends and valued colleagues, engaging with individuals and collectives in the pursuit of better strategies, procedures, and outcomes.

Conclusion

At the beginning of this chapter, we reminded ourselves of the three overarching *Carpe Vitam* framing values: professional integrity, moral purpose, and critical friendship. All are conjoined and come into play, heightening the exercise of professional discretion. Another essential element of our expanded view of professional integrity is a commitment to social justice principles expressed in UNESCO's Rights of the Child and in its statement on democratic values. In particular circumstances, all of these may interact when those leading learning are faced with decisions which require reason and judgement when seeking solutions from amongst acceptable and unacceptable alternatives. Particular dilemmas arise in situations where policies and politics constrain opportunities to "do the right thing" by the child.

In these circumstances, decisions may have to be taken which challenge convention and conventional wisdom. This may entail discarding approaches considered unacceptable because they undermine the integrity of the profession. Professional discretion is abused and professionalism is violated when decisions taken sidestep the implicit and explicit norms of behaviour which define professional integrity. These integrity norms, at the very least, champion the *moral purpose of education*, act painstakingly in the interests of learners, and maintain a focus on the *breadth of learning* necessary to enhance a citizen's *capability to function* and to make decisions that uphold *social justice, children's rights* and the essential democratic principle of *parity of participation*. The embedding of these in the LfL cases we have described is a reminder of the critical importance of context. This underlines again the importance of adapting professional practices which respond to particular circumstances without compromising their essential intent.

So, what does our explanation of professional integrity hold for those seeking to take a challenge up to policy? Five actions are immediately apparent.

First, senior school leaders and teachers, acting with professional integrity, will take every opportunity to remind politicians and policymakers that education is a moral enterprise, serving the interests of children and young people. Where other priorities detrimental to children's interests threaten, it is crucial to reiterate an uncompromising moral purpose. Centre stage in both leading and learning is the shared commitment to helping those young people to recognise and use their talents to enrich their lives and the lives of others.

Second, principals and teachers acting with integrity become the guardians of learning in breadth, particularly in the primary years' curriculum. They use their discretion to ensure that structures, curriculum, timetabling, and pedagogy work in harmony to offer opportunities for rich, innovative, and comprehensive learning experiences, such as those described in Chapter 6. They would argue that doing so promotes strategies which enable children to perform well, within and beyond mandated testing environments. Preparing for life with the capabilities to function as informed and capable citizens is their guiding principle. They are able to view test scores and comparative measures with a critical and enlightened eye. They welcome, promote, and participate actively wherever possible in formal and informal learning outside the school. Their defence against narrowing the school curriculum to what is measurable is deep seated and instinctive. Actions such as these are likely to bring principals and teachers into conflict with policymakers and system authorities, and on to an unequal policy "battleground". Rising to the challenge is the test of their professional integrity and commitment to what is right and just.

Third, acting with professional integrity requires headteachers and teachers to take an unshakeable position on critical issues of social justice. Central to this is a commitment to education for all, no matter their circumstances. Again, this fundamental stance requires professionals who understand the power of cultural affiliation as well as the debilitating effects of disadvantage, dispossession, and marginalisation. Dealing with difference in inclusive and proactive ways requires sophisticated cultural "readers", able to understand young people's desire for recognition, acceptance, and inclusion. Acting with integrity also leads irrevocably to the equitable allocation and use of resources. Sometimes this may bring headteachers into contested debates about equity, but always with recourse to the question: "Whose interests are being served?" The latitude and discretion for leaders to act on this question will vary widely in differing political and policy contexts. In places where there is scope and license for leaders who hold the purse strings, integrity demands some forms of redistributive redress. In other circumstances which allow very little "wriggle room", the leadership imperative is a modelling of behaviour and value commitment which permeates the ethos of day-to-day priorities.

Fourth, democratic values and what they imply for children's rights, challenge principals and teachers to create the conditions in which education may take place, from the ground up. Seeing and explaining the world from a child's point of view is a process which takes us back to our own childhoods, the relishing of the present and nurturing hopes for a better life. We share the aspiration that, from an early age, learning should open up opportunities and promise a fulfilling future. Professionals who recall the opportunities and obstacles in their own upbringing, expect those in positions of trust to act with integrity and to stand up for a child's right to an education which is free from fear. They recognise often hidden talents and implicit abilities and create the conditions for children and young people to progress as far as they are able. Those acting with professional integrity encourage the free expression of ideas by young people in peaceful exchanges, respecting the ideas of others.

Fifth, headteachers and teachers who value their professional integrity acknowledge the importance of listening to the voices of those who have an interest in the child's education, including the child himself or herself. They consult openly with parents, teachers, children, caregivers, and members of school communities, ensuring that the parity of participation principle prevails. Excluding the unpalatable voices of some, so that the acceptable voices of others may dominate, violates these democratic principles and undermines professional integrity.

Taking the challenge up to policy needs a profession which is willing to publicise its stance, wherever possible, and whenever that stance is placed in jeopardy by politicians and policymakers. Principals and teachers are in the front line of defence against compromise and corruption. They require grit and determination to defend their professional integrity and its essential principles in the interests of those who, knowingly or unknowingly, depend on them.

References

Alexander, R., Armstrong, M., Flutter, J., Hargreaves, L., Harlen, W., Harrison, D., … Utting, G. (2009). *Children their world, their education: Final report and recommendations of the Cambridge Primary Review.* London: Routledge.

Australian Primary Principals Association. (2009). *Australian Primary Principals Association position paper on the publication of nationally comparable school performance information.* Kaleen, ACT: Author.

Bishop, R., Berryman, M., Cavanagh, T. H., & Teddy, L. (2009). *Te Kotahitanga: Addressing educational disparities facing Māori students in New Zealand*. Amsterdam: Elsevier Ltd.

Costa, A. L., & Kallik, B. (1993). Through the lens of a critical friend. *Educational Leadership*, *51*(2), 49–51.

Cullen, P. (2010). *Submission to senate inquiry into the administration & reporting of Naplan testing*. Retrieved from http://primaryschooling.net/?page_id=1672

Dempster, N. (2009). Leadership for learning: A framework synthesising recent research. *Edventures*, Paper 13, Australian College of Educators, Canberra.

Education Scotland. (2012). *The curriculum for excellence: Building the curriculum 3. A framework for learning and teaching*. Retrieved from http://www.gov.scot/resource/doc/226155/0061245.pdf

Eraut, M. (1994). *Developing professional knowledge and competence*. London: RoutledgeFalmer.

Fraser, N. (2007). *Abnormal justice*. Retrieved from http://www.fehe.org/uploads/media/Fraser_Abnormal_Justice_essay.pdf

Fullan, M. (2001). *Leading in a culture of change*. San Francisco, CA: Jossey-Bass.

Galton, M., & MacBeath, J. (2015). *Inclusion: Statements of intent*. A Report to the National Union of Teachers on the current state of special educational needs and disability provision. London: National Union of Teachers.

Ghana Education Service (GES). (2014). *Leadership for learning: A manual/handbook for headteachers and circuit supervisors*. Accra, Ghana: GES, Teacher Education Division.

Gilbert, R., Keddlie, A., Lindgard, R., Mills, M., & Renshaw, P. (2013). Equity and education research, policy and practice: A review. In A. Reid & L. Reynolds (Eds.), *Equity and education: Exploring new directions for equity in Australian education* (pp. 16–40). Carlton: VIC: Australian College of Educators.

Grace, G. (1995). *Beyond education management*. London: Taylor and Francis.

Guskey, T. R. (2002). Professional development and teacher change. *Teachers and Teaching: Theory and Practice*, *8*(3), 381–391.

Hedges, H. (2010). Blurring the boundaries: Connecting research, practice and professional learning. *Cambridge Journal of Education*, *40*(3), 299–314.

Homel, R., Dempster, N., Freiberg, K., Branch, S., Tilbury, C., & Johnson, G. (2016). Creating the conditions for collective impact: Improving wellbeing and educational outcomes for children through community prevention coalitions in disadvantaged communities. Paper presented at ECER 2016, Leading Education: The Distinct Contributions of Educational Research and Researchers, Dublin.

Johnson, G., Dempster, N., McKenzie, L., Klieve, H., Flückiger, B., Lovett, S., Riley, T., & Webster, A. (2014). *Principals as literacy leaders with Indigenous communities: Leadership for learning to read – 'Both ways'*. Canberra: The Australian Primary Principals Association.

Jull, S., Swaffield, S., & MacBeath, J. (2014). Changing perceptions is one thing…: Barriers to transforming leadership and learning in Ghanaian basic schools. *School Leadership & Management*, *34*(1), 69–84.

Louis, K. S. (2003). Democratic schools, democratic communities: Reflections in an international context. *Leadership and Policy in Schools*, *2*(2), 93–108.

MacBeath, J., & Dempster, N. (Eds.). (2009). *Connecting leadership and learning: Principles for practice*. London: Routledge.

MacBeath, J., & Swaffield, S. (2011). *Leadership for learning in Ghana*. Paper presented at the 24th International Congress for School Effectiveness and Improvement (ICSEI), Limassol, Cyprus, 4–7 January.

MacBeath, J., & Swaffield, S. (2013). Living with the colonial legacy: The Ghana story. In S. Clarke & T. O'Donoghue (Eds.), *School level leadership in post-conflict societies* (pp. 49–63). London: Routledge.

MacBeath, J., Frost, D., Swaffield, S., & Waterhouse, J. (2006). *Making the connections: The story of a seven country odyssey in search of a practical theory*. Cambridge: University of Cambridge Faculty of Education.

MacBeath, J., & Swaffield, S., with Oduro, G., & Hassler, B. (2016a). *Leadership for learning: Handbook for facilitators*. T-TEL Professional Development Programme. Theme 6: Leadership for Learning (Handbook for Facilitators). Published by the Ministry of Education (Ghana), under Creative Commons Attribution- ShareAlike 4.0 International. Available online at http://oer.t-tel.org. Version 1, December 2016.

MacBeath, J., & Swaffield, S., with Oduro, G., & Hassler, B. (2016b). *Leadership for learning: Handbook for PD coordinators*. T-TEL Professional Development Programme. Theme 6: Leadership for Learning (Handbook for PD Coordinators). Published by the Ministry of Education (Ghana), under Creative Commons Attribution- ShareAlike 4.0 International. Available online at http://oer.t-tel.org. Version 1, November 2016.

MacBeath, J., & Swaffield, S., with Oduro, G., & Hassler, B. (2016c). *Leadership for learning: Professional development guide for tutors*. T-TEL Professional Development Programme. Theme 6: Leadership for Learning (Professional Development Guide for Tutors). Published by the Ministry of Education (Ghana), under Creative Commons Attribution- ShareAlike 4.0 International. Available online at http://oer.t-tel.org. Version 1, December 2016.

Malakolunthu, S., MacBeath, J., & Swaffield, S. (2014). Improving the quality of teaching and learning through 'Leadership for Learning': Changing scenarios in basic schools in Ghana. *Educational Management Administration and Leadership*, *42*(5), 701–717.

Ministry of Education. (2010). *Headteachers' handbook* (2nd ed.). Accra, Ghana: Ministry of Education.

Ministerial Council for Education, Early Childhood Development and Youth Affairs (MCEECDYA). (2008). *The Melbourne Declaration for Educational Goals for Young Australians*. Retrieved from http://www.curriculum.edu.au/verve/_resources/National_Declaration_on_the_Educational_Goals_for_Young_Australians.pdf

Oduro, G. (2010, January). *Headteacher development in Ghana: the leadership for learning (LfL) model*. Paper presented at the Commonwealth Secretariat School Leadership Review Workshop, London.

Organisation for Economic Co-operation and Development (OECD). (2008). *Improving school leadership. Volume 1: Policy and practice*. OECD Publishing.

Rawls, J. (1971). *A theory of justice*. Cambridge, MA: Belknap Press of Harvard University Press.

Robinson, V. M. J. (2007). *School leadership and student outcomes: Identifying what works*. Winmalee, New South Wales: Australian Council for Educational Leaders.

Robinson, V. M. J. (2009). Fit for a purpose: An educationally relevant account of distributed leadership. In A. Harris (Ed.), *Distributed leadership: Different perspectives* (Vol. 7, pp. 219–240). Netherlands: Springer.

Ryan, W. (1976). *Blaming the victim*. New York: Penguin, Random House.

Sen, A. (1992). *Inequality reexamined*. Oxford: Oxford University Press.

Swaffield, S. (2017). Supporting headteachers in a developing country. In R. Maclean (Ed.), *Life in schools and classrooms: Past, present and future* (pp. 277–292). Singapore: Springer.

Swaffield, S., Jull, S., & Ampah-Mensah, A. (2013). Using mobile phone texting to support the capacity of school leaders in Ghana to practise leadership for learning. *Procedia – Social and Behavioural Sciences*, *103*, 1295–1302.

The Scottish Education Office. (2016). The purpose of the curriculum. Retrieved 07 March, 2016, from www.educationscotland.gov.uk/learningandteaching/thecurriculum/whatis curriculumforexcellence/thepurposeofthecurriculum/

UNICEF. (1990). *A simplified version of the United Nations Convention on the Rights of the Child.* Retrieved from http://www.unicef.org/rightsite/files/uncrcchilldfriendlylanguage.pdf

United Nations Human Rights, Office of the High Commissioner. (1990). *Convention on the Rights of the Child.* Retrieved from http://www.ohchr.org/EN/ProfessionalInterest/Pages/CRC.aspx

Zame, M.Y., Hope, W. C., & Respress, T. (2008). Educational reform in Ghana: The leadership challenge. *International Journal of Educational Management, 22*(2), 115–128.

5

LEADERSHIP AS PRACTICE

Leadership as role and status or as activity and practice? What is the essential difference between these descriptions? Role and status say little about agency which lies at the very heart, not only of teacher professionalism, but also of young people's engagement with learning, while "activity" and "practice" take us closer to the essence of leadership and to the essential purpose of education. Consider the following representations:

> School life is always a "hive" of activities in which leadership is deeply embedded but rarely opened to critical scrutiny by its everyday agents.
> *(Swaffield & MacBeath, 2009, p. 49)*

> When leadership is conceptualised as activity, it builds social capital.
> *(Swaffield & MacBeath, 2009, p. 45)*

> Leadership for Learning is a distinct form of educational practice that involves an explicit dialogue, maintaining a focus on learning, attending to the conditions that favour learning, and leadership that is both shared and accountable. Learning and leadership are conceived of as "activities" linked by the centrality of human agency within a framework of moral purpose.
> *(Swaffield & MacBeath, 2009, p. 42)*

These three representations – school life as a hive of activities, leadership conceptualised as activity, and leadership for learning (LfL) as a distinct form of educational practice – add considerable substance to the general depiction of what leaders do. The following characterisation from the *Carpe Vitam* Project is an adaptation of Leithwood and Riehl's (2003, p. 7) earlier definition:

> School leaders, understanding and harnessing the contexts in which they operate, mobilise and work with others to articulate and achieve shared intentions that enhance learning and the lives of learners.
>
> *(MacBeath & Dempster, 2009, p. 22)*

In other words, leadership is about people in everyday settings, whether or not holding positions of power, working together on common goals; in short, a melding of the three concepts of purpose, context, and human agency. While this depiction may appear almost as a matter of fact, the real world is often much more messy and unpredictable than the world of aspirational prose and ambitious nostrums. For example, an agreed purpose may not be immediately apparent, even though there are people in the same place confronted with issues or challenges they may want to address; or some of the people who might become engaged in an activity may be reluctant; or unravelling the complex dynamics in a school's context may be politically difficult; or the "bigger" purpose of improving the lives of learners might be overtaken by a child's bad behaviour which, for a time, diverts a teacher's attention from that higher goal. Over the course of the LfL Project which took us into schools, and continues to do so, the complexity and "messiness" of classroom life challenges us to resolve the discontinuity between the aspirational and the lived reality. The fictionalised vignettes contained in this chapter have been chosen to illustrate the tensions, to help us tease out what actually occurred, and to show how people grapple with what might appear, on the surface, to be reasonably straight-forward activities.

As a prelude to these vignettes we summarise ideas from a selection of literature on leadership as activity or practice to provide scaffolding for a discussion of what is illustrated in the vignettes.

Towards understanding leadership as practice

In education and elsewhere (Crevani, Lindgren, & Packendorff, 2010; Endrissat & von Arx, 2013), there is growing interest in a conceptualisation of leadership as a practice or as an activity, grounded in organisational realities. Those who hold this view (Crevani, 2015; Raelin, 2016) argue that it is less helpful to "see" leadership from a particular theoretical perspective than to see it as activity teased out from what is happening around the people working together in an organisation. It is less helpful to see leadership with an individual focus than to view it as a social act requiring collective human agency. It is less helpful to see it as a commodity to be delegated by a person of position than to come to an understanding of it as occurring amongst people motivated by a particular and shared purpose. Leadership from this point of view is a pragmatic concept, always influenced by an organisation's context and the motivations, understandings, and actions of the people striving to achieve agreed ends. But more than this, it is a practice embedded in the flow of daily activity, influenced by what is happening in the here and now as well as in the underlying motivations which people bring to their shared interactions with others.

The growing interest in seeking deeper understandings of leadership in action through a leadership-as-practice lens is helpfully discussed in recent work by Barbara Simpson (2016) and others (Gergen & Herted, 2016; Raelin, 2016). Simpson's work uses a three-part typology first advanced by John Dewey and Arthur Bentley (1949) in their book *Knowing and the Known*. Using this typology, they describe three different categories of action: self-action, inter-action, and trans-action. Simpson explains:

- the central assumption of self-action is that things, or entities act under their own powers (p. 160);
- the notion of inter-action owes much to the modernist epistemology of Sir Isaac Newton, for whom the world is an extended mechanism comprising material entities acted on by simple forces to produce instrumental outcomes (p. 162); and
- trans-action puts process first. Its starting point is a world that is active and in continuous flow, a world filled with agency (p. 165).

Simpson (2016, p. 173) has extrapolated a comparison of different practice perspectives of leadership from the Dewey/Bentley typology, reproduced below (Table 5.1). This comparison offers a helpful organising framework for a commentary on a broad corpus of past, present, and emerging school leadership literature. As Table 5.1 shows, Simpson draws from the concept of self-action, a "leader-practitioner" perspective, from inter-action, the perspective of "leadership as a set of practices", and from trans-action, she derives a "leadership in the flow of practice" perspective. She compares how each of these perspectives approaches agency, power, context,

TABLE 5.1 Comparison of different practice perspectives of leadership

Category of action	The leader-practitioner Self-action	Leadership as a set of practices Inter-action	Leadership in the flow of practice Trans-action
Agency	Exercise of free will	Influencing others	Ongoing coordinated accomplishment of work
Power	Power to...	Power over...	Power with...
Context	Irrelevant	Structure as a fixed container within which action takes place	Context and trans-actors are mutually engaged in an emergent whole
Relationality	Irrelevant	Dyadic and network inter-linkages	Mutually constituting temporally unfolding relationships
Temporality	Irrelevant	Time as an independent variable	Temporal experience is enfolded in and emergent with trans-actions

(Adapted from Simpson, 2016, p. 173)

relationality, and temporality. In her original table, she added the ontological assumptions underlying each perspective. A brief explanation of the features of the three perspectives follows.

The leader-practitioner

Simpson's (2016) tabular analysis shows that, typically, the leader-practitioner perspective highlights leader-centrism, the self-action and individualism of the "heroic" leader with the will, power, and personal agency to make things happen as she or he would like. Doing so is the result of the individual's capacity, his or her traits, characteristics, personal charisma, and positional authority or recognised expertise. Leadership from this perspective is not so much context dependent as it is leader dependent. Relationships are not a primary focus nor is time, other than the timing of action required by the leader-practitioner to ensure that outcomes are achieved. The extension of so-called "school autonomy" in the education systems of many OECD countries in recent years (OECD, 2008) acts as a mask for privileging leader-centric views of school leadership. These developments have a tendency to cement in place peak positional hierarchies and certainly affect how leadership activities are construed at lower levels within those hierarchies. The school leadership and management literature is replete with studies of the principal and the qualities he or she should bring to the role. As Simpson notes, "this self-actional orientation remains dominant in contemporary social science thinking, and indeed it is precisely this dominance in the field of leadership that has prompted the call for new approaches such as that promised by leadership-as-practice" (p. 160).

Leadership as a set of practices

In the second perspective defined by Simpson (2016) in Table 5.1, leadership is described as a set of practices. Here, inter-action between leaders and followers is the norm, with leaders harnessing their collective capacities to pursue agreed ends. This highlights the leader's power over others, exercised through networks and linkages, either assuaging or sharing that power through inter-agency endeavour. Context is influential in this perspective though it is seen as "fixed", providing the concrete circumstances in which a set of practices is enacted.

Much of the recent work on generic leadership practices in education (Day et al., 2010; Leithwood et al., 2006), while exemplifying this perspective, does not go far enough in challenging some of the inherent assumptions within which the notion of "distributed" leadership continues to reside. As Simpson (2016) contends, distribution may simply be a means of reinforcement of traditional hierarchies inherent in school systems and in schools themselves. Powerful forms of teacher leadership are needed to challenge those hierarchical structures and their embedded assumptions.

> Teacher leadership symbolizes distribution because it provides teachers the opportunity of exercising leadership beyond the limits of formal hierarchical

leadership models within the school. It involves "not just a matter of delegation, direction or distribution of responsibility, but rather a matter of teachers'
agency and choice in initiating and sustaining change whatever their status"
(Frost & Durrant, 2003, p. 174).

(MacBeath, Oduro, & Waterhouse, 2004, p. 15)

Agency, choice, and initiative are powerful ideas but leadership without hierarchy
seems a long way off, writes Simpson, questioning the notion of agency as residing
with the individual and arguing for a more radical form of conjoint agency:

> Those seeking a more plural, less individualized expression of leadership have
> explored the possibilities of leadership that is collective, collaborative, par-
> ticipative or distributed, where agency still resides in individuals, but perhaps
> only temporarily, or in ways that are delimited by other inter-actors.

(p. 62)

Given the abundance of research and writing on leadership as a set of practices
embracing collaborations, a diversion into a summary of findings selected from this
body of work illustrates the prevalence of this perspective in scholarly articles and
contemporary empirical studies of leadership in education.

A diversion into research on collective, collaborative, participative, or distributed leadership

Leadership construed as collective and collaborative runs so much against the grain
of long-established practice that many commentators and frustrated researchers
conclude that it is an unequal contest. "Many more forces (e.g. history, inertia) to
hold structures in place are in play than there are to loosen and dissolve structural
bonds", wrote Murphy, Smylie, Mayrowetz, and Louis in 2009 (p. 185). Investigating
the role of principals in fostering the development of distributive leadership, they
found a "reluctance to change", and suggested that "structural arrangements" in
schools were not "especially malleable" and that developing teacher leadership was
not "instinctive". They pointed to social and organisational structures in schools
which carry a long history together with long-standing political sanctioning. This
creates a context in which leadership seems inevitably linked to hierarchy, authority, and position rather than arising in spontaneous activity amongst peers.

Heck and Hallinger (2010, p. 231) seem to soften somewhat the individualism of
the positional leader by proposing focused research into a reciprocal effects model
of leadership. They argue that their preferred approach:

- does not make untenable assumptions about the heroic role of leadership in
  bringing about change;
- presents leadership for learning in dynamic relationship with other organizational processes; and

- offers a new empirical description of collaborative leadership and academic capacity building as mutually reinforcing, parallel change processes.

(p. 245)

"Reciprocal effects", they say, result from collaborative leadership which has a simultaneous impact on the capacities of teachers and leaders alike as they work to make changes to improve practice. Heck and Hallinger see the role of the leader as essential to collaboration and, while they offer a disclaimer signalling a stepping back from "untenable assumptions" about heroic leaders, they nevertheless implicate positional leaders prominently in capacity building.

Heck and Hallinger's (2010) work finds support in a large-scale study led by Louis and colleagues (Louis, Leithwood, Wahlstrom, & Anderson, 2010) arguing that:

> The recent flurry of attention to a broader spectrum or distribution of leadership has begun to sensitize us to the remarkable array of people who exercise formal or informal leadership in schools and districts. We cannot push our understanding of leadership influence much further without considering the many sources of leadership in the education system and also the web of interaction created by these sources.
>
> *(p. 11)*

Amongst the findings from this research, two conclusions stand out, reinforcing the view that positional leaders continue to have a powerful hold on the inter-actions of leadership activity, no matter how it is shared or distributed:

- Collective leadership has a stronger influence on student achievement than individual leadership.
- Principals and district leaders have the most influence on decisions in all schools; however, they do not lose influence as others gain influence.

(p. 19)

The enduring power of people in positions, or in Simpson's (2016) terms, leader-practitioners, is exposed by Louis et al. (2010) in the following:

- The degree of influence exercised by these people and groups reflects a traditional, hierarchical conception of leadership in organizations.
- Teachers rate the influence of traditional sources of leadership much higher than they rate non-traditional sources.
- Among teacher roles, the more formalized the leadership expectation, the greater the perceived influence.

(p. 32)

The co-construction of distributed leadership practices was the focus of research by Park and Datnow (2009). Again, in this study, the interaction between positional leaders and followers was highlighted, with significantly greater influence attributed to position holders than to teachers themselves. This was evident in the fact that leaders:

> distributed decision-making authority in a manner that empowered different staff members to utilise their expertise. From the system perspective, teachers were not necessarily granted full autonomy; rather, they were responsible for developing effective instructional practices while the central office held themselves accountable for providing resources and developing learning opportunities.
>
> *(p. 491)*

From a conceptual study of school leadership and management with a distributive perspective, Spillane, Healey, Parise, and Kenney (2010) advocate caution in accepting causal connections between leadership of this kind and enhanced school outcomes.

> A distributed perspective frames practice in a particular way, not simply as individual actions but rather as a product of the interactions ... among school *leaders, followers* and aspects of their *situation* ... the practice of leading and managing is stretched over the work of two or more leaders and followers. Interactions, not just actions, are central to investigating practice.
>
> *(p. 161, emphasis in original)*

As he argues elsewhere (Spillane, 2006), it is important to make a distinction between distributive leadership which focuses on the actions of individuals and a much less intuitive concept of conjoint agency which focuses on interactions among individuals and groups of "actors" – in other words, focusing on leadership as activity.

This view resonates with Simpson's (2016) explanation of leadership as a set of practices embracing the agency of inter-actors. Spillane (2006) concedes that one of the actors is more often than not the headteacher or principal. Nevertheless, this understanding accords agency to everyone engaged in distributive leadership activity, offering a shared purpose as the motivation for inter-action and downplaying, for a time, hierarchical status.

A more pragmatic argument for leadership distribution is suggested by Hartley (2010), emphasising its capacity to assist hard-pressed senior leaders to deal on a day-to-day basis with the work overload they face. This is not a position given much credence by Bush (2013) who has described distributive leadership as "the model of choice in the 21st century". He takes a line much more consistent with Spillane's (2006) inter-active view, contending that leadership may arise for any one of a number of purposes anywhere in the organisation and that it is not necessarily confined to formal leaders.

This is not immediately consistent with an earlier view, perhaps closer to Hartley's pragmatic position, in which, with Glover (Bush & Glover, 2012, pp. 21–36), he challenges the claim that leadership may appear "anywhere in the organization" unassisted by those in positions of power. Indeed together, they argue that their work is an important manifestation of distributed leadership and that their research shows "that high-performing leadership teams are characterised by internal coherence and unity, a clear focus on high standards, two-way communication with internal and external stakeholders and a commitment to distributed leadership" (p. 21).

While the research findings are unsurprising given that senior leadership teams are almost self-evidently more effective than the individualistic or heroic head, the "power over" others and the unequal agency signalled by Simpson (2016) may, more often than not, serve to reinforce hierarchical structures, potentially disempowering a genuine sense of collective agency.

What we take from the Louis-led study (2010) is a reaffirmation that distributive or collective leadership is perceived by those in senior positions as an important way of influencing the practice of teachers who do not automatically perceive themselves as leaders. There are familiar echoes here with Lieberman and Friedrich's (2007) work with teachers in the United States and Barzano and Brotto's (2009) similar findings in an Italian context. In these two highly divergent cultural and policy contexts, these researchers describe teachers' reticence to share their practice and thinking, reluctant to step out of their assigned role as it would be regarded by their superiors as presumptuous and by their colleagues as arrogance.

Working with small groups of teachers in the United States, Ann Lieberman described how they learnt over time to overcome the entrenched bureaucratic norms of the school and institutionalised notions of leaders. It was seen as crucial to their credibility with their peers that these teachers were simultaneously challenging and improving their own practice, understanding the systemic pressures that their peers faced, and recognising what these teachers had to offer by way of leading learning within and beyond their own classrooms. As teachers developed their expertise and visibility they became the "go to" people for advice and support. Three key strategies emerging from this work were:

- creating collaborative forums in which teachers work together and make their practice public;
- publicising and celebrating others' good work; and
- navigating the school culture and supporting others in effecting change.

As the researchers described it, these teachers needed the stimulus from an external source and continuing support to challenge deeply ingrained practice. It was only through working with the research team that they gained the confidence to exercise initiative, to develop strategies for building community, and to find ways of drawing on and sharing expertise and sharing leadership with others. "It encouraged them to work collaboratively and to go public with both their successes and their questions" (Lieberman & Freidrich, 2007, p. 49).

The cultural context in which Giovanna Barzano and Francesca Brotto worked with teachers in Italian schools could hardly have been more different from their

American counterparts, yet the hierarchical, bureaucratic pressures and micropoliti-cal issues were very similar. The challenge, as they described it, was to help teachers move from a deeply embedded view of *essere per* (being for) to *stare con* (being with), in which the cultural shift was from a vertical sense of upward accountability to a horizontal, or collegial mindset marked by "contagious listening, empathy, team-work and sense-making, allied with 'being for' as mutual empowerment and service to one another" (2009, p. 235).

There are echoes here of Katzenmeyer and Møller's (1996) reference to "awak-ening the sleeping giant of teacher leadership", an apt metaphor as it captures both the dormant qualities of an undervalued profession and the massive potential for leadership lying unexploited. While we have been conditioned to view "agency" and "leadership" as distinctive concepts, they are closely related, yet the term lead-ership is so imbued with positional models that teachers are often reluctant to see themselves as leaders or as exercising leadership. Even when they do exercise initia-tive beyond their own classrooms, they tend to use a different language register to describe their actions.

In Latin-American countries – Ecuador, Chile, Mexico, and Paraguay – each with its own quite different political and socioeconomic histories, there appears to be a common understanding growing that teachers should be less passive recipients of others' directions, of policy mandates, and become more active participants in shaping the educational process both within their own schools and in collaboration more systemically (Aguerrando & Vezub, 2011).

When teachers exercise their agency beyond the classroom, with colleagues, with parents and other agencies or with policy, they exercise leadership. When they do so as part of a collective endeavour leadership becomes a shared activity. Despite a body of writing on teacher leadership, much of it fails to grasp or explore the connections between individual agency and the collective. Teacher leadership is construed as a role or as status within the institutional hierarchy rather than cap-tured in the flow of activities. "The roles and activities of leadership flow from the expertise required for learning and improvement, not from the formal dictates of the institution" (Elmore, 2008, in MacBeath, 2012).

Summary

The key issue in this diversion into the collective, collaborative, participative, or distributed leadership literature is that generally, the findings and conclusions are consistent with Simpson's (2016) theoretical analysis. In distributive leadership, agency is about leaders influencing others and harnessing their collective capaci-ties to pursue specific ends. The leader retains power over others, though groups, networks, and affiliations are formed which temporarily share that power through inter-agency. The bureaucratic and hierarchical context is fixed and highly influ-ential, providing the concrete circumstances in which collaborative or participative practices are at work. At its best, leadership becomes, for a time, an authentic shared undertaking. On the downside, it may rely too heavily on the power of individuals whose influence is enhanced, whose hierarchical status is confirmed, and whose actions may lessen the agency of non-positional inter-actors.

Having taken a brief detour into some of the influential distributed leadership literature, we return now to the third of the perspectives of leadership presented by Simpson in the tabulation included earlier in the chapter – *leadership in the flow of practice*.

Leadership in the flow of practice

Returning to Simpson's (2016) table, we can see that *leadership in the flow of practice* links agency to the coordinated accomplishment of work. Power is seen as exercised *with* others rather than over them; actors are engaged intrinsically with their contexts where mutual relationships unfold in the moments in which trans-actions occur. The outcomes of trans-actions are, more often than not, unanticipated. In Simpson's terms, they are "emergent" and quite possibly novel (p. 67). She goes on to encourage us to think of this trans-actional view of practice as the "ongoing dialogical accomplishment of meaning" (p. 68). She further argues that dialogue is essential to this leadership perspective. As an aside, this provides an additional justification for the significance of the LfL principle in relation to dialogue and the process we have called "disciplined dialogue" described in Chapter 2 (about which more is said in Chapter 6).

For Simpson, leadership in the flow of practice encourages more intuitive and spontaneous agency than occurs through self-action or inter-action and as such creates enhanced opportunities for more widely defined achievements. As agency is exercised mutually in and through trans-actions, "they [the trans-actions] are arguably saturated in power and influence" (Simpson, 2016, p. 69). This is defined by Raelin (2016) as "collaborative agency". In discussions of leadership as practice, he describes another of the essential benefits of trans-actions: "The parties committed to a practice enter an authentic dialog to reproduce or transform the very practice in which they are engaged" (p. 133). Raelin goes on to stress that practice is forward looking, asking people to "create knowledge as they improvise around the problems they are confronting" (p. 134). This reinforces Simpson's view that novelty or innovation emerges from trans-actions in the here and now of quotidian activity. At the same time, there is unanimity in Simpson's and Raelin's views on the locus of power in trans-actions produced "through the individual and collective agency of those affiliated in everyday practice" (Raelin, 2016, p. 134). In relation to power, Raelin writes:

> Leadership is more about *where, when, how* and *why* leadership work is being done than about who is offering visions for others to understand and perform the work in question. ... Ultimately, leadership becomes a consequence of collaborative meaning making in practice; in this way, it is intrinsically tied to a collective rather than to an individual model of leadership.
>
> *(p. 134)*

In the discussion to this stage, we have referred to the thinking of authors from disciplines outside education. That said, it would be remiss to leave this section of the chapter without acknowledging some of the work of educational leadership scholars who lean towards the perspective of leadership in the flow of practice. Several, such as Robert Glatter, Peter Gronn, and Peter Woods are helpful here, though the stimulus for their critiques lies in studies of distributive leadership, rather than specifically leadership in the flow of practice.

Although without explicit reference to this same concept, Glatter (2009, p. 226) articulates the gist of it, referring to leadership as "a complex and interactive process", expressed through relationships amongst actors undertaking specific tasks in practical contexts. These contexts are often complicated and couched in uncertainty. Glatter does not, however, take understanding of this complex process further, returning to the inter-action and influence of leaders with followers and the skills leaders should develop to manage complexity. Woods and Gronn (2009, p. 447) do not shy away from the description of interactive complexity. They write that participation, so essential for democratic practices, shapes a "radical form" of distributive leadership, raising questions about the relationship between individual agents and the groups in which inter-agency occurs. They conceptualise this radical form of distributive leadership as "concertive action" – action between individual agents and the social and organisational structures around them. They go further to argue that "[d]emocracy can be seen as the working out of this relationship so that people *consciously* and as *ethical agents* participate in the co-creation of their environment" (p. 447, emphasis in original).

In complementary work on leadership configurations, Gronn (2009) suggests that:

> By treating pluralities of leaders as numerically equivalent or all-of-a-piece, for example, an aggregated understanding makes little allowance for different levels of leadership and for qualitative differences among leading units. In a number of empirical accounts of distributed leadership, however, individual leaders still figure prominently as agents of influence, although they frequently do so in company with a variety of emergent "small number" formations. For this reason, the totality of such arrangements represents a time-, space-, context- and membership-bound configuration of influence-based relationships, the dynamics of which, due to the mixed patterning of the formations, are most accurately characterized as "hybrid".
>
> *(p. 381)*

If Simpson's (2016) perspective of leadership in the flow of practice were taken literally, hybridity would disappear to be overtaken by agents engaging as peers, unencumbered by mixed patterning or formal hierarchy.

Summary

In summarising this section of the chapter on the use of Simpson's (2016) perspectives of leadership, it is important to emphasise that the typology has enabled us to show clear distinctions between self-action, inter-action, and trans-action as the baseplates for understanding leadership as practice. However, both the leader-practitioner perspective and the perspective of leadership as a set of practices confirm the power and influence of positional leaders at the expense of those seen as led. In schools, the "led" are typically teachers and students, ensuring that principals and other position holders inside the school and in system positions retain agency ascendancy. While spontaneous agency, the hallmark of leadership in the flow of practice, is not yet commonplace, there are encouraging leanings in that direction. Its potential contribution to more egalitarian and democratic participative leadership promises more than heroic or distributive forms of leadership can ever offer. The words of Crevani et al. (2010) concisely draw these issues together, pointing a pathway towards unfettered collective leadership trans-actions.

> Going beyond dominating heroic conceptions of leadership as lodged in single individuals, the suggested perspective [leadership in the flow of practice] will enable us to gain new understandings of how leadership activities emerge in social interaction and of how institutionalized notions of leadership are brought into – and re-constructed in – these same activities. Given this reasoning, we suggest that the empirical study of leadership should be based in a process ontology, focused on leadership practices as constructed in interactions – embedded in a cultural context where societal notions of "leadership" are both taken for granted and under re-construction.
>
> *(p. 77)*

The vignettes which follow describe what we have observed in LfL research projects from schools in two different countries. The first is from Austria followed by a second from Australia. What do each of these vignettes offer as insights to further our understanding of the three perspectives of leadership already explained: the leader-practitioner, leadership as a set of (distributed) practices, and leadership in the flow of practice?

Vignette 1

Leadership learning in Austria

A Leadership Academy was established in Austria in 2004 under the direction of Michael Schratz and Wilfred Schley. Its stated purpose was to enhance leadership at all levels within the system, "a joint learning process" in which the whole educational system would be involved. This bold initiative required endorsement and funding from the Ministry. In the beginning, the educational authorities of the regions and the local authorities were sceptical and opposed innovative opportunities in the historically conflicting structure between central decision-making and decentralised accountability. It is a tension and source of conflict that, historically, has often prevented school reform in Austria due to the dominating policy culture (Pelinka, 1996).

The Ministry buy-in was both gratifying and challenging. Capacity building on such a scale was unprecedented but immensely helped by the presence of the Minister herself in regional workshops, admitting to experiencing a learning curve with regard to issues, innovative ideas, and a shared sense of purpose and principles. The scale of the challenge could not, however, be underestimated.

One of the primary tasks was to address "eclectic government interventions" which were causing an overload problem by "piling disconnected policies one upon one another" (Schmid et al., 2007), leading to a sense of confusion and uncertainty not only among staff in the schools, but also at different levels within the school system (regional, district, local levels). This fragmentation within the system was creating leadership dilemmas, pulling school managers in different directions between their sense of duty, or compliance (*sollen*) and what they believed they would like to be doing (*wollen*).

As Fullan has argued, "We need a radically new mind-set for reconciling the seemingly intractable dilemmas fundamental for sustainable reform: top-down versus bottom-up, local and central accountability, informed prescription and informed professional judgment, improvement that keeps being replenished" (2005, p. 11). It is not enough to renew or improve schools, as Hentig argued in 1993. He called for rethinking school, demanding a new mindset as to how we do and might envisage school. In research, theoretical and methodological discussions have taken place in the process of reframing the "classical approach" to changing patterns of schooling at large, and teaching and learning in particular (e.g., see Vosniadou, 2008).

This required a reframing process, no longer "downloading" patterns from the past, as Scharmer (2007, p. 119) has argued. To do so prevents us from creating a shift of pattern from best practice to next practice. For new patterns to emerge, it was crucial to open up perspectives by leaving the trodden path. This did, however, initially cause insecurity and instability. Old patterns of mind were no longer functioning smoothly while new ones had not yet gained stability – an experience similar to an incubation phase for the emergence of the new. Creating a mindset of sustainable change was to be a key concept permeating all the phases of the LEA (local education authority). Bringing together leaders from all parts of the system was helpful in sharing the discomfort and the challenge of engaging everyone in a mutual development process, leading to new ways of thinking and acting. The LEA investment in capacity building was a way of strengthening systemic leadership by shifting reform policy away from a mere top-down process toward a network-based development.

Network coordinators in all Austrian provinces function as the regional support system, ensuring regional networking. The networking character of the LEA aims at creating a new mentality of leadership, one which rests on trust and authenticity rather than on positional power. Its ultimate goal lies in sustainably improving the preconditions and processes of young people's learning. Networking serves capacity building, qualification, and empowerment of leaders through the whole of the Austrian educational system. Leaders are motivated to strategically target complex development tasks through priority setting, focusing on solutions, individual development projects, and creating organisation profiles. As work develops over time participants learn to translate challenges into innovative development processes, enticing and empowering staff to achieve outstanding performance.

Bringing representatives from all sections of the system together is a prerequisite for creating system thinkers in action. In the LEA, the social technology of collaborative team coaching (CTC) (Schley & Schley, 2010) was the vehicle for practising system thinking in action, each CTC team consisting of heterogeneous groups of six participants working together within a mandated structure, one designed to foster a solution-oriented approach rather than a problem-oriented one. In each collaborative team coaching session, one participant as "actor" is guided from the "problem space" in which they are caught, moving toward a "solution space". Goal orientation, creativity, and inventiveness are the foundation and factors of the philosophy of the CTC.

This collaboration in the CTC enables a studied diagnosis of key issues – issues for the development, leadership, and management of an organisation, offering concrete possibilities for solutions and their implementation. It enhances a team's intellectual, creative, and emotional potential; fosters entrepreneurial and goal-oriented thinking and acting; and encourages the forging of new paths and development of new strategies. After a period of searching for the key issues comes the breakthrough in "seeing the seeing" and "seeing from the whole" (Scharmer, 2007). Between the forums, leaders "take home" back to their schools this continuous learning and development process of colleagues by colleagues. As it is learnt and practised it becomes an integral part of an organisation's culture and a significant strategy for building a learning organisation.

What Vignette 1 tells us

Turning to Simpson's (2016) table, we can see immediately that there has been a deliberate and observable shift in the approach to LfL in Austria. In Bentley and Dewey's terms, there has been a move from *self-action* with its focus on the individuality of the leader-practitioner to a commitment to the inter-action essential for leadership as a set of shared or distributed practices. The power of position, so dominant at the time the Academy was introduced into the Austrian system, has been significantly supplemented and somewhat overtaken by the power of networked collective action.

There is no absolutely clear-cut division between management and leadership, and yet their features are distinct. There is no "either – or" but an "as well as". Management, which has been pre-eminent in Austrian educational discourse, carries elements of leadership and vice versa. Management is more a state of behaviour referring to norms; leadership, more a (moral) attitude of influence. Behaving (managing) without a moral attitude is just as problematic as leading without adhering to (given) norms. Competency in management is easier to acquire than the capability of leadership, which requires action to enable staff to rise to their individual challenges and meet them with appropriate measures. Leadership can only be effective insofar as leaders are willing to take on, and work to, their own moral (and policy) agendas. These do need, however, to be grounded within the political framework in which their education systems operate, and it is just so in Austria.

From the outset, the value of sharing was emphasised by the Academy and conceived as "a joint learning process", "colleague by colleague", so that leading and learning together simply became part of the organisational culture. With such a collegial ethos, we are reminded by Simpson (2016) that leadership should never be a solo act, but rather, a social activity imbued with moral purpose. When learning and leading rest on genuine trust and authenticity rather than on positional power, a sharing of moral purpose comes to the fore. It is made explicit and becomes a reference point for dialogue and ongoing self-evaluation. There is little need for prompting because it resides within the mutuality of the moral culture.

This mutuality is readily apparent in the adoption of CTC. Here the Austrian initiative comes closest to the implementation of the trans-actional, the hallmark of the peer-related power so necessary to make a difference on persistent problems. However, the top-down cultural influences on the Austrian system are strong, as the vignette shows, with the trust and authenticity of principals tested as they go about "enticing" staff members to take up the collaborative leadership challenge. The tensions between duty and discretion, the *sollen* and *wollen* highlighted above, will be felt as collaborative inter-action on issues to improve both leadership and learning is undertaken.

Vignette 2

Oral language development

Tough Times Primary School lies in one of the poorest areas in one of Australia's southern states. Its socioeconomic index rating is at the low end of the bottom quartile. This number signals high unemployment, much of it intergenerational, heavy reliance on social security payments and welfare housing, higher than average criminal activity and convictions, low work-life aspirations, higher than average smoking, drug, and alcohol usage, and rates of obesity, all of which lead to higher than average medical and general physical and mental health issues. In combination, these community conditions make Tough Times' catchment a very challenging one for the principal and teachers and indeed, the children themselves.

When it comes to literacy, children tested in 2015 for their oral language skills by the visiting speech pathologist showed marked deficiencies for youngsters prior to entering Year I. In fact, this first-time test showed that just under 70% of Kinder children (30) were assessed as exhibiting "mild to severe" language problems (and these were all children born of English first-language-speaking parents). For example, when shown the pictures of a truck, a bird, and a river, one 5-year-old was unable to say what they were. His teachers could not but speculate on why this youngster was so language deprived. In their search for answers they consulted the internet to find on one site dedicated to "tackling the 'vocabulary gap' between rich and poor children", the following quotation from Hilary Clinton:

> Studies have found that by age four, children in middle and upper class families hear 15 million more words than children in working-class families, and 30 million more words than children in families on welfare. This disparity in hearing words from parents and caregivers translates directly into a disparity in learning words. And that puts our children born with the fewest advantages even further behind. Among those born in 2001, only 58 percent of poor children started school ready to learn, compared to 75 percent of children from middle-income families.
>
> *(www.psychologytoday.com/blog/the-athletes-way/*
> *201402/tackling-the-vocabulary-gap-between-rich-and-poor-children)*

Teachers also noted that in some low-SES (socio-economic status) families, little time was spent in conversing with children. Rather, many children experienced the predominantly procedural language of command and sanction and this with high frequency: "Get back to bed", "Come here", "Don't do that", "Do that again and you'll cop it", "I told you to shut up!". When these one-way instructions occur with debilitating regularity, often accompanied by profanities, they reduce the child's exposure to a wide general-knowledge-informed vocabulary.

Another little girl was described by the teachers as having "speech refusal" (probably selective mutism). This disorder is often attributed to anxiety, shyness, and timidity in social situations and is linked to speech development problems. Although she seemed to understand much of what was being said to her, no one at the school, teachers or children, had ever heard her speak.

The plight of these two children highlighted the need for urgent action which the principal, James, knew was critical. He had recently been reminded in an LfL professional development program that one of the most important platforms for the development of reading skills is the quality and extent of the child's oral language (Bayetto, 2014; Konza, 2011). The figure of 69% really startled James, his deputy principal, Janet, and the Kinder and Year 1 teachers, Marie and Melanie, and together, after discussing an idea suggested by Melanie, they decided to do something about it. From this point on, we pick up the remainder of the story from Dempster et al. (2017, pp. 230–233).

> Together, the team agreed on a strategy aimed at bringing oral language experiences back onto centre stage for all Kinder and Year 1 students. This was the beginning of a partnership that was to grow and strengthen over the ensuing year.

This strategy required James's positional authority because time, opportunity, and financial resources were necessary to support a series of fortnightly oral language excursions designed to enhance students' general knowledge, vocabularies, and confidence in speaking and listening about their shared experiences. The teachers, Marie and Melanie, thoroughly planned what would happen on these excursions and prior to departure developed students' background knowledge about the venues. In support of this planning a discussion paper about oral language, outlining the research and practical approaches, was shared with them (http://www.appa.asn.au/wp-content/uploads/2015/08/Oral-Language-article.pdf). After returning from the oral language excursions the teachers had students talking, writing, and reporting about what had occurred and their responses.

By the third excursion, James acknowledged that the two teachers had assumed the lead in the oral language project and he, like the Deputy Principal, saw himself as providing active support to them. James visited classrooms after each excursion and engaged with individual students as they wrote and spoke about what they had seen and experienced. He described himself as a learner heavily reliant on Marie and Melanie's knowledge. The Deputy Principal created connections with parents by posting photographs of the students on excursion and recounting their excursion when back at school. With a number of parents known to be reluctant about involvement with the school, the use of social media provided an immediate connection. Indeed, this was a welcome addition to their repertoire, spoken of with relish by the partnership. Such was the impact of the oral language excursions on teachers' planning, students' learning, and willingness to talk about their travels that the partnership took the decision to move with an oral language program progressively up the school, starting the following year. The evidence they had collected from samples of students' writing, but more importantly, in the video capture of improvements in oral presentations to their peers, acted as convincing evidence about the value of their strategy. Moreover, others in the school took up advocacy for the oral language program. No better example of this was the role played by the school janitor, Henry, who doubled as bus driver for the excursions. His understanding of the need for all adults to model effective speaking was translated into practice through use of the microphone on bus trips when he pointed out places of interest and landmarks. Interestingly, many of the words he used were often reproduced in students' conversations and writing.

Throughout the year James, Janet, Marie, and Melanie met on a regular basis: when the university researchers visited and again when their follow-up reports arrived. They used these meeting times to examine the evidence provided to plan the next steps in the program and to hear from the researchers about helpful documents such as one used as a basis for development of their assessment rubric. The meetings were also a time to share successes. James was particularly keen on talking about individual students and both Marie and Melanie were enthusiastic about the real change in one child who had begun to talk at school for the first time. All in all, James was prepared to continue to support oral language development not only because of what he was noting about students' burgeoning speaking and listening but also in their overall improved behaviour. On his arrival three years earlier, students in Kinder and Year 1 were known as "runners" – students who would run out of the classroom for no apparent reason and head for home. This was no longer occurring and although the change could not necessarily be fully attributed to the oral language excursion program, all four in the team believed that it had helped to create calmer and more learning-focussed classrooms.

[In the second year, Tough Times Primary School extended] the reach of its program across the school to make concrete the first of the BIG 6, namely, *early and ongoing oral language experiences*. James and his team know it will take an unremitting commitment because of the circumstances these students have in their families and in the local community. James knows that he will have to juggle the limited resources at his disposal, and the early year teachers know that new challenges will come through the classroom door year after year but they believe they're ready for them.

What Vignette 2 tells us

Dewey and Bentley's three forms of action and the three leadership perspectives that Simpson (2016) has derived from them are all evident in the oral language vignette, though the first two are the more apparent. Leadership as self-action shows up in the initiative taken by James, the leader-practitioner, to find a way of addressing the less than desirable oral language capability of a significant proportion of his young pupils. But from that point on, inter-action and a set of distributive leadership practices take over quite fluidly. This is definitely aided by James's apparent willingness to put his power as principal on the "back burner". A four-person team is formed to discuss and agree on a strategy or strategies to improve the scope and depth of children's oral language. Gronn's "hybridity" is evident in the combination of positional leaders (James and Janet) with grassroots teachers (Marie and Melanie) but hierarchy is not prominent in their exchanges other than in the authorisation by James for the use of school resources such as the school's bus, dedicated timetable slots and the school's Facebook page.

That the strategy adopted was suggested by Melanie is further evidence of the non-hierarchical nature of the team, at least while the four were engaged in developing and implementing the program of excursions. The temporary shedding of the principal's power is also noticeable in the "learner" role James adopted, as he followed up the outcomes of each excursion in classroom visits with children so that he might show support for his students and learn more about their oral language experiences.

This role of learner applies to all four in the team, as Melanie and Marie drew on information from research papers and online searches to add to their growing bank of knowledge about oral language capacity. The learning of deputy principal Janet centres on understanding the feasibility and significance of social media in making better connections with parents in the lead up to and following excursions. The welcome of the janitor to the team is added confirmation that hierarchy was not on overt display from the earliest engagement in the project. More than this, it is an example of how leadership in the flow of practice arises. Transaction in the everyday circumstances faced by those at Tough Times Primary opened up members of staff to the possibility and power of collective action. This ultimately resulted in wider interest in oral language and the initiative led by Marie and Melanie to engage others in making oral language experiences for all children in the school a part of each teacher's pedagogical repertoire.

Dialogue about the children's development was undertaken mostly in informal staffroom conversations as teachers discussed the problems they faced in improving children's reading in particular and literacy in general. Marie and Melanie were instrumental in bringing their new-found knowledge to these conversations and to the growing collaboration with their fellow teachers. Self-action by the leader-practitioner comes into view a second time when James's authority is required to confirm the teachers' desire for curriculum change to include oral language experiences explicitly at every grade level.

It is clear from this vignette that leadership action by Marie and Melanie would not have arisen without the initiative and backing of their principal. This confirms the authority embedded in the role, even when leadership is being shared. However, James, who seems to want to reduce the power distance between himself and his teachers, leads a school to believe that in future, spontaneous leadership action in the face of persisting problems may well come from the ground up. It is speculation only, but James may well believe that teacher LfL would be the outcome.

Conclusion

All three perspectives on leadership referred to in this chapter find a home in school settings. The leader–practitioner looms large, almost as a fixed "object" in education systems, intractably hierarchical with layers of positional leadership dominating organisational structures. These are unlikely to be discarded while one person in each school is designated as the accountable officer for what takes place there. The shifts being made in recent years to conceptualise and implement leadership as a set of (distributed) practices retain and often enhance the influential role of the school principal. His or her business it is to "gird the loins" of followers in order to undertake tasks which contribute to the leader's vision, albeit with others who share in its pursuit. While the positional leader may want to define himself or herself as "first among equals", this appears to us to be rather more rhetorical than real in the light of a decade of research into distributed, collaborative, or shared leadership. As we have shown, however, such a "norm" may, in fact, materialise.

Movement towards the idea of leadership emerging in the flow of practice, when and where activity occurs, invests a collective power in those who want to put pedagogical practice under scrutiny. This contributes to enhanced understanding, influencing future practice, adding meaning to one's own agency, and the concept of leadership itself in the process. Put succinctly, our thinking about the three perspectives, when applied to LfL in schools, suggests that we would all be better off with less of the first perspective and more of the second and third. This is particularly important where there is a genuine thirst for understanding leadership and learning and the connections between them.

What then are the challenges to policy we have raised in this chapter?

The most obvious challenge to policy is the lessening of the ubiquitous influence of the heroic leader-practitioner while simultaneously increasing the influence of the great bulk of the profession, the non-position holders, on their everyday activity. The generality of teachers, the "rank and file" of the profession often impugned by contemporary politicians and policymakers, should dare to embrace what leadership in the flow of practice can mean for their shared experience, research, and critical friendship. Freed from hierarchical mindsets, communities of practice can become a reality. The creation of convivial networks would then promote innovative solutions to troublesome problems, and teachers' professional judgement then would become more highly valued than it is at present. In its turn, professionalism would be greatly enhanced. We expand on these themes and the importance of dialogical processes in better understanding LfL in the flow of daily practice in Chapter 6.

We are realistic enough to acknowledge that grassroots leadership and the learning that accompanies it will not occur in highly structured school systems without policymakers and principals recognising the tangible benefits that can follow from relinquishing the power of position. While the embrace of collective agency may be more aspirational than realistic, were it to be realised, we could envisage a much-enhanced learning profession. It would see teachers coming together as colleagues, improving educational practice and challenging the limitations of current social and organisational structures. Such an outcome requires voluntary agency, exercised in the interests of students as a first priority, in the interests of an enhanced profession as a second, with the interests of the system acknowledged and addressed as a third. As we have argued in Chapter 3, voluntary agency and these priorities are essential elements of professional integrity. They are matters to which we return in Chapter 7, "Enhancing teacher professionality".

References

Aguerrando, I., & Vezub, L. (2011). Leadership for effective school improvement: Support for schools and teachers' professional development in the Latin American region. In

T. Townsend & J. MacBeath (Eds.), *International handbook of leadership for learning (Part 1)* (pp. 691–715). Dordrecht: Springer.

Bayetto, A. (2014). *Oral language.* Australian Primary Principals Association. Retrieved from https://www.appa.asn.au/wp-content/uploads/2015/08/Oral-Language-article.pdf

Barzano, G., & Brotto, F. (2009). Leadership, learning and Italy: A tale of atmospheres. In J. MacBeath & Y. C. Cheng, *Leadership for learning: International perspectives* (pp. 223–240). Rotterdam: Sense Publishers.

Bush, T. (2013). Distributed leadership: The model of choice in the 21st century. *Educational Management Administration & Leadership, 41*(5), 543–544.

Bush, T., & Glover, D. (2012). Distributed leadership in action: Leading high-performing leadership teams in English schools. *School Leadership & Management, 32*(1), 21–36.

Crevani, L. (2015). Is there leadership in a fluid world? Exploring the ongoing production of direction in organizing. *Leadership, 0*(0), 1–27.

Crevani, L., Lindgren, M., & Packendorff, J. (2010). Leadership, not leaders: On the study of leadership as practices and interactions. *Scandinavian Journal of Management, 26,* 77–86.

Day, C., Sammons, P., Hopkins, D., Harris, A., Leithwood, K., Gu, Q., & Brown, E. (2010). *Ten strong claims about successful school leadership.* Nottingham: National College for School Leadership and Children's Services.

Dempster, N., Townsend, T., Johnson, G., Bayetto, A., Lovett, S., & Stevens, E. (2017). *Leadership and literacy: Principals, partnerships and pathways to improvement.* Cham, Switzerland: Springer.

Dewey, J., & Bentley, A. (1949). *Knowing and the known.* Boston, MA: Beacon Press.

Endrissat, N., & von Arx, W. (2013). Leadership practices and context: Two sides of the same coin. *Leadership, 9*(2), 278–304.

Gergen, K. J., & Hersted, L. (2016). Developing leadership as dialogic practice. In J. A. Raelin (Ed.), *Leadership-as-practice: Theory and application* (pp. 178–197). London: Routledge.

Glatter, R. (2009). Wisdom and bus schedules: Developing school leadership. *School Leadership and Management, 29*(3), 225–237.

Gronn, P. (2009). Leadership configurations. *Leadership, 5*(3), 381–394.

Hartley, D. (2010). Paradigms: How far does research in distributed leadership 'stretch'? *Educational Management Administration & Leadership, 38*(3), 271–285.

Heck, R. H., & Hallinger, P. (2010). Collaborative leadership effects on school improvement: Integrating unidirectional- and reciprocal-effects models. *Elementary School Journal, 111*(2), 226–252.

Katzenmeyer, M., & Møller, G. (1996). *Awakening the sleeping giant: Helping teachers develop as leaders.* Thousand Oaks, CA: Corwin Press.

Konza, D. (2011). *Understanding the reading process.* Research into Practice Series. Retrieved from http://www.decd.sa.gov.au/literacy/files/links/link_157541.pdf

Leithwood, K., Day, C., Sammons, P., Harris, A., & Hopkins, D. (2006). *Seven strong claims about successful leadership.* Nottingham: National College for School Leadership.

Leithwood, K., & Riehl, C. (2003). *What we know about successful school leadership.* Philadelphia, PA: Laboratory for Student Success, Temple University.

Lieberman, A., & Friedrich, L. (2007). Changing teaching from within: Teachers as leaders. In J. MacBeath & Y. C. Cheng (Eds.), *Leadership for learning: International perspectives* (pp. 41–64). Rotterdam: Sense Publishers.

Louis, K. S., Leithwood, K., Wahlstrom, K. L., & Anderson, S. E. (2010). *Investigating the links to improved student learning: Final report of research findings.* Retrieved from http://conservancy.umn.edu/bitstream/11299/140885/1/Learning-from-Leadership_Final-Research-Report_July-2010.pdf

MacBeath, J. (2012). *Future of teaching profession.* Cambridge, UK: Education International Research Institute and University of Cambridge, Faculty of Education.

MacBeath, J., & Dempster, N. (Eds.) (2009). *Connecting leadership and learning. Principles of practice.* London: Routledge.

MacBeath, J., Oduro, G. K. T., & Waterhouse, J. (2004). *Distributed leadership in action: Full report.* Nottingham: National College for School Leadership.

Murphy, J., Smylie, M., Mayrowetz, D., & Louis, K. S. (2009). The role of the principal in fostering the development of distributed leadership. *School Leadership & Management, 29*(2), 181–214.

Organisation for Economic Co-operation and Development (OECD). (2008). *Improving school leadership. Vol. 1: Policy and practice.* Paris: OECD Publishing.

Park, V., & Datnow, A. (2009). Co-constructing distributed leadership: District and school connections in data-driven decision-making. *School Leadership & Management, 29*(5), 477–494.

Pelinka, A. (1996). Die (veränderte) Kultur bildungspolitischer Entscheidungen. In W. Specht & J. Thonhauser (Eds.), *Studien zur Bildungsforschung & Bildungspolitik. Schulqualität.* Entwicklungen, Befunde, Perspektiven (Vol. 14) (pp. 22–37). Innsbruck: Studien Verl.

Raelin, J. (2016). Imagine there are no leaders: Reframing leadership as collaborative agency. *Leadership, 12*(2), 131–158.

Scharmer, C. O. (2007). *Theory U. Leading from the future as it emerges.* Cambridge, MA: SOL.

Schley, V., & Schley, W. (2010). Handbuch Kollegiales Teamcoaching – Systemische Beratung in Aktion, Innsbruck, Austria: Studienverlag.

Simpson, B. (2016). Where's the agency in leadership-as-practice? In J. A. Raelin (Ed.), *Leadership-as-practice: Theory and application* (pp. 159–178). London: Routledge.

Spillane, J. (2006). *Distributed leadership.* San Francisco, CA: Jossey-Bass.

Spillane, J. P., Healey, K., Parise, L. M., & Kenney, A. (2010). A distributed perspective on learning leadership. In J. Robertson & H. Timperley (Eds.), *Leadership and learning* (pp. 159–171). London: SAGE Publications.

Swaffield, S., & MacBeath, J. (2009). Leadership for learning. In J. MacBeath & N. Dempster (Eds.), *Connecting leadership and learning: Principles for practice* (pp. 32–52). London and New York: Routledge.

Vosniadou, S. (Ed.). (2008). *Educational psychology handbook series. International handbook of research on conceptual change.* New York: Routledge.

Woods, P. A., & Gronn, P. (2009). Nurturing democracy: The contribution of distributed leadership to a democratic organizational landscape. *Educational Management Administration & Leadership, 37*(4), 430–451.

6

THINKING DIFFERENTLY ABOUT LEARNING AND TEACHING

Teachers are good at telling pupils what to do but never very good at telling them why they're doing it. Nor do we give pupils time to reflect on a finished activity.

Why do we need to think differently about learning and teaching? Why should this assume such a high priority in the challenge to government policies? Why is there not a more robust and sustained critique of policies which constrain teaching and inhibit learning? The answer to these questions is to be found in the wider global environment, in the consensus and contradictions among international agencies, policymakers, teachers, and young people themselves as to what is worth learning and what is prescribed.

Over a protracted period, both before and since the turn of the century, we have been persuaded to see learning as performance against mandated standards which may be measured and compared. A focus on the individual and his or her needs has meanwhile become lost in quantitative combinations and simplistic comparisons of attainment amongst schools, systems, and countries. What is measured then becomes the major focus for teaching, with attainment standards the ultimate warrant of classroom pedagogy. As the age-old axiom has it, "Who examines controls", so that the measure of the best teachers is about those who are most adept at eliciting authorised performance from their captive clientele.

We expect policy to set standards. No education systems could survive without a clear commitment to standards, to monitoring achievement, and alive to international comparisons. The creation and development of performance indicators, in which the OECD has played a major role over three decades, was designed to inform the profession and the public as to how well school systems were serving their clientele and where room for improvement might lie. While there are strong arguments for the value and potential benefits of such information, it was inevitable that governments would compete in what would progressively become a high-stakes "game". It was, perhaps, also inevitable that the subjects and forms of learning less amenable to quantification would lose out and that "hard" subjects would provide the most robust of comparative measures.

So, the curriculum, the defining body of content, skills, and dispositions that all children should master, has become inexorably shaped by what we are required to assess, in what ways that should be effected, and its assumed value – not so much for children as for the national economy. We may debate the relative merit of art as against mathematics, science versus music, physical education or grammar, but this becomes a wholly academic pursuit when what matters is what counts and what can be counted. This implicit hierarchy of values is accompanied by an uneasy silence, or at best a nodded acknowledgement, to engagement, intrinsic interest, stimulation, and emotional growth. Cooperation, collaboration, mutuality, empathy, and service are, apparently, to be encouraged but achievement is individually defined and achieved by self-interested competition. We may even learn to sympathise with, while enjoying, others' misfortunes.

So, spontaneity and serendipity in the classroom disappear. Stress becomes an attendant aspect of teachers' lives but now also endemic among young people and children as young as five. Who said education was fun? As Charles Fadel from the Centre for Curriculum Redesign at Harvard University says in conversation with Jo Earp (2017, p. 1):

> What is required is a massive rethink about modernising what students learn as an imperative. Where Science, Technology, Engineering and Maths (STEM) matter increasingly but Humanities and Arts remain essential, each borrowing from the other, for a deeply versatile education. Where working with others, at school, in the community, and in the workplace is as vital as ensuring growth at every level, allowing top students to thrive while assisting all students in areas where they are struggling. Where young people are given the skills and qualities they need to thrive in work and life. There is general acknowledgement around the world that to equip young people for success we need to shift from a knowledge-only based education towards incorporating skills such as creative problem solving, collaboration and character skills such as resilience, agility, compassion and respect. These elements are central to new success.

What is worrying about this challenge is its familiarity. We may well argue that we have been thinking "massively" for more than a decade while little actually changes in the policy world, except perhaps for the rhetoric.

As long as policy dictates and shapes what is learnt, how it is learnt, and how it is evaluated, it is likely that change will be, at best, slow and reluctant. In England in 2017, Education ministers were still lauding the curriculum reforms of 2013 which took teachers back to the curriculum of half a century ago when rote learning, memorising dates of great battles, and drawing rivers on blank maps defined what was worth knowing, although only temporarily.

While this brave old world necessarily included homework, its value and quality remained unquestioned. It was of itself seen as a good discipline while, regardless of home circumstances, failure to complete the requisite task would incur sanctions and further disaffection not only with school but, more fundamentally, with learning. At the same time, courageous school leaders were questioning the value of ritual homework while inventive teachers were experimenting with creative tasks and shared projects.

The intensification of learning in the classroom carried over into the home can prove counterproductive, given a deep misunderstanding in the policy community of contexts, motivations, and the social nature of learning. The relentless focus on standards often excludes or discounts parents and families as leaders of learning together with an obliviousness as to the teaching, learning, and leadership opportunities that exist in the wider community. It is time to think, and act, differently.

PricewaterhouseCoopers's study (2001) described some of the constraining conditions of classroom learning, together with teachers' expectations of what could realistically be achieved within the limiting parameters of the school day. It was echoed in Graham Leicester's (2011) doleful image of squeezing the last drop of professionalism and ownership out of the profession. The following are some of the peculiar pressures on learning and teaching from the viewpoint of teachers interviewed.

> There was relatively little contact with other adults so that some teachers had virtually no time for a conversation with another adult during a whole day.
>
> Not being in control of their work was a salient cause of stress. This was brought about by the pace and manner of change with insufficient support to meet those changes and a resentment about having to engage in tasks which did not support learning.
>
> There were also many tasks which could be carried out by support staff rather than by teachers, or addressed more efficiently using ICT. When these tasks carried over into weekends, it was an additional source of resentment and disaffection for teachers.
>
> At the core of the job was the need to put on a "performance" for many hours each day. This, while it could at times be exhilarating, was also often exhausting.
>
> Pressures were intensified by an inappropriate expectation of what schools and teachers could achieve, especially in a social context of deteriorating pupil behaviour and a lack of parental support.

In a 2003 article in *Educational Leadership*, Rick Weissbourd describes the "steady drizzle of helplessness and hopelessness that can wear teachers down". He writes:

> Although a mountainous literature exists on depression, psychologists have remarkably little understanding of disillusionment. They don't even have a vocabulary for talking about it. But disillusionment – especially the loss of

belief that they can make a difference in students' lives – is one of the biggest reasons that nearly one half of teachers in the United States leave the profession within their first five years of teaching … Disillusionment becomes pernicious when it slides into helplessness and passivity – when teachers don't have the confidence, support, or opportunities for the creativity needed to master those realities.

(p. 4)

At its roots is what Dollard, Winefield, and Winefield (2001) describe as "emotional dissonance", the mismatch between felt emotions and what are seen as "required" emotions. Why teachers are at greater risk of suffering from emotional dissonance than most other human service workers, write Dormann and Kaiser (2002), is due to the heavy emotional investment that they make in their students. "The more important that care is to a teacher, the more emotionally devastating is the experience of failing to provide it" (Hargreaves & Tucker, 1991, p. 496).

Similar themes are echoed in many countries. This is the context for many teachers where governments are, as Leicester writes, squeezing out their last drop of professionalism. These issues have to take a back seat for teachers already caught in the vice of competitive performance tables, oblivious to ethnic, cultural, and political issues, drawing selectively on highly contested data, applying further pressure on schools and teachers to emulate South Korea, Japan, Finland, or whatever country is the current aspirational benchmark. Visits to South Korea and Japan by a group of international school-based researchers shed a whole different light on policy and the possible.

Case study: The Learning School

If this seems too far-fetched a scenario, consider the case of The Learning School, now in its 14th year of operation. The brainchild of an assistant headteacher in Anderson High School in the Shetland Islands, the creation of The Learning School in 1999 was designed to expand the horizons of young people living on an island to the north of Scotland, geographically and culturally disconnected from "the mainland". For a whole school year, a group of young people leave their classrooms behind and travel the world, visiting, observing, participating, and researching in classrooms, schools, and communities.

In early September, young people from six or seven countries come together to the Shetland Islands, usually in pairs, for orientation and training in research methodology. This is followed by four to six weeks in each of the different countries, allowing time for deeper exploration of where culture and schooling meet, or fail to meet. Living with families offers experience of life at first hand – village life in the Czech Republic, living with a Japanese family who speak no English, and the privations of a South African township demand a continuing reframing of expectations, assumptions, and values.

Sophie, who lived with a black family in a South African township, recounts the shock on her first day when the daughter of her own age expressed her dislike for white people, a shock for Sophie, who had never before had to face such explicit racism. This experience was instrumental in helping Sophie reflect on her own prejudices, acknowledging her own ignorance as a root of bigotry, and coming to value the harshness of this experience – as she later wrote, "an important lesson for life". Her fellow traveller, Jolene, aged 16, summarised her experience in these words – "I have probably learnt as much in these 10 months as I did in 13 years of school".

The 2003 book on The Learning School contains powerful testimonies such as the following:

> This year has been a massive education to us all, an almost vertical learning curve. I often worried that I was not using this opportunity to learn as much as I could, but now after having stepped back indefinitely from this particular journey I can see how by watching and feeling another culture from within you cannot help but learn infinite amounts. It is the greatest educational tool ever to have at one's disposal. Teaching things schools will never be able to teach, through first-hand experience, feeding a desire to understand the world in which we live. This year has given me a real thirst to continue to test myself academically and to become more aware of different societies, cultures and people, as I am sure it has to everyone who was a part of Learning School 2.
> *(Colin, in MacBeath, Sugimine et al., 2003, p. 36)*

Summarising their own learning in their book, students list some of the skills they have acquired and attitudes that have changed; in summary – thinking differently.

- challenging your own values and assumptions;
- learning to see things from different perspectives;
- working as a member of a team exercising leadership;
- learning to compromise;
- observing with discrimination;
- working to deadlines;
- taking difficult decisions;
- making presentations to large, and critical audiences;
- exercising initiative;
- writing for different audiences;
- increasing self-knowledge; and
- learning to deal with conflict.

Geography, Social Studies, and History are no longer "subjects" but lived experiences unlikely ever to be forgotten, as the following visit to a site of major historic significance vividly illustrates:

> The opportunity to accompany these young people to the Memorial Museum in Hiroshima was a profoundly moving occasion. German, Scottish and Swedish students were confronted together with the role of their own

nations in one of history's most devastating events. Its impact was brought to bear in the remnants of everyday things – charred clothes, relics of abandoned toys, a melted tricycle to which a child's shoe still adhered. While their discussion around the exhibits had the effect of sharpening national identities, it also brought to the surface, and elucidated, values that were deeply shared. The following observation from a Scottish student brings a new meaning to the concept of "potential", which is used in such a limiting way in current school discourse. As Jolene wrote later "This year has allowed me to see things from a different angle and to realise that sometimes we place limitations on ourselves and that there is so much more that we can do".

(MacBeath, Sugimine et al., 2003, p. 38)

The question raised by these various ventures is whether it requires an escape from the classroom in order to expand mental horizons. Why, having created an institution for educating children, do we need to then get out of it in order to learn? Wasn't the essential purpose of schooling to allow virtual experiences and imaginative travel beyond the immediate present?

What we have learnt

Expanding horizons

The question raised in this case study is the extent to which schools and classrooms can all too easily constrain and narrow horizons and to what extent does escape require a physical or virtual release from the timetable, curriculum, and assessment? What were the essential elements that contributed to Colin and his colleagues' testimony that they had learnt more in these 9 months than in all the previous years of classroom-bound learning? Colin writes about "feeding a desire to understand the world in which we live". Is this not the purpose of schools?

While all five *Carpe Vitam* principles (see Chapter 3) are exemplified in this venture, perhaps above all a sense of agency was pre-eminent. Their full story told in their own book recounts a sequence of episodes of risk-taking initiative, venturing well beyond their comfort zones, testing the latent power and authority which their schools had never allowed them. As learning was released from its directed confines a huge amount was learnt about leadership, and about individual and shared accountability, recast as reciprocal and arising naturally from living and learning together over a number of months. Conceptions of ability and potential were challenged, rethought, and reframed. As young people returned to their schools they brought with them an enhanced understanding of schooling and education and the differences between them.

Thinking differently

What does it mean to think differently, to challenge convention, to escape from the classroom, to change the habits of a lifetime? Can we change what Carol Dweck

(2007) has described as our "mindset", a settled approach to our own minds and how we think about ourselves? It has been characterised as keeping a running account of what's happening to us, an internal monologue to explain why we can and can't do things, why we rise or don't rise to a challenge. To what extent is this a product of what our parents, our teachers, or schooling in general, tell us about ourselves, our "ability", our "potential", our likely destination in life? Thinking differently starts, we believe, with a reconnection with the primary educators of our children – parents and extended family members – and the situations and circumstances in which they raise their offspring: Doing what comes naturally. Mick Waters, formerly Director of the Qualifications and Curriculum Authority in England, cast it in these terms:

> Children's learning is best when they do the natural things and we help them to cross thresholds as a result. They make, do and mend, they have adventures, they produce plays and shows, play instruments, speak different languages, and they grow things, care for creatures and have collections. All of these are gateways that teachers make into turnstiles to a brighter future.
>
> *(Report to the Children's University)*

Thinking differently about families and learning

Recent policies in Western countries have encouraged closer links between schools, homes, and communities. On the surface, policy reform might appear to embrace new ways of thinking about the roles that parents and communities play in leading learning, but such a perception is open to question. An analysis of school–family partnership policies in the industrialised economies of the OECD shows that parent and family engagement with schools is based largely on assuring them of the extent to which school accountability standards are being met.

Paradoxically, the policy rhetoric is for school principals to lead productive partnerships with parents. But what assumptions drive the conceptualisation of "productive learning partnerships"? What counts as parental engagement? Who is included in the partnership and on what terms, for what ultimate purpose? These questions cannot be meaningfully addressed, however, when the school is centre stage, with parents and families cast in a subsidiary or supporting role. While the move to increased family engagement in children's learning has been recognised and attempts have been made to construct a genuine dialogue between home and school, the beneficiaries have tended to be the better educated, often white, middle-class families. A different story is to be told about those from marginalised communities, often immigrants, refugees, or first nations' people, who might not speak English as a first language and whose school experiences are less memorable.

The reasons for parental disaffection are easy to discern. It is schools who determine the nature of home–school–community engagement. It is schools who expect that parents will dutifully endorse the value of their child's classroom experiences. It is parents' obligation to prioritise and support what is being taught and ensure their children's compliance. It is their duty to engage their children with prescribed reading, to sign their homework or offer an explanation for their failure to do so. It is then too often assumed that non-English speaking parents are disengaged and unconcerned about learning and so carry the blame for their apparent disengagement and lack of concern as to their children's achievement. School principals and teachers become dispirited when they fail to engage what they describe as these "hard-to-reach" parents. This further emphasises the need to think differently about what this means and why that issue runs so deep, to be asking the question, is it schools that are hard to reach and if so, why? Mapp and Soo's (2010) work helps to re-vision schools' views on parent engagement by debunking the myth of hard-to-reach parents.

Goodall and Montgomery (2014) have argued that a key reason for the failure of policy reform to answer the above questions and to address the underlying issues stems from an unbalanced conception of power relations and of agency. Parents are requested to be auxiliary providers of the school curriculum, as evidence of their engagement with schools. When parents are unable to provide such a service, for a variety of reasons, they are considered disengaged, disaffected, or disinterested in their children's learning.

Thinking and acting differently about parental engagement

To think differently would be the prelude to engaging leaders, teachers, and families as active participants in professional learning. Its success would be measured by its impact on those families most constrained by current practice. This would be a first step in changing the perception, the rhetoric, and the reality of hard-to-reach families. Such a shift in understanding has to be founded on the knowledge gained from and with parents, in which family and community strengths are the focus and foundation of capability building (Auerbach, 2012) – and, ultimately, leadership of learning.

An early example of a shift to such parent agency may be seen in a pilot study where Spanish-speaking migrant farm workers, parents of preschool children, sent drawings of their family activities to their children's classrooms to supplement a bi-language reading program (Caesar & Nelson, 2014). Language strengths, not deficits, were on show here.

Bolivar and Chrispeels (2011) take this kind of shift seriously in their research into community action, empowering low-income families to engage in, and advocate for, children's success at school. They see parents as resuming their pivotal role in children's education by seeking school support for what is important to them and their families. The partnerships shaped through this type of action are more likely to take place where there is a genuinely equal footing, one which enables the powers of the school and the agency of home to complement each other.

While enlightened school leaders are looking for ways to shift the discourse and practice from exclusion to inclusion, doing so remains difficult when it appears, from an outside-school perspective, that the agenda is institutionally controlled. Two important strategies enlist "institutional agents" and "cultural brokers". Stanton-Salazar (2011) describes institutional agents as high-status, non-kin agents who have relatively high status within the system, allowing them to provide essential forms of social and institutional support. In a similar vein Jezewshi (1990), from an ethnographical perspective, describes cultural brokers who serve as intermediaries at the most basic level – bridging the cultural gap by communicating differences and similarities between cultures. They may also serve in more sophisticated roles, mediating and negotiating complex processes within organisations, government, and communities, and between interest groups or countries. As Jezewshi suggests, these intermediaries may:

- assess and understand their own cultural identities and value systems;
- recognise the values that guide and mould attitudes and behaviours;
- understand a community's traditional beliefs, values, and practices and changes that occur through acculturation;
- understand and practise the tenets of effective cross-cultural communication, including the cultural nuances of both verbal and non-verbal communication; and
- advocate for the client, to ensure the delivery of effective child welfare services.

Both concepts have the potential to act as levers for change "both ways" in how children learn inside schools, in homes, and out in their communities. The role of cultural brokers in supporting children's learning has been seen to work productively when the broker is trusted and respected by school staff as well as by families and communities (Johnson et al., 2014). The work of the broker can be seen as disrupting and reforming the divide between how schools, families, and communities view learning. Brokering has the potential to build capabilities for collaboration both ways, inside and outside schools, so that the nature and extent of learning becomes place based and open to negotiation.

The practices of institutional agents might become more closely aligned to the cultural broker's role, with a further reconsideration of power and agency. For such an alignment to occur, cultural brokers need access to institutional and social capital. Too often this is the missing link. In many cases, the position of cultural brokering has been offered to, and taken up by, community members who are tasked by the school with "fixing" behavioural and attendance issues, without any thought to empowering them to critique the situation and the discourses that underpin the problem.

Before we can expect different thinking about learning, schools need to challenge long-held cultural assumptions underpinning the perceived problems impeding children's achievement. Learning the school's way is the status quo, reinforced by successive bouts of policy reform. Learning both ways is less familiar, but possible, through the alignment made accessible in "culturing broking" and "institutional agency".

Communities and NGOs

Emerging evidence on relationships between schools and their communities challenges much of what has been assumed about the role of schools, parents, and communities. There are still places bearing signs such as "no parents beyond this point" while in some other venues, parents are welcomed into classrooms and work alongside teachers and with students. The determined reach into the school by community groups and not-for-profit non-government agencies (NGOs) is testimony to a grass-roots recognition that learning and teaching are responsibilities that must be taken seriously both within and beyond the school site. Yet, there remains a long way to go.

A program driven by the work of the NGO The Smith Family (TSF), in a remote Australian town, has demonstrated a move in this direction. In practice, TSF employed coaches (in this instance, qualified social workers) to work full-time in dedicated rooms on the school site in supporting and empowering middle-school girls to attend school more regularly, to engage in learning and in different forms of leadership, to develop positive social interactions, and to graduate to high school. Many of the girls are from low-income families and a high proportion of them are Aboriginal and Torres Strait Islanders. The coaches' roles are as "institutional agents", inducting girls and their families into new social and educational networks and learning inside and outside the school curriculum. The coaches' work as supportive agents is significant in so far as it is performed by adults who are not family or school staff but are in a position to broker both-ways relationships for learning.

The success of the brokerage is such that families have reported new-found confidence in forming relationships with school staff and other families in supporting their children's appetite for learning (see Johnson & Wheeley, 2016). There is a way to go before the families are empowered to challenge the status quo and introduce culturally relevant ways of learning into the school curriculum. When this happens, it will bring together and demonstrate a fusion of institutional agency and cultural brokerage.

Notwithstanding developments like those described above, the question remains: why have we educators failed to engage parents and the wider community in a fuller understanding of what learning means? Could it be that our growing knowledge of a child's cognitive and emotional development is invariably left to the popular media to educate the public, rather than coming from educators themselves? Is it not we who have a clear professional responsibility to interpret and apply what we know about the brain, learning individually and socially, learning disabilities, and what current research about them is telling us?

Modes of knowing and being

We owe much to Jean Piaget and fellow researchers who took time to closely observe and painstakingly document how children learnt at different stages of development. It was a revelation for teachers to learn why so much of teaching was based on an adult-centred view of the world. While child-centredness was to come in for considerable criticism, Piaget's studies provided the groundwork for Jerome Bruner to offer a less age-based, sequentially deterministic "theory of instruction", and for Kieran Egan (1997) in Canada to revisit Piaget with new insights.

Egan (1997) points to the fallacy in stage theory, or its application, as with developing intellectual and emotional maturity we do not, he argues, put away childish things. Rather, we have access to a wider range of modes of thought. He offers an alternative theoretical stance. While accepting many of the valid insights from stage theories, he has problematised and reframed these, depicting them as modes of knowing which need to be applied more fluidly to children and young people's progressive learning journey.

In his book *The Educated Mind*, Egan (1997) outlines a theory which, although broadly developmental in nature, is also recursive, so that whether as children or as adults, we constantly revisit ways of knowing, building not so much on what we know but on how we know. As what we know becomes more deeply layered and more finely textured by the mental modes with which we engage, we become more insightful and sophisticated in the way we apprehend and process knowledge; in other words, we get better at learning how to learn.

Egan's five cognitive tools

Egan proposes five modes of understanding and cognitive tools which broadly follow a developmental sequence and although most are characteristic of certain ages and stages, all are facets of human beings' attempts to comprehend their world.

Somatic understanding is in evolutionary and developmental terms the most primitive form of interpreting the world, yet essential to continuously feeling our way through life. It is memetic, a representational mode which does not rely on language but uses bodily sensation, rhythm, and musicality to learn and communicate with others.

Mythic understanding is a fundamental mode of thought, most characteristic of early childhood in which the world is constructed of binary oppositions – good and evil, truth and lies, black and white. It is dominated by affective images rather than words, appealing to metaphor which graphically opens up new ways of apprehending causality and relationships.

Romantic understanding has its roots in the real world, made available by the tools of literacy and therefore offering a more distanced and complex version of events. The simplicity of binary oppositions is problematised and relationships are complexified. For young children it is "the trek out of Eden to the adult's more prosaic world". Yet it is a reality in which wonder, the exotic, and the extreme exert a particular fascination.

Philosophic understanding is a product of a search for intelligible replicable truth that lies beneath the surface appearance of things. It is concerned with norms and the rules of argument, logic, and evidence. It is systematic, abstract, and dispassionate and moves beyond an interest in the particular to the general and generalisable.

Ironic understanding does not settle for the explanations of logic and science. It is reflexive and quizzical. It seeks to question not just what we know but how we know it. It recognises the tension that exists between an inherent sceptical approach to knowing and the need for a general knowledge schema within which we make sense out of non-sense. Irony without philosophic capacity, however, is impotent.

Understanding in any one of these modes, argues Egan (1997), does not fade away to be replaced by the next, but rather each properly coalesces in significant degree with its predecessor. So, as adults we have access to all modes, including somatic understanding which, although to the fore in infancy, continues to be deployed in adulthood. We accrue a wider repertoire of ways of understanding and a more highly developed social sensitivity as to when the somatic, mythic, romantic, philosophical, or ironic mode is most appropriate. This ability to move around among modes of thinking is what systems theorists refer to as the principle of requisite variety. It describes the intellectual tool called into use so as to conform with the complexity of what it represents. In complex problem solving, whether by scientists, philosophers, inventors, or business executives at the cutting edge, learning is very often playful and romantic as well as philosophic and ironic, as much given to wrong answers as to right ones.

As adults, we may find ourselves socially embarrassed when caught out in childish modes of behaviour, indulging the child in the adult, yet no matter how grown up we are, we invent alternative magical worlds, fantasise and dream, enjoy adult fairy stories, science fiction, and horror movies, and go to fancy dress parties. And even as philosophic and ironic adults, argues Egan (1997, p. 162), very often "magic trumps science". An alien paying a visit to a large newsagent might construct a theory of what preoccupies earthlings by scanning the 101 covers of adult magazines.

As adults, we also create challenges for ourselves – in music, leisure, the arts, and sport, which we pursue with obsessive dedication, much of it competitive against others, much of it competitive against our own previous best. We pursue what Csikzentimahlyi (1990) terms "flow" experiences, the psychological high we get from the meeting point of challenge and skill. We seek out cognitive challenges, through Sudoku, crosswords, jigsaw puzzles, chess and bridge problems, pub quizzes, and video games, because the progress from cognitive dissonance to cognitive resolution is intrinsically rewarding. Often persisting into adulthood are the collections we started as children – stamps, coins, comics and magazines, dolls, Dinky toys and train sets, military artefacts, and other memorabilia to which we form a deep emotional attachment. The desire, or need, to collect, to complete the set, to reach the next level, is a powerful emotional driver.

It seems that human beings are never truly satisfied with the status quo and pursue higher levels of attainment and intelligence through the range of tools they have at their disposal. When we have access to what Vygotsky (1962, 1978) terms "mediating intellectual tools" it opens up new ideas and alternative ways of understanding the world. Our restless inquiry prompts us not to settle for immediate reality, or the too-easily known. The drive for novelty is always in tension, however, with the comfort of the familiar. As Mark Twain puts it, "what gets us in trouble is what we think we know but it just ain't so".

Vygotsky describes the zone of proximal development (ZPD) to represent the sphere of knowing beyond our current understanding. The stimulus to move beyond what we currently know, or think we know, may come from the scaffolding of teachers but also from peers or parents or from our own psychological need to achieve, to know more, to do it better. In formal settings and conventional curricula, the ZPD is often interpreted as the next linear step represented by predetermined targets, rather than, as Vygotsky intended, as a horizon of possibilities which may take us in new and uncharted directions. The Scottish Futures Forum has, over a period of a decade, worked on potential scenarios, taking issue with McKinsey and Company (2010) whose visions for the future are essentially extensions of what already exists. Leicester writes:

> I suggested that the real challenge for schools in an age of rapid change is to prepare our young people "for jobs that don't yet exist, using technologies that have not been invented, in order to solve problems we don't even know are problems yet". No school system in the world has adequately addressed this challenge, even though all of them know they must do so.
>
> *(2011, p. 2)*

As Leicester argues, it will take a special kind of innovation to move to new paradigms. These as yet unknown needs will not be met simply by "squeezing the last drop of performance or efficiency out of the systems we already have – even though the political clamour, especially in the age of austerity, is to do precisely that".

Against this more unconstrained view of people as learners, rather than as the student compliant to school norms would suggest, we acknowledge the reality of institutional learning and teaching as one point on a much-expanded learning compass. About which, we need to think differently.

Thinking differently about school learning and teaching

While our mindset may be shaped by our family and community experiences before we first enter a classroom, to what extent does the school experience reinforce and exaggerate our internal monologue and limit our ability to rise to new challenges? While, on the one hand, praise for simply being clever may lead to complacency, it may also inhibit effort and accomplishment. So, children learn to invest their time in "documenting their intelligence or talents instead of developing them" (Protocol Education, 2014).

We are still, year by year, learning more about the human mind, its hitherto unsuspected capacities which challenge our understandings of "intelligence" and performance in and beyond the classroom. The most exceptional and dramatic examples of mindsets come from children we deem to have "complex special needs", their unique views of the world and expression of emotion frequently misunderstood or misinterpreted. Asperger syndrome, for example, can take a variety of forms and not always be easy to discern, including in many people with high intellectual capacity and intense, highly focused interests, often evident from a fairly young age.

At Cambridge University, Simon Baron-Cohen's (2008) groundbreaking studies of Asperger syndrome have found that for every three cases, there are two which have not been identified. He writes that "while cognitive empathy is impaired, affective empathy may be intact, while for a small sub group – with alexithymia – these children and young people appear not to understand their own feelings and lack the words to describe their feelings to others" (p. 15). Referring to a rare form of Asperger's – the "savant syndrome", in which "special needs" encompasses people who display extraordinary abilities – Hiles (2001, 2002) writes, "we will never truly understand human memory and cognition until we understand the savant" (para 1).

While cases such as these are exceptional, they do tell us something about the hidden capacities of the human mind. Yet the compartmentalisation of our brains does serve an important purpose. While limiting our encyclopaedic memory, it acts as a protection against knowing too much and thinking too wildly. But that still leaves a hugely unknown and untapped creativity which exposes the easy rhetoric of "fulfilling potential".

Fulfilling potential is too elusive a goal for the social institutions we have created. It is in the very DNA of schools and schooling to bring some form of order and sequence into our learning so that the wildness of our thinking is tamed and compartmentalised. So, over time, English, Geography, History, Physics and Chemistry, Art and Music become subjects against which memorisation and attainment are measured. The gold standard is less about comprehension, internalisation, and mastery than it is about couching performance in terms of attainment benchmarks and relative comparisons with our age-related peers.

More significant and more deeply embedded in schools are the lessons we learn about authority – the authority of knowledge, of relationships, of our capacities and destinies. In Robert Mackenzie's (1965) book *Escape from the Classroom*, he describes not only his pupils' physical release from the constraints of the timetable but more significantly, an escape from the conventions of the mind. His was not a de-schooling agenda but a way of expanding physical and intellectual parameters so that return to the classroom was always invested with new insights, new ways of seeing.

In the words of the OECD, *school* and *classroom* do not offer a satisfactory architecture for framing learning environments, as these "construction sites" are essentially institutional and partial. These two key aspects of schools as we know them account for the process by which learning becomes institutionalised, and the selective process by which inclusion and exclusion make inquiry captive – or in David Perkins's phrase, "taming the wild". In 1998, Starrat wrote:

> Teachers may suggest a connection between learners' interests and experience and the school curriculum, but that is more of a ploy to motivate learners to absorb the meat and potatoes of the academic curriculum. Tests rarely

ask for personal connections or commentaries; they want the curriculum rendered back in its pure academic form, untainted by personal associations.

(p. 245)

Every 4 years, the OECD tests roughly half a million children in the principal industrialised countries, not simply in order to check whether students have learnt what they were recently taught, but to examine the extent to which students can extrapolate from what they have learnt and apply their knowledge and skills in novel settings. This has been consistently shown to be problematic. As Carol Dweck wrote a decade ago (2007), to be truly skilful outside of school, young people must develop situation-specific forms of competence. While much of school learning is generalised and abstracted from the context of its use, very little, she concludes, can be applied directly from in-school to out-of-school contexts. Resnick (1987) extends on this claim by making the following contrasts:

- **Individual cognition in school versus shared cognition outside.** The success of most learning and performance in school is judged on an individual basis rather than a group basis. In the world outside school, intelligence may be described as "distributed". We learn with and through others so that ideas and new ways of thinking are not necessarily individually "owned".
- **Pure mentation in school versus tool manipulation outside.** In school, the greatest premium is placed on "pure thought" – what individuals can do without the external support of books and notes, calculators, or other complex instruments. Testing and exams typically require retrieval or creation alone, in a time-limited, barren, and totally silent environment. In contrast, the accomplishment of activities outside of school usually requires access to a range of tools or artifacts in order to accomplish a particular task.
- **Symbol manipulation in school versus contextualized reasoning outside.** Jerome Bruner (1966) described the enactive, iconic, and symbolic forms of learning, highlighting the dysfunction created as progress in school, from too early an age, places a premium on symbolic forms. Learning becomes less playful and more abstract. The use and manipulation of symbols as representations of real objects contrasts with using objects themselves, as ways of solving problems in a meaningful way.
- **Generalized learning in school versus situation-specific competencies outside.** Classroom work, homework, field and project work, require situation-specific forms of competence. Given the more abstract and generalized nature of what we learn in the classroom, "very little can be transported directly from school to out-of-school use" (p. 15). Each new situation encountered, individually and socially, in the home, or in work, or informal activities may require rethinking and re-adapting to the changing context in which we find ourselves.

In day-to-day school routine, children have become used to waiting to be told what to do, a conditioned response to the peculiar environment of the classroom where authority and initiative clearly lie with the teacher. Pupils often respond well to those teachers who command unquestioned authority, who from day one lay down the rules of what happens "in my classroom". They welcome the fact that there is no latitude for misbehaviour and that they are allowed simply to get on with their work. At the same time, this raises the question of ownership and initiative, of children and young people waiting to be taught and freed of responsibility for their own learning.

The opportunity to learn from our mistakes, and the freedom to make them, is often denied by the premium placed on getting it right first time. Carol Dweck (2007) has found that getting the answer wrong creates greater activity in the brain than when someone gets the answer right. The cognitive dissonance which this provokes is, in a supportive environment, a positive stimulus to try again and, as one teacher put it, "fail better".

Thinking differently about learning in the community

The opportunity to be perceived differently, to be or to become a different person, has benefited from initiatives in which different kinds of activities, in different locations, with a range of people of varying ages and interests, help to redefine identity and impulse. Stepping back to get a better view of schooling, learning, and their interrelationship, we can, in the words of the OECD, observe "an holistic eco system that functions over time and context and includes the activity and outcomes of learning" (2013, p. 23). We are invited to revisit the all-too-familiar and overused term "context" as something neither defined by the school nor as something external, but as "integral to the main environment players and variables, most obviously the learners who enter in already with particular social profiles, family experiences, knowledge and expectations, and cultural experience and values" (p. 23).

The critical variable in all of this is the extent to which the learning environment is open or closed, predetermined or shaped and reshaped by the agency which teachers and students exercise, or fail to exercise. How often do teachers and students discuss the immediate context of their learning, the physical arrangements of school and classroom? How unusual is this Dutch teacher's introduction to his incoming class in which his first encounter with his students is to invite them to explore his classroom as a place for learning – to open drawers, arrange and rearrange desks or perhaps dispose of them altogether, and then to discuss the relationship of the physical architecture and its impact on the learning architecture? In the same spirit of critical inquiry, students may be invited to consider the proposed curriculum diet, the roles of teacher and students, the nature of assessment and its purposes, intrinsic and extrinsic.

Outward Bound is the name given to courses for young people that look beyond the immediate environment and attempt to surmount the boundaries of schooling. With a range of challenges in outdoor locations, its aims are to help young people develop self-efficacy, optimism, resilience, perseverance, self-esteem, emotional well-being, and life satisfaction: in sum, a growth mindset.

We aim to develop the skills that young people need to cope with adversity, and to persevere when they encounter difficulty. We help them to develop a "growth mindset", which enables them to see challenges as an opportunity to improve and learn. Successfully tackling and overcoming challenges provides young people with a memorable experience of "being able to do it" and promotes confidence and determination to rise to challenges again and again. The experience gives them a feeling that "anything is possible", which helps to raise their aspirations for what they can achieve in the future.

(The Outward Bound Trust, 2014, p. 15)

Outward Bound might have been an apt description for the government initiative in Hong Kong described as Other Learning Experiences. Each of these three words carries a challenge to convention. "Other" refers to alternative ways of thinking and acting; "learning" brings us back to essential purpose, grounded less in being taught than in "experiences". Its stipulation that 15% of the curriculum should be devoted to experiences external to the school and classroom was designed to expand both physical and conceptual horizons.

Students take part in activities in the community, in children's centres, hospitals, community centres, and charities, not simply as community service but as a learning experience to be documented, analysed, discussed, and credited. The activities engaged in have a present focus and a long-term objective. While learning is often individual in nature it is embedded in a social context, active and exploratory, with the purpose of developing skills and dispositions that transcend the context in which they are acquired so as to be applied lifelong and lifewide.

Transcending context

Built on the same principles, its more ambitious counterpart in the United Kingdom is known as the Children' University (CU). By offering educational activities out of school hours and in sites such as museums, art galleries, and cultural and community centres, the CU has opened up for thousands of children and young people an alternative future. It has, for many, proved to be a path out of conflict, both physical and psychological. Now also established in the Netherlands, Germany, Malaysia, and Australia, the CU has been described as a place where there is learning without limits, where "you can become clever", "where you learn for yourself", where "you don't get bullied", a place free from much of the conflict that occurs in the classroom and in the playground. The virtual absence of intimidation, teasing, and petty disagreements, as described by so many young people, is explained by being in more open and adult environments, by opportunities to experience success rather than invidious comparisons and constant reminders of failure.

A key feature of the CU is the growing number of learning destinations, places validated by the CU as offering genuine and, typically, collaborative learning experiences. Across the United Kingdom, the number of learning destinations runs close to 3,000 located on an online map of the United Kingdom allowing the user to click on the symbol and get details of what is on offer at that site – ranging from the Houses of Parliament to theatre companies, museums, military establishments, sporting clubs, wildlife parks, titles offices, and so on. Many of the sites have been suggested by children themselves.

Complementing visits and short-term activities, children have been able to take part in more extended and challenging "Rich Tasks". For example, a 10-week learning program with a focus on the heart was carried out by a team of 13–14-year-olds along with Biology, Physical Education, and Home Economics teachers and a number of medical staff. It included visiting the local hospital health suite and a variety of health professionals and persons with specific heart-related conditions to supplement sessions held in school. Reviewing the program, students spoke enthusiastically about the opportunity to enjoy collegial, conflict-free learning. Active participation and full engagement with all stages of the task from development through to delivery and evaluation, along with direct contact with the wider community, were vital factors in contributing to the impact of the program. Much of the success of the CU has been attributed to the change in environment and, as children testify, "learning in a new and different way".

The creation of passports, which give entry to learning destinations and merit a stamp for every validated learning hour, has proved a major success. After 30 hours of validated learning, children may "graduate" and receive a bronze certificate, with a silver award after 60 hours and a gold award after 90. Certification and graduation are symbolic milestones, marking progress and achievement. Around a quarter of a million passports have now been issued. Graduations take place in universities very often presided over by the Vice Chancellor himself or herself, handing out certificates to children begowned and wearing tasseled mortarboards.

Not only is the incidence of disruption, bullying, and anti-social behaviour noticeably absent in CU activities, but there is also a marked impact on schools and classrooms. The evidence from the Cambridge University evaluation is that children are now more engaged in classroom learning due to a boost to their confidence and self-esteem. A comment from one 10-year-old speaks for many: "Before, if I was stuck I wouldn't have asked for help. Now because of C.U. activities I know more about what I'm actually good at and what I'm not good at and when I need to ask for more help". And, "These activities are not only fun and keep you out of mischief but they make you like school more, help you get on better with other people and give you more confidence to do your class work and your homework" (MacBeath, 2013, p. 2).

The seven "A"s

The evaluation of the CU in 2002 resulted in conclusions beginning with the letter A, seven of which provide a challenging set of criteria for evaluating the impact of school and classroom learning.

Attitudes. Perhaps the most significant of all the seven, our attitudes to learning, to ourselves, to society predict most accurately the nature and likelihood of success, or failure.

Ambition. Virtually inseparable from attitudes, ambition may be set high or low and take the form of a self-fulfilling prophecy – once a flower girl always a flower girl, or alternatively, a belief that virtually nothing is beyond our reach.

Aspiration. A desire to reach beyond what you already know and can do. Aspiration sees beyond the present horizon of possibilities and refers to an ability to rise above low expectations, criticism, and the limited goals that others (teachers, friends, or family) may set for us.

Adventure. A characteristic built into our genes and perhaps the most prevalent characteristic of childhood. Exploring, taking risks, pushing the boundaries of the possible is what children do and it is a trait which is never left behind by successful entrepreneurs and adventurers.

Advocacy. A measure of the unrestrained enthusiasm of children and young people who want to tell their learning story, to infect and enlist others in adventure. Advocates promote and publicise what they have found fulfilling – the "can't wait to tell others" factor.

Adaptability. Refers to a critical skill, contextually dependent, measuring the ability to read a situation, to know what is required, what to hold on to, what is worthwhile and to know what to leave behind. It is a hallmark of effective learners, employees, and self-starters in a world that's changing so fast that adaptability is necessary rather than desirable.

Agency. A term not always understood, given its more technical or academic origins, but when understood as the individual power to effect change in self, in others and even society, it may be ranked highest of all the "As". It may be defined as acting rather than being acted upon. It recaptures the self-belief in very young children for whom there are no limits to their ability, their desire to fly to the moon and be whatever they may aspire to.

Storyline: Telling and creating stories

Do schools by their very nature require a more sober and serious approach? Hard work and the end of fun? An end to mythic and romantic understanding? Yet we find exceptional teachers and exciting classrooms in which romance is not dead and the engagement of storytelling fires the imagination.

In Scotland in the 1970s before the Educational Dark Ages, many primary schools used an approach called Storyline. It was founded on the belief that all learning is a form of narrative quest for deeper meaning and that all, or the greater part of learning could be construed as a type of storytelling. This was a thematic approach, engaging children so as to make connections between the external knowledge of the world and the inner world of their creative imaginations. The classroom, indeed the whole of a school, might become an Amazon rainforest, a Victorian village, an island community, or an urban street, the sterility of barren walls and regimented desks transformed into inspirational places, social places in which learning takes on the character of a shared adventure. Classrooms become sites of surprise, welcoming of the unexpected and the unplanned. Now practised in 30 countries of the world, the approach brings teachers together biannually for conferences at which stories are shared and re-enacted. As an early years teacher explains:

> The Storyline method poses problems and asks questions of pupils rather than giving the answers to questions they have never asked. The pupils and the teacher explore ideas together. This approach draws the curriculum together using the environment and social subjects as a stimulus to explore, and using expressive arts and language as a means of discussing, describing and explaining. Research and reference skills are extended as pupils are encouraged to search for answers.
>
> *(http://www.storyline.org/history/index.html)*

The following example is from a school in Stockholm.

> The theme chosen for the first course was the Hotel. In groups, teachers designed and constructed a frieze showing the Romb Star Hotel which, as the name suggests, was built using a variety of exciting shapes and these were explored and discussed. Key questions were then posed – what kind of staff would we need? How would they be recruited? Interviewed? Trained? Each student then created a character working in the hotel giving them an identity a role and a personality. With a "Setting" and "Characters" in place attention could turn to explore the mathematical implications of running a Hotel business. Plans of bedrooms and the penthouse suite were designed to scale. Opportunities were given for teachers to suggest how many useful and relevant mathematical challenges could be presented to the students based on the running of the Hotel – proof that mathematics is all around us.
>
> We claim that Storyline is not only about knowledge and skills but also involves feelings and attitudes because the students become the characters in the story. Every Storyline ends on a "high point" and amongst the suggestions made was for a Grand Opening Ceremony (a Parents' Evening) which would give the students an opportunity to show their work and describe the mathematics they had used and what they had learned.

Having invested their energies in the creation of their characters, their families, and their schools and communities, they typically express deep feelings when taken out of their comfort zone such as, for example, proposing plans for a new motorway to cut through the community, demolishing buildings, requiring letters to the local council, visiting the planning department, examining costs and opportunities.

Critics may argue that there comes a time for serious endeavour, putting away childish things because learning can't always be fun. Yet a professor in Hamburg University, Ulf Schwanke, demonstrated with his postgraduate students that somatic, mythic, and romantic understanding could all be exploited, using a Storyline approach. Students created classrooms in a large "shoebox", following the classic Storyline tradition of creating characters, giving them identities and biographies, and, with a classroom established, creating a local community and history. This is followed by critical incidents in which decisions have to be made, sanctions discussed, and differing values explored in a multiracial classroom. The impact of immigration in Germany over the last few years presented both a particular challenge and a rich knowledge seam to be explored.

Stories are not just for children. "We live in a storied world", writes Patrick Lewis. Without the story form, "humans would have endless unconnected, chaotic experiences" (2007, p. 1). Such a view receives confirmation from neuroscientists who describe the cortex's narrative drive, its intrinsic need to make sense of, and weave stories out of, our disparate experiences. In Jerome Bruner's words, we have a "readiness or predisposition to organize experience into a narrative form" (Bruner, 1990, p. 45). Unless teachers are able to effect this and schools are structured as storied worlds, children's experience of learning is liable to remain unconnected and dislocated.

Sticky knowledge

What is it about Storyline that stays in the memory and is able to travel beyond the immediacy of the classroom? For teachers, getting knowledge to "stick" proves to be a perpetual challenge. We do know that knowledge is indeed sticky but in a quite different sense of that term. As David Hargreaves characterised it in a lecture to Cambridge students, the transmission of information between a teacher and student gets stuck in many places en route. It gets stuck in misconception because there is no prior knowledge on which to build. It remains faithful to old mental models because there is resistance to new or disturbing ideas. It fails to adhere because there is no emotional glue to hold it fast. It sticks because there is no disposition or apparent need to commit to the learning moment. It sticks because young people are deeply affected by the attitudes of their peers and wish to remain detached and "cool". As Maurice Galton found,

> If they volunteered too many acceptable answers too quickly, they could earn the reputation of being a "boff". If they offered too few answers they might be regarded as "thick". It was much safer, therefore, to get teachers to answer their own questions.
>
> *(Galton, 2007, p. 62)*

Perhaps above all, though, knowledge sticks fast because it is located deeply and singularly in the context of the classroom. "Knowledge to go", as David Perkins and Gavriel Salomon (2012) put it, is deeply problematic. Put simply, children can be taught with a high degree of reliability to solve problems when those problems are structured appropriately by the teacher and presented to students in the classroom context. Indeed, it may be possible to achieve 100% success with well-designed problem-solving tasks in the classroom. However, in an unstructured "open field" outside of school, the success rate may fall to as low as 5%, says Perkins. This is due to three key factors. One, students have to be able to spot the problem. Two, they need to be motivated to want to engage with the problem. Three, they then need to have the ability to select and use the most appropriate tools and strategies to solve the problem. This is why Perkins places so much emphasis on dispositions, because without a desire to engage, learning will always be at second hand with a pitiable half-life in memory.

Howard Gardner (1993) reports similar findings. Research with college students on physics courses found that they could not solve the most basic problems if posed in a context slightly dissimilar to the one in which they first encountered it. Gardner found that even successful students responded to problems with the same confusions and misconceptions as young children, reverting to their own implicit theories formed in childhood. This is depressing news for teachers, trying vainly to deploy every device and strategy to entice children into learning. Are their efforts frustrated because the legacy of schooling is to limit classroom endeavour to just one of Howard Gardner's "multiple" intelligences? Is it because we reserve expression of intelligence to drama and the "creative subjects", those at the periphery of the curriculum or relegated to the "extra" curricular domain?

We return to the work of The Smith Family in Australia for an example of unconventional ways of building multiple intelligences with at-risk middle-school girls. Much of this NGO's work in broadening what counts as knowledge is relegated to the extracurricular domain. For example, a before-school "Breakfast with a Mentor" program hosts guest speakers, usually professionals from the community, who are invited to talk about their lives and career pathways via their personal stories. Arguably, these opportunities for social networking and learning outside the regular school curriculum play a significant part in building the girls' aspirations for completing school and actively seeking interesting opportunities for work and further study inside and outside their community. An interesting benefit has been a change to more positive attitudes towards the girls, demonstrated through offers for internships and employment. Traditional high-stakes assessment would not rate the girls' participation in these breakfasts highly, yet resultant internships and employment and engagement in the processes are testimony to how unconventional learning outside school can work cohesively with school targets for attendance and engagement in learning.

Conclusion

Entitling an address to faculty staff at the University of Cambridge, "Learning in the Wild", David Perkins contrasted a spontaneous, untutored, and personally driven process on the one hand with the linear, "ruthlessly cumulative" process of learning "in captivity". If indeed, as much research tells us, the spontaneity of learning is stifled by regime and conformity, is conflict not therefore inherent and inevitable?

From a government viewpoint, tougher, stricter, and "zero tolerance" measures have an obvious appeal, yet as we know, containment and compliance are short-term responses. On the other hand, when teachers, schools, local agencies, and teacher associations take initiatives to broaden the scope of learning, there is, in Perkins's phrase, a "wilding of the tame".

Although written nearly half a century ago, Freire's (1976) critique of the "banking" concept (in which information is deposited in children for a limited period, to be later withdrawn in tests and exams) has depressingly current relevance. Policymakers tend to dislike complexity, while short-life governments, wary of losing touch with the electorate, prefer to stay with the tried (but rarely tested) approach to "business as usual".

Schools are, by their very constitution, all about growth and change. It is in the DNA of an educational experience to challenge preconceptions, to offer new pathways to learning, to encourage collaboration in the creation and sharing of knowledge in ways that help minimise competitive tensions. This would, however, require a fundamental challenge to the notion of schools as places in which "teachers teach and children learn". To challenge this reactionary view of learning and promote the agency of the young will require a genuine commitment to deep personal, collective, and networked learning with the full engagement of the whole school and the community it serves.

References

Auerbach, S. (2012). Conceptualizing leadership for authentic partnerships: A continuum to inspire practice. In S. Auerbach (Ed.), *School leadership for authentic family and community partnerships: Research perspectives for transforming practices* (pp. 29–52). New York: Routledge.

Baron-Cohen, S. (2008). *Autism and Asperger Syndrome.* Oxford: Oxford University Press.

Bolivar, J. M., & Chrispeels, J. H. (2011). Enhancing parent leadership through building social and intellectual capital. *American Education Research Journal, 48,* 4–38.

Bruner, J. S. (1966). *Toward a theory of instruction.* Cambridge, MA: Belkapp Press.

Bruner, J. S. (1990). *Acts of meaning.* Cambridge, MA: Harvard University Press.

Caesar, L. G., & Nelson, W. N. (2014). Parental involvement in language and literacy acquisition: A bilingual journaling approach. *Child Language and Therapy, 30*(3), 317–336.

Csikzentimahlyi, M. (1990). *Flow: The psychology of optimal experience.* New York: Harper and Row.

Dollard, M. F., Winefield, H. R., & Winefield, A. H. (2001). *Occupational strain and efficacy in human service workers.* Dordrecht, The Netherlands: Kluwer Academic Publishers.

Dormann, C., & Kaiser, D. M. (2002). Job conditions and customer satisfaction. *European Journal of Work and Occupational Psychology, 11*(3), 257–283.

Dweck, C. (2007). *Mindset, the new psychology of success.* New York: Ballantine Books, Random House.

Earp, J. (2017). Global education: 21st century skills. *Teacher Magazine.* Retrieved from www. teachermagazine.com.au/article/global-education-21st-century-skills

Egan, K. (1997). *The educated mind: How cognitive tools shape our understanding.* Chicago: University of Chicago Press.

Freire, P. (1976). *Pedagogy of the oppressed.* London: Penguin Books.

Galton, M. (2007). *Learning and teaching in the primary classroom.* London: Sage.

Gardner, H. (1993). *The unschooled mind: How children think and how schools should teach.* London: Basic Books.

Goodall, J., & Montgomery, C. (2014). Parental involvement to parental engagement: A continuum. *Educational Review, 66*(4), 399–410.

Hargreaves, A., & Tucker, E. (1991). Teaching and guilt: Exploring the feelings of teaching. *Teaching and Teacher Education, 75*(5/6), 491–505.

Hiles, D. (2001, 2002). *Savant syndrome.* Retrieved from http://www.psy.dmu.ac.uk/drhiles/Savant%20Syndrome.htm

Jezewski, M. A. (1990). Culture brokering in migrant farmworker health care. *Western Journal of Nursing Research, 12*(4), 497–513.

Johnson, G., Dempster, N., McKenzie, L., Klieve, H., Flückiger, B., Lovett, S., Riley, T., & Webster, A. (2014). *Principals as literacy leaders with Indigenous communities: Leadership for learning to read – 'Both ways'.* Canberra: The Australian Primary Principals Association.

Johnson, G., & Wheeley, E. (2016). *Towards a model of professional learning: Enhancing Indigenous and non-Indigenous girls' engagement in middle school.* Final report. Brisbane: Griffith University, Griffith Institute for Educational Research.

Leicester, G. (2011). Turning the McKinsey model on its head. International Futures forum.com.

Lewis, P. J. (2007). *How we think but not in school.* Rotterdam/Taipei: Sense Publishers.

MacBeath, J. (2013). *Evaluating provision, progress and quality of learning in the Children's University 2012,* University of Cambridge.

MacBeath, J., & Sugimine, H., with Sutherland, G., Nishimura, M., and the students of the Learning School (2003). *Self evaluation in the global classroom.* London: Routledge.

Mackenzie, R. (1965). *Escape from the classroom.* London: Collins.

McKinsey & Company. (2010). *How the world's most improved school systems keep getting better.* McKinsey & Company.

Mapp, K. L., & Soo, S. (2010). Debunking the myth of the hard-to-reach parent. In S. L. Christenson & A. L. Reschly (Eds.), *Handbook of school-family partnerships* (pp. 345–361). London: Routledge.

Organisation for Economic Co-operation and Development (OECD). (2013). *Innovative learning environments* (Educational Research and Innovation). Paris: OECD Publishing.

The Outward Bound Trust. (2014). *Social impact report 2014.* Cumbria: Author.

Perkins, D., & Salomon, G. (2012). Knowledge to go: A motivational and dispositional view of transfer. *Educational Psychologist, 47*(3), 248–258.

PricewaterhouseCoopers. (2001). *Teacher workload study.* A Report of a Review commissioned by the DfES. London: PricewaterhouseCoopers.

Protocol Education. (2014). Helping students to develop a growth mindset. Retrieved from https://www.protocol-education.com/news/helping-students-to-develop-a-growth-mindset-99606862822

Resnick, L. B. (1987). The 1987 presidential address: Learning in school and out. *Educational Researcher, 16*(9), 13–20 + 54.

Stanton-Salazar, R. D. (2011). A social capital framework for the study of institutional agents and their role in the empowerment of low-status students and youth. *Youth and Society, 43*(3), 1066–1109.

Starrat, R. J. (1998). Grounding moral educational leadership in the morality of teaching and learning. *Leading and Managing, 4*(4), 243–255.

Vygotsky, L. (1962). *Thought and language.* Cambridge, MA: MIT Press.

Vygotsky, L. S. (1978). *Mind in society: The development of higher psychological processes.* Cambridge, MA: Harvard University Press.

Weissbourd, R. (2003). Creating caring schools. *Educational Leadership, 60*(6), 6–11.

7

ENHANCING TEACHER PROFESSIONALITY

In Chapter 3, we highlighted integrity as a cornerstone of professionalism and described how it has been eroded in an era characterised by performativity and new public management. In a recent book edited by two Dutch teachers (Evers & Kneyber, 2015), neoliberal thinking is identified as the source of a prevailing malaise in the teaching profession. The effect on the profession is profound and mostly negative. Teachers find themselves working under unprecedented levels of intensification, leading to emotional pressures and stress. As competition between teachers and subject teams increases, schools lose their sense of community. Professional discourse is impoverished, partly because of the lack of time for reflection and, in part, because of the unforgiving focus on performance (Ball, 2003; Kneyber, 2015). In this chapter, therefore, we are concerned with what some might refer to as teacher professionalism and how it can be enhanced although, as explained below, we prefer the term teacher professionality (Evans, 2008; Hoyle, 1974).

Teacher quality, effectiveness, and standards

The issues are not limited to Organisation for Economic Co-operation and Development (OECD) countries such as the United Kingdom and the Netherlands, but are part of a global transformation which, for policymakers the world over, presents an irresistible challenge (Steiner-Khamsi, Silova, & Johnson, 2006). While school autonomy is one of the shibboleths of neoliberal policies, teacher autonomy tends to be given much less consideration. Nevertheless, policies aimed at educational success are focusing with renewed vigour on the centrality of what teachers do. While we know that socioeconomic factors play a major role in determining access to, and success in learning, together with the appropriateness of curricula and the quality of school leadership, it is argued that the most influential factor is the quality of what teachers do in their classrooms (Hanushek, 2011; OECD, 2005;

UNESCO, 2014). However, while there may be agreement as to the importance and impact of teaching, far more challenging is the question of how the quality of teaching may be improved.

The bringing together of experts from across the world for a succession of Cambridge Seminars focused attention on the commitment in many policy contexts to professional standards. As one participant said: "How can you expect teachers to be professional unless you tell them what they should know and what they should be able to do?" At first glance this is common sense, but as Judyth Sachs pointed out some time ago (2003), this uncritical approach is an obstacle to considering the most important question: are professional standards about teacher development or about regulation? On the face of it, clear specifications of what teachers should know and be able to do seem plausible, exemplified in documents such as the Australian National Professional Standards for Teachers (AITSL, 2011). Undue emphasis on such statements is, however, unhelpful. Rather, what is important is what education systems, schools, and teachers actually *do* to improve the quality of educational practice.

Underpinning the standards mindset is the school effectiveness paradigm in which researchers seek to correlate specific forms of behaviour with measures of attainment. School effectiveness research, which we have critiqued in the past (MacBeath, 2002), has contributed to research such as John Hattie's in which the links between particular practices and quantifiable outcomes are demonstrated (Hattie, 2009). His earlier study of teacher expertise features analysis of dimensions of expertise which are presented in behavioural terms and under these headings:

- can identify essential representations of their subject;
- can guide learning through classroom interactions;
- can monitor learning and provide feedback;
- can attend to affective attributes; and
- can influence student outcomes.

Here we see the logic of the school effectiveness tradition.

> My search is driven by the goal of ascertaining the attributes of excellence – because if we can discover the location of these goal posts, if we can understand the height of the bar of the goal posts, we then have the basis for developing appropriate professional development, the basis for teacher education programs to highlight that which truly makes the difference.
>
> *(Hattie, 2003, p. 1)*

In this way of thinking, it is assumed that professional development can be externally directed and designed to correspond with what experts believe about teachers' needs or deficiencies. It tends to lead to a training model which focuses attention on behavioural outcomes rather than on the nature of the processes through which teachers, both singly and collectively, develop their professional expertise.

Leaving aside for the moment the question of whether such training actually makes a difference, one obvious shortcoming is that teachers tend not to value it and, in some cases, find it disempowering. This technical approach to professional development fails to acknowledge the need to build teachers' capacity to lead and manage innovation, to have an active voice in change, and to experiment with and reflect on their practice at school level (Guven, 2008). This delivery model of teacher development is, unsurprisingly, both unpopular with teachers and ineffective in changing practice (Sari, 2006). In many European countries, dissatisfaction with outmoded forms of professional development is reflected in the low numbers of teachers attending professional development events (OECD, 2009) even when they are provided by or accredited by the government and are free of charge. Many teachers would rather participate in alternative programs at their own expense.

At the heart of the problem is the lack of understanding of two key dimensions: professional identity and moral purpose, which are, of course, closely linked. They both rest on the centrality of human agency. As we have argued in the past (MacBeath & Dempster, 2006) and reassert above, essential features of authentic learning and teaching are agency and moral purpose. This argument is supported by a number of American researchers (Goddard, Hoy, & Woolfolk-Hoy, 2000; Tschannen-Moran & Barr, 2004), by the McKinsey Report (Barber & Mourshed, 2007), and by a more recent OECD report to the International Summit on the Teaching Profession (Schleicher, 2016). What they all agree on is that what makes the difference is teachers' motivation and belief in their own ability to make a difference. Teachers' self-efficacy is emerging as a key factor in educational success, as evidence from a secondary analysis of TALIS data demonstrates (Scheerens, 2010). This was cited in an LfL report for Education International which explored the relationships between teachers' self-efficacy, voice, well-being, and leadership (Bangs & Frost, 2012).

Professionalism, professionality, and professional identity

In his memoirs, *The Naked Civil Servant*, the celebrated eccentric Quentin Crisp (1968) justified his dedicated approach to being a life model, saying that he regarded anything done for money as sacred. He was expressing a sense of moral obligation to fulfill the expectations of the artists for whom he posed. Although in our present highly consumerist age some might regard this as admirable, it does represent a particularly narrow view of professionalism.

In the 1970s, Eric Hoyle wrestled with the theme of professionalisation and has, more recently, reflected on that early work (Hoyle, 2008). In the 1970s, he coined the term "extended professionality", "in contradistinction to professionalism" which had connotations of strategies to enhance status. Hoyle wanted to avoid giving ammunition to the sceptical view as expressed in George Bernard Shaw's famous aphorism that the professions are "conspiracies against the laity". It was a view endorsed by Margaret Thatcher a few decades later and with a more potent political impact.

For Hoyle in the 1970s professionality was either restricted or extended:

> A restricted professional was construed as a teacher for whom teaching was an intuitive activity, whose perspective was restricted to the classroom, who engaged little with wider professional reading or activities, relied on experience as a guide to success, and greatly valued classroom autonomy. An extended professional was construed as a teacher for whom teaching was a rational activity, who sought to improve practice through reading and through engaging in continuous professional development, who was happily collegial, and who located classroom practice within a larger social framework.
>
> *(Hoyle, 2008, p. 291)*

While this was a very influential contribution, there remained a lot to be said, for example about the nature of professional knowledge, support for continuous professional development, and the relationship between these two.

What counts as knowledge

The question of what counts as knowledge has always been contested, especially in relation to professional contexts. In the 1980s, the concept of experiential learning (Kolb, 1984) had been widely discussed and the importance of reflection to the development of practice was highlighted by Schön in a similar period (1983). In the early 1990s, Eraut recognised the socially situated process of knowledge acquisition which led to a broader consideration of ways in which professional knowledge is created (Eraut, 1994). Learning from experience is a key dimension of professional knowledge but for Eraut, this could be "non-formal" or "deliberative" (Eraut, 2000). He built on what Polanyi (1966) had identified many years earlier, exploring the relevance of "tacit knowledge". In the light of this debate, enhancing our understanding of professional knowledge and the ways in which it is shared and developed, it is surprising that rather simplistic training models of support for continuing professional development have retained such a firm grip within our education systems and in the minds of policymakers.

The Leadership for Learning alternative

Within the leadership for learning (LfL) arena we have been concerned with the question of how best to enable teachers to construct for themselves professional identities that go beyond Hoyle's (2008) "extended professionality" so as to embrace advocacy, activism, and leadership. These dimensions are critical in the effort to improve professional practice in the here and now, as well as enhancing the stock of professional knowledge in educational systems.

In LfL related projects and initiatives we have worked in collaboration with schools – rather than as researchers enjoying the luxury of academic critique – because we know that schools play a key role in creating the conditions in which extended professionality can flourish. Research evidence to support the idea that the context of the school affects the development of professional identity has been accumulating (Beauchamp & Thomas, 2009; Beijard, Verloop, & Vermunt, 2000; Flores & Day, 2006), confirmed and enhanced in a recent small-scale action research study (Creaby, 2016).

A convenient rhetorical device for promoting extended professionality is the term "teacher leadership". The idea of teacher leadership was part of the developing discourse of professionalisation in the United States in the 1980s (York-Barr & Duke, 2004). Major reports such as *A Nation at Risk* (National Commission on Excellence in Education, 1983) and *A Nation Prepared: Teachers for the 21st Century* (Carnegie Corporation, 1986) called for a reinvigoration of the teaching profession in the United States. Teacher leadership was seen to be the key lever for this reinvigoration (Lieberman, 1992; Little, 1988). Significant momentum for this work was evident in the literature through the 1990s both in the United States and Australia (Crowther, Kaagan, Ferguson, & Hann, 2002; Katzenmeyer & Møller, 1996).

In the United Kingdom, the term "teacher leadership" had been rendered somewhat redundant by the growth of increasingly diverse organisational structures that assign special responsibilities and attendant authority to those with designated posts. In England, the recently retitled National College for School Leadership provided training courses and other forms of support focusing on "middle leadership" and "emergent leaders". These have tended to pay attention to building the capacity of heads of departments and other team leaders to manage their teams more productively (Naylor, Gkolia, & Brundrett, 2006). More recently, this approach has been examined and lauded in a report by an American researcher who visited the United Kingdom to look at what he called the "lattice for school leadership" (Supovitz, 2014, 2015) in the English system. He noted these features:

- multiple leadership positions within a school;
- a broadly recognised set of leadership competencies;
- formal and network learning opportunities;
- widely recognised certifications for school leaders; and
- the leadership function integrated into the broader accountability system.

Supovitz identified benefits such as the capacity for "instructional improvement efforts", for targeted support for professional development, career incentives, and pressure to advance leadership competencies. From a policy perspective, it is perhaps easy to see how this might sound like "apple pie" to those accustomed to the American context in which schools tend to be flatter organisational hierarchies and where school principals are exhorted to engage in "instructional leadership"; however, there remains a major question as to whether this complex pattern of multiple responsibilities has actually been transformative in England.

Given the contrast outlined in the UK and US reports mentioned above, it is understandable that the developing clamour for teacher leadership has been strongest in the United States. In May 2011 this reached something of an apotheosis in the form of the publication of a set of "model standards" for teacher leaders, the result of an extended discussion involving a consortium of state authorities, universities, and teacher organisations. The report was intended to engage and to further discussions about teacher leadership, a helpful step forward in terms of public recognition of the leadership roles that teachers can and ought to play. The standards proposed were organised into seven domains as set out below.

The domains of competence for teacher leaders

- Fostering a collaborative culture to support educator development and student learning;
- accessing and using research to improve practice and student learning;
- promoting professional learning for continuous improvement;
- facilitating improvements in instruction and student learning;
- promoting the use of assessments and data for school and district improvement;
- improving outreach and collaboration with families and community; and
- advocating for student learning and the profession.

These are doubtless important and useful activities, but the assumption in the document remains that teacher leadership is about designated roles. The model standards document says of teacher leaders that "they need recognized responsibilities, authority, time to collaborate, and support from school administrators to assume leadership roles" (Teacher Leadership Exploratory Consortium, 2011, p. 12).

Common to all the approaches referred to above is the idea of designating or appointing a minority of teachers as "teacher leaders". This contrasts somewhat with the multiplicity of leadership roles to which Supovitz (2014) has drawn attention, yet still emphasises leadership role rather than leadership practice.

The following two contrasting approaches to teacher leadership illustrate the thrust of the differences we have identified. The first comes from Florida where the idea of the teacher leader has been sponsored systemically, implicitly informed by the national standards referred to above. The second example draws from a grassroots or bottom-up approach to teacher leadership, active in Hertfordshire and Cambridge (HertsCam) in the United Kingdom.

Case 1: The Teacher Leader Fellowship in Florida

> People will respond to your advocacy if they trust you, if they perceive a moral purpose. … It cannot happen without a culture of trust.

These words taken from the evaluation of the Teacher Leader Fellowship Program in Florida emphasise three essential values – advocacy, trust, and moral purpose. These are the values in what is described in Florida as a reframed leadership paradigm focused on teachers and learning "at every level within schools, neighbourhoods and districts" (MacBeath & Alexandrou, 2016, p. 4).

In affiliation with the University of Florida's Lastinger Center and funded by the state, this intervention program ran from 2015 to 2017. It was designed to mobilise teacher expertise, "leveraging their formal and informal influence over supervisors, colleagues, and members of the school community through collaborative relationships that improve teaching and lead learning practices in schools" (MacBeath & Alexandrou, 2016, p. 7).

Over a 3-year period, University of Florida faculty members worked with a group of 40 fellows and 200 critical friends, selected primarily on their effectiveness as classroom practitioners and their apparent capacity for leadership. Their commitment was to address key pedagogical issues within their classrooms and schools. The essential criterion was the promise they offered as a potential resource for their colleagues and for the system as a whole, laying the groundwork and the foundations for building a community (or communities) of practice. Designed to help participants construct an extended professional identity, the program set the bar high in respect of expectations, readiness, and maturity to engage with the multiplicity of roles, role modelling, and the role partners that teacher leadership requires.

"Growing teacher leadership", as it was used in Florida, is a compelling metaphor because it seems to encourage a flatter leadership process rather than one reinforcing a hierarchy with positional status resistant to challenge. This growth process was described as "a new brand of teacher leadership, where the state's most effective classroom practitioners exercised leadership in spreading the teaching expertise, with a focus on learning", "managing the space" between formal leadership structures and informal and ad hoc leadership, so that leading could be exercised and understood in new ways. Essential to this was "co-constructing the public narrative", challenging a story that has been told and retold in which leadership is seen as individual, hierarchical, and powerful. "Challenging the story", as referred to in the program, required a fundamental reframing, a different lens through which to examine leadership as practice, to draw on the five LfL principles to ascertain where the focus on practice lay and to assert and reassert the primacy of learning through dialogue about the nature of practice, making it explicit, discussable, and transferable through active collegial inquiry.

The context of the Teacher Leader Fellowship Program in Florida at the time was one in which new state standards required what were described as "instructional shifts", that is, not simply new ways of teaching but new ways of making the connections among the "how" and "why" of learning and leading. To achieve this, the Fellowship intervention program set its sights high, ambitious and layered, comprising multi-day institutes, out-of-state residential experiences, regional leadership meetings, and virtual teacher collaborative communities of practice. These were designed to provide a coherent and integrated approach, described in the documentation as "blended learning", each facet of the program building on and mutually enhancing the others.

Regional leadership meetings allowed University of Florida staff to guide and support the fellows on a consistent basis (every 6–8 weeks) on site, specifically addressing how their work as a teacher leader could be both specific to their own school, but applicable and influential at district level. The endpoint was to co-construct a public narrative, capturing ways in which shifts in practice through teacher-led networks created, documented, and archived their teacher leadership practice and how these stories might influence others to change. Another objective was to incorporate these public narratives in a larger systemic production of Teacher Leaders' Value-Creation Stories.

Workshops provided a testing ground for teacher leaders, nurturing the capacity to lead one's colleagues but in an environment quite different from that of the school, with all of its attendant pressures, hierarchies, and competitiveness. The evidence from the Cambridge-led evaluation suggests that the program's ambition has been realised in the creation of an environment for learning which is collegial and supportive, where it is safe to experiment, and where teachers felt safe to admit to and learn from failure. The disclosure of personal dilemmas is both an acknowledgement of the very nature of teaching and, for participants, a crucial opportunity to explore the causes, contexts, and consequences of those dilemmas – a necessary prelude to addressing them effectively.

> It was hugely important, valuable, to me, to be able to air some of my problems, issues, shortcomings, if you like, with people who I know are not going to leap immediately to judgement and who will actually listen to what I have to say. That alone is worth the investment in this programme.

Sustaining such a commitment does, however, require both resilience and support mechanisms, the ability to deal with the demands of the "real" day-to-day world of school, its micropolitics, and the triumph of the urgent over the important. Addressing attrition and sustaining enthusiasm, collegiality, and commitment so vibrant in the workshops and in their accompanying social activities was an ongoing pressure for the success of the initiative. The evaluation referred to above found, in interviews and focus groups, a number of teachers who confessed to struggling with the questions asked by their peers and in some cases, the instructions from senior leaders when they returned to their schools.

At the heart of the Teacher Leader Fellowship and a contributor to its outcomes, however, has been its commitment to an evidence-based approach, an emphasis on leading and learning and, as a professional educator, being able to engage with the sources of evidence; to critically evaluate the application of differing theories of practice; to use evidence to inform and to change practice; and to effect this not only individually but to influence and inspire colleagues as leaders of learning.

What do we see in the Florida Teacher Leader Fellowship Program?

The Florida Teacher Leader Fellowship Program has proved successful in enhancing teachers' capacity for reflection and challenge to routine practice while necessarily tied into organisational structures and procedures. It is always difficult to escape the expectations of the funding authorities to whom accountability ultimately resides. It is also critical to the success of programs such as this that there is, from the outset, a buy-in from senior school leaders and a willingness to embrace a "flatter" leadership paradigm.

A further positive is the adoption of an extended view of professionality which exposed participants to research-informed practice through support from university staff members. This support opened participants to knowledge beyond personal experience, essential to our view of extended professionality. When systems sponsor and support innovation, it is well to ask whose interests are being served. In this case, it is clear that system personnel judged that gains could be made through the dissemination of the "public narratives" prepared and advocated by the 40 fellows. These would also have been of great benefit to schools as informing documents, potentially influential in sparking internal debates as to specific practices. Hierarchy is an endemic and ever-present factor in any attempt to create and sustain flatter leadership, especially within a national, or local, "top-down" authority. This raises a question as to how such a position may be achieved, the matter addressed in the following account from a teacher leadership initiative in the United Kingdom.

Case 2: The HertsCam Network approach to teacher leadership

The teacher leadership approach developed within the HertsCam Network was founded on the values of LfL. The view taken there was that the role-based approach puts limits on the development of leadership capacity. When the LfL principles, such as shared leadership and mutual accountability, are applied, a more inclusive and democratic approach to teacher leadership is called for. The key to understanding the HertsCam approach is the concept of professionality outlined above. Based on Hoyle's (2008) prototype, the shared understanding in the HertsCam Network sees it as desirable for teachers to see themselves as:

- members of a professional community rather than individual practitioners;
- agential, engaging in innovation rather than complying with prescription from above;
- guided by educational principles and a sense of moral purpose rather than by standards, rules, and externally defined deficits;
- creators of professional knowledge through inquiry, development work, and networking rather than relying on initial training and continuous updating provided by expert outsiders; and
- someone who seeks to influence others by exercising leadership rather than simply being led.

This set of descriptors resonates to some extent with David Hargreaves's argument in 1994 about "the new professionalism". An important aspect of this was his proposition that "there is little significant teacher development without school development" (Hargreaves, 1994, p. 436). His argument was echoed a couple of years later in a specification by Goodson and Hargreaves (1996) under the heading of "7 principles of new professionalism". In both these contributions we see the highlighting of the importance of collaboration yet no reference at all to the idea of leadership. In contrast, it is axiomatic that the kind of professionality promoted in the HertsCam Network embraces the practice of leadership on the part of all practitioners – an integral dimension of their professional identity.

It is commonly argued that teacher effectiveness requires technical skill and know-how. Underpinning this is what Muijs et al. (2014) refer to as being "adaptive experts", using inquiry to build knowledge about teaching. However, without a strong sense of moral purpose, these skills are relatively meaningless. Ultimately, what is needed are teachers with a commitment to the best possible outcomes for young people. Moral purpose and commitment are essential, but an important dimension of a truly transformative conceptualisation of teacher effectiveness is contained in Michael Fullan's (1993) warning in an influential article, predating offerings from Hargreaves and Goodson and Hargreaves.

> Moral purpose without change agency is martyrdom; change agency without moral purpose is change for the sake of change. In combination, not only are they effective in getting things done, but they are good at getting the right things done.
>
> *(Fullan, 1993, p. 3)*

Building on this, it can be argued that the quality of education depends on teacher professionality which has at its core a heightened sense of moral purpose. It is accompanied by the strategic nous that enables the teacher to act as a change agent, exercising leadership purposefully and skilfully in order to develop practice. In the HertsCam Network the term "non-positional teacher leadership" (Frost, 2013) is used to denote this.

Operationalising non-positional teacher leadership in the HertsCam Network

Over the last 10–15 years, HertsCam has gradually developed mechanisms for self-governance, eventually establishing itself as an independent network led by teachers themselves. The organisation is constituted as a charity with the explicit aim of improving public education. This is pursued by supporting teachers as agents of change, leading innovation in their schools and building knowledge about teaching and learning across schools. Experienced teachers in the network facilitate school-based support groups, teach their own master's degree course, and organise network activities based in schools. Participation enables teachers to lead collaborative development projects that improve the quality of teaching and learning. HertsCam's core activities include the Teacher Led Development Work (TLDW) Program, the MEd in Leading Teaching and Learning Program, and the Networking Program which includes international engagement.

HertsCam recognises the potential of all teachers to exercise leadership as part of their professional role. This was illustrated and exemplified in the book *Transforming Education Through Teacher Leadership* (TETTL, Frost, 2014) containing accounts of teacher leadership which, collectively, explicate a theory of teacher professionality and educational transformation through teachers' narratives. The theory of non-positional teacher leadership is illustrated in Figure 7.1 and then discussed in outline.

The rhetoric of teacher leadership was adopted by HertsCam as a way of transcending the limitations of concepts such as continuing professional development, practitioner research, and action research. "Teacher leadership" had the potential to be more empowering. In formulating our understanding, we were drawn to Fullan's argument in the early 1990s that every teacher is an agent of change and that this is part of being "new professionals" (Fullan, 1993). This is well expressed by Val Hill, a teacher, in the book (TETTL) referred to earlier:

([W]e) propose that leadership could be a dimension of all teachers' professionality ... we argued for an approach to teacher leadership, which does not assume that leadership is linked with positions in the organisational hierarchy of the school. Instead it recognises the potential of all teachers to exercise leadership as part of their role as a teacher. We believe that all teachers and education practitioners have some leadership capacity. After all, leadership is a dimension of being human. In HertsCam and the wider International Teacher Leadership (ITL) network, we argue that it should be seen as an essential part of teachers' professionality.

(Hill, 2014)

The vision portrayed in the TETTL book is of an approach which is inclusive and democratic, offering the means by which any practitioner is enabled to develop their leadership capacity. Leadership in this context is conceptualised as influence, a defining characteristic of leadership practice (Yukl, 2010).

FIGURE 7.1 The theory of non-positional teacher leadership

The TLDW Program supports teacher leadership in primary, secondary, and special schools by enabling teachers and other educational practitioners to plan and lead projects designed to develop the quality and effectiveness of teaching and learning in their own schools. Each participant designs and leads their own development project over the course of one academic year. Successful completion leads to the award of the HertsCam Certificate in Teacher Leadership. TLDW groups are facilitated by members of the HertsCam tutor team, all experienced teachers. This program has been running continuously since 2004 when it was initiated in just four schools.

The MEd in the Leading Teaching and Learning Program is designed, planned, and taught entirely by practitioners. This 2-year, part-time program, like TLDW, enables teachers to plan and lead development projects in their schools. The MEd differs from the TLDW Program by demanding a higher level of scholarship and critical analysis, drawing on relevant literatures and domains of knowledge. Following various conference papers and presentations, the first published account of this program appears as a chapter in the book *Empowering Teachers as Agents of Change* published by LfL, Cambridge (Frost, 2017). This account draws attention to ways in which enhanced professionality may be manifested. This refers not only to the way in which participating teachers develop their leadership capacity but also to how their more experienced colleagues (as tutors of the program) are able to employ what they call "a pedagogy for empowerment" (Ball, Lightfoot, & Hill, 2017). The first of the seven pedagogical principles that underpin the teaching of this program is "Principle 1: The cultivation of moral purpose as a dimension of extended professionality". This shared understanding is outlined in the chapter alluded to earlier.

> Our central purpose is improving the life chances of the young people in our schools. Enhanced moral purpose is a key dimension of the type of professionality the course promotes (Frost and Roberts, 2013) and is made explicit to candidates during the selection interview.
>
> *(Ball et al., 2017, p. 74)*

Participation in this particular "community of practice" (Wenger, 1998) is dependent on an explicit compact focused on the type of professionality described above.

The Networking Program includes a series of six network events each year and an annual conference. Typically, between 50 and 150 teachers participate in each event, displaying posters about their development project or leading workshops in which they give an account of their project, engaging participants in discussion. Towards the end of the academic year the entire network comes together for an annual conference. This program of activities enables teachers and other education practitioners to participate in what the HertsCam team like to call "knowledge building" (Frost, 2013). This is a term which suggests that professional knowledge is not simply codified and disseminated but is to be discerned in the flow of the dialogue, and facilitated through networking. What is also distinctive about this view of professional knowledge is its focus not only on pedagogy but also on leadership. Therefore, a teacher participating in a workshop led by another teacher in the network might expect to learn something not only about classroom practice but also about leadership strategies which draw colleagues into a collaborative process of review, deliberation, and innovation.

But does the HertsCam idea travel?

It might be assumed that the approaches to enhanced professionality in these two case studies are only likely to flourish in successful schools in privileged education systems. When Andy Hargreaves distinguished between "professional learning communities" and "performance-training sects", he argued that the former is a luxury afforded only to those schools where levels of student attainment are sufficient to relieve the pressure of accountability, whereas schools in disadvantaged communities are more likely to have their freedom to innovate curtailed by such pressure (Hargreaves, 2003). However, there is evidence to suggest that non-positional teacher leadership has the power to enhance professionality in schools that face the challenge of disadvantage. The crucial variables are the quality of the facilitation and the extent to which the senior leadership of the school acts strategically to create favourable conditions for that to be effective.

It might similarly be assumed that such an approach would not succeed in quite different cultural and political milieux. Commentators often criticise the implementation of educational reform strategies spawned in the West – so called "policy-borrowing" (Phillips & Ochs, 2003; Steiner-Khamsi, 2004) – but the experiences in both the Florida and the International Teacher Leadership initiatives demonstrate that some educational ideas really do travel.

Evidence to support this is presented in the EFFeCT Project which is a study of collaborative professionalism in six European countries. The UK branch of this research involved a series of case studies drawn from HertsCam's programs and included one of the iterations of the International Teacher Leadership (ITL) initiative based in Bosnia and Herzegovina (Roberts & Woods, 2017). The ITL initiative established teacher leadership programs across the Western Balkans in 2009 when Open Society Foundations invited HertsCam to present the non-positional teacher leadership approach to a network of civil society organisations at a meeting in Belgrade. One of the key aims of the ITL project was "to explore how the development of teachers' professional identity and their modes of professionality can contribute to educational reform in a variety of cultural/national contexts" (Frost, 2011, p. 2). The case of Bosnia was particularly challenging due to social, cultural, and political factors that contrasted sharply with those pertaining in the United Kingdom. Following the Dayton peace agreement in 1995, the country was still struggling to keep the peace. There were 13 separate ministries of education with elaborate bureaucracies representing three ethnic groups: the Bosniaks, Croats, and Serbs (Vranješević & Čelebičić, 2014). Nevertheless, the team from proMente Social Research, an NGO based in Sarajevo, was able to develop a very successful program which empowered teachers from all parts of the country and even enabled members of the different ethnic groups to collaborate.

Having said that the HertsCam approach was based on LfL values – for example, shared leadership and dialogue – it was nevertheless surprising to find that the interest in non-positional teacher leadership from the Balkans was more explicitly focused on democracy. The peace agreement had established the legal framework necessary to keep the peace, but the challenge remained to build a democratic way of life that Dewey (1937) had envisaged. Teacher leadership offered the potential to promote democratic values in relation to institutional life and professionality. It was hoped that such developments could, in the long run, contribute to the enrichment of society.

Subsequent to the development of non-positional teacher leadership in the Western Balkans, Greece, Turkey, and Portugal, we have seen it take hold in the Middle East. Programs in both Egypt and Palestine, although small in scale, are nevertheless flourishing and demonstrating that there is an appetite for enhanced professionality (Ramahi & Eltemamy, 2014). This claim is supported in an LfL study for Education International in which teachers and union officials in 12 countries around the world were surveyed. The overall message from this exercise was that, universally, teachers are frustrated by the feeling that they remain "ghosts at the feast" and want to have far greater influence on the direction of education policy and on the development of practice in their schools (Bangs & Frost, 2012).

In Ramallah, the HertsCam approach was adapted as the basis of the Teachers Leading the Way Program which, although conducted in just one school, was nonetheless revealing. The program was productive in enabling teachers to release their creativity and solve professional problems by posing their own questions and devising new strategies. A good example is the project initiated and led by Rana Daoud who developed methods for improving the quality of student relationships in the school (Daoud & Ramahi, 2017). She involved students, teachers, support staff, and parents in working to increase her colleagues' confidence in, and commitment to, strategies that produced a noticeable decrease in student aggression. While solving problems such as this was a breakthrough for school improvement, the experience was transformative in a broader sense. This is illustrated by Munir, another participant in the Teachers Leading the Way Program in its first year.

> Our society doesn't allow us to think on our own or express our individual thoughts. All of a sudden [through involvement in the program] I'm going to solve my problems. I'm the owner of the idea and the solution ... it contradicts the local environment. It's from this reality that one has low confidence. I have confidence in a lot of things but I'm doing this for the first time and God willing it will develop and succeed.
>
> *(Quoted in Ramahi, 2016, p. 8)*

Hanan Ramahi's own account draws attention to the successful operation of the program demonstrating that, given the chance, teachers in Palestine are able to exercise leadership. She argues that mobilising this untapped energy is essential for human and societal renewal for Palestinians and everyone else across the Middle East and North Africa regions.

The sheer number of teachers and their manifest impact on student achievement demands that government officials, policy makers, social activists, parents and citizens acknowledge, empower and mobilise teacher leadership in the drive towards education reform.

(Ramahi, 2017, p. 117)

Here we see the thread that connects what seems to be, at first glance, a mere school improvement strategy to a more profound transformation of professional identity.

Individual and collective agency in enhancing professionalism

What have we learnt from our discussion with respect to enhancing professionalism from the activities in the US and the English examples? There are at least five encouraging insights.

First, both personal and collective agency are required to enhance professionalism. It has been shown in both of these examples that this is possible when non-positional teacher leadership becomes an integral aspect of a professional learning culture. It is clearly understood that the control of school resources rests with headteachers/principals and others beyond the school, in local authorities or district offices. For the most part, they determine what opportunities will be made available for the professional development of teaching staff. When this occurs, personal agency is bypassed, replaced by positional power over the profession – the "heroic" self-action of leaders we noted in Chapter 4. However, when teachers themselves assert their personal agency, a different professional learning agenda comes into play, one steeped in the context of everyday practice and in the shared leadership of equal actors.

Second, dialogue amongst peers constitutes the engine room for improved practice. The focus of interaction emphasises what is in the interests of students, opening up the critical discourse regardless of position or hierarchy. This has historically been one of the major strengths of Nordic countries where there is an absence of hierarchy and deference to institutional authority. In Norway, serving as a mentor, as in Sweden, participating in mentoring, is associated with self-efficacy. Having a mentor as well as serving as a mentor has a positive association with job satisfaction, as the TALIS data show (OECD, 2014).

Different dialogical processes are more likely to come to the fore when hierarchy is absent, when there is, as emphasised in the Florida case study, a culture of trust. Dialogical processes assume a new character when there is a common focus on moral purpose, one aimed at improving the lives and life chances of children and young people through a transformative quality of learning. Pedagogical practices are the means at the disposal of teachers intent on realising their moral purpose, so classroom activities, strategies, and experiences become the core business, activating leadership for learning.

Third, the very fact that innovations and improvements which result from teachers' combined efforts are shared with others nationally and internationally is testimony to Eraut's (1994) tenet that professionals reflect on their practice personally and contribute their knowledge collaboratively, so improving the practice of the profession as a whole. This is immediately evident in the work and modus operandi of HertsCam, for example, and made evident in its allegiance to Hoyle's (2008) view of extended professionality.

Fourth, the pairing of personal and collective agency is powerful. The one without the other is inimical to enhancing professionalism. This duality places a degree of onus on individual teachers who identify themselves as professionals, to take up the challenges of LfL unaided by position and status. Being a teacher leader is a fluid and flexible role enabling transactions between agents as they search together for improved professional practice. The individualism, or self-action as we have described it in Chapter 5, is expanded in the collectivism of interaction and transaction as Dewey and Bentley (1949) have shown. However, collective agency is necessary if the primacy of organisational social structures such as positional hierarchies is to be set aside or ignored.

Fifth, the emphasis over recent years by education systems on improving the quality of school leadership (AITSL, 2011; Pont, Nusche, & Morman, 2008; Robinson, Hohepa, & Lloyd, 2009) has an unfortunate unanticipated consequence. It has a tendency to cast a shadow over teachers as self-directed agents. The implication is that teachers are directionless without strong principals and that improvement in school performance is, inevitably, a top-down matter. This implies a deficit model of the teaching profession and denies the capacity for grass-roots transactional approaches to leadership as shown in Simpson's (2016) typology in Chapter 5. Logic would tell us that the capacity to enhance professionalism lies where the greatest bulk of the profession is located – amongst classroom teachers in schools. The paradox, though, is that such is the policy compliance demanded by systems, and such is the abhorrence of criticism and difference, that individual teachers are unlikely to exercise the power of their own personal agency unless those in positional authority create the conditions for it to flourish. What we have seen in both case studies is that a professional collective supported by peer facilitators is necessary to enable teacher leadership to emerge. Recognising the importance of this for ongoing collaborative support within the collective occurs when Fraser's (2007) "parity of participation" principle is honoured. These actions help to ensure that enhancing teacher professionality will take place in spite of bureaucratic hierarchies.

Conclusion

The term "professional development", in the world of education at least, has become commodified. It tends to be used to refer to a program of one kind or another rather than the development of the teacher as a professional. At best, it can be seen to be something that is provided for teachers and at worst as something done to them. In professional contexts, the use of acronyms to refer to such provision adds to the reification. In the United Kingdom, terms such as CPD (continuing professional development) and INSET (in-service education and training of teachers) usually refer to an event or a series of activities in which teachers might participate voluntarily or as part of their "directed time". In New Zealand, the preferred term is PLD (professional learning and development). In the United States, simply PD (professional development) is more common. Such provision varies in respect of a number of dimensions. For example, it may be focused on agendas set by central government or more locally by schools or districts; it may be designed and led by organisations external to the school or by senior leaders within the school; it may operate in a very instructional, training mode or in a more constructivist, exploratory mode; its purpose may be to "update" teachers' specialist knowledge or to prepare them for new roles. Whatever the design features of professional development programs, the common weakness is the lack of focus on the development of teachers' professionality. A report in New Zealand addresses this by arguing for the term "professional learning" (Timperley, Wilson, Barrar, & Fung, 2007). Shifts in terminology are of themselves, however, unlikely to address the substantive issues. If we are truly interested in enhancing teachers' professionality, a first priority is to engage senior school leaders and teachers in a re-examination of the policy discourse and its impact on school and classroom practice. If our commitment is to an enhanced school experience and more meaningful measures of achievement, a precondition is to remind ourselves of teachers' moral purpose, their agency in addressing professional issues, and their ability to co-construct professional knowledge.

Secondly, we need to apply LfL principles to the question of teachers' professionality. This entails enabling teachers to:

- maintain their focus on learning as an activity;
- work developmentally on conditions that favour learning as an activity;
- participate in dialogue about learning, leadership, and the connection between these;
- share in the practice of leadership; and
- engage in mutual, collegial forms of accountability.

It is not proposed here that these principles should be merely a guide to the design of professional development programs. On the contrary, the third challenge is to put an end to the ghettoisation of teachers' professional learning. For schools to become truly transformative we need to integrate teacher development, practice development, and school development. They should be seen as dimensions of how schools and education systems operate in ways that mobilise teachers' capacity to improve the effectiveness of teaching and the quality of learning.

References

Australian Institute for Teaching and School Leadership (AITSL). (2011). *Australian professional standards for teachers*. Retrieved from http://www.teacherstandards.aitsl.edu.au/

Ball, S. (2003). The teacher's soul and the terrors of performativity. *Journal of Educational Policy, 18*, 215–228.

Ball, S., Lightfoot, S., & Hill, V. (2017). A breakthrough in support for school and teacher development: A profession-led masters programme. In D. Frost (Ed.), *Empowering teachers as agents of change: A non-positional approach to teacher leadership* (pp. 72–78). Cambridge: LfL: the Cambridge Network.

Bangs, J., & Frost, D. (2012). *Teacher self-efficacy, voice and leadership: Towards a policy framework for Education International.* Brussels: Education International.

Barber, M., & Mourshed, M. (2007). *How the world's best-performing school systems come out on top* (The McKinsey Report). Washington, DC: McKinsey & Company.

Beauchamp, C., & Thomas, L. (2009). Understanding teacher identity: An overview of issues in the literature and implications for teacher education. *Cambridge Journal of Education, 39*(2), 175–189.

Beijaard, D., Verloop, N., & Vermunt, J. (2000). Teachers' perceptions of professional identity: An exploratory study from a personal knowledge perspective. *Teaching and Teacher Education, 16,* 749–764.

Carnegie Corporation. (1986). *A nation prepared: Teachers for the 21st century. The report of the task force on teaching as a profession.* New York: Carnegie Corporation.

Creaby, C. (2016). *A study of the relationship between professional development strategies and teacher professional identities.* Unpublished doctoral thesis, University of Cambridge Faculty of Education.

Crisp, Q. (1968). *The naked civil servant.* London: Jonathan Cape.

Crowther, F., Kaagan, S., Ferguson, M., & Hann, L. (2002). *Developing teacher leaders: How teacher leadership enhances school success.* Thousand Oaks, CA: Corwin Press.

Daoud, R., & Ramahi, H. (2017). Developing strategies to improve relationships between students in a school in Palestine. In D. Frost (Ed.), *Empowering teachers as agents of change: a non-positional approach to teacher leadership* (pp. 18–24). Cambridge: LfL: the Cambridge Network.

Dewey, J. (1937). Democracy and educational administration. *School and Society, 45*(April 3), 457–467.

Dewey, J., & Bentley, A. F. (1949). *Knowing and the known.* Boston, MA: Beacon Press.

Eraut, M. (1994). *Developing professional knowledge and competence.* London: Falmer Press.

Eraut, M. (2000). Non-formal learning and tacit knowledge in professional work. *British Journal of Educational Psychology, 70,* 113–136.

Evans, L. (2008). Professionalism, professionality and the development of education professionals. *British Journal of Educational Studies, 56*(1), 20–38.

Evers, J., & Kneyber, R. (Eds.). (2015). *Flip the system: Changing education from the ground up.* London: Routledge.

Flores, M., & Day, C. (2006). Contexts which shape and reshape new teachers' identities: A multi-perspective study. *Teaching and Teacher Education, 22,* 219–232.

Fraser, N. (2007). *Abnormal justice.* Retrieved from http://www.fehe.org/uploads/media/Fraser_Abnormal_Justice_essay.pdfFrost, D. (2011). *Supporting teacher leadership in 15 countries: The international teacher leadership project, phase 1 – a report.* Cambridge: LfL: the Cambridge Network.

Frost, D. (2013). Teacher-led development work: A methodology for building professional knowledge. *HertsCam Occasional Papers,* April. HertsCam Publications.

Frost, D. (Ed.) (2014). *Transforming education through teacher leadership.* Cambridge: LfL: the Cambridge Network.

Frost, D. (Ed.) (2017). *Empowering teachers as agents of change: A non-positional approach to teacher leadership.* Cambridge: LfL: the Cambridge Network.

Fullan, M. G. (1993). Why teachers must become change agents. *Educational Leadership, 50*(6), 12–17.

Goddard, R., Hoy, W., & Woolfolk-Hoy, A. (2000). Collective teacher efficacy: Its meaning, measure, and impact on student achievement. *American Research Journal, 37*, 479–508.

Goodson, I. F., & Hargreaves, A. (1996). *Teacher professional lives*. London: Falmer Press.

Guven, I. (2008). Teacher education reform and international globalization hegemony: Issues and challenges in Turkish teacher education. *International Journal of Social Sciences, 3*(1), 8–17.

Hargreaves, A. (2003). *Teaching in the knowledge society: Education in the age of insecurity*. New York: Teachers College Press.

Hargreaves, D. (1994). The new professionalism: The synthesis of professional and institutional development. *Teaching and Teacher Education, 10*(4), 423–438.

Hanushek, E. A. (2011). The economic value of higher teacher quality. *Economics of Education Review, 30*, 466–447.

Hattie, J. A. C. (2003, October). *Teachers make a difference: What is the research evidence?* Paper presented at the Building Teacher Quality: What does the research tell us ACER Research Conference, Melbourne, Australia. Retrieved from http://research.acer.edu.au/research_conference_2003/4/

Hattie, J. A. C. (2009). *Visible learning: A synthesis of over 800 meta-analyses relating to achievement*. London: Routledge.

Hill, V. (2014). The HertsCam TLDW programme. In D. Frost (Ed.), *Transforming education through teacher leadership* (pp. 73–83). Cambridge: Leadership for Learning.

Hoyle, E. (1974). Professionality, professionalism and control in teaching. *London Educational Review, 3*(2), 42–54.

Hoyle, E. (2008). Changing conceptions of teaching as a profession: Personal reflections. In D. Johnson & R. Maclean (Eds.), *Teaching: Professionalization, development and leadership* (pp. 285–304). The Netherlands: Springer.

Katzenmeyer, M., & Møller, G. (1996). *Awakening the sleeping giant: Helping teachers develop as leaders*. Thousand Oaks, CA: Corwin Press.

Kneyber, R. (2015). On neo-liberalism and how it travels: Interview with Stephen Ball. In J. Evers & R. Kneyber (Eds.), *Flip the system: Changing education from the ground up* (pp. 39–44). London: Routledge.

Kolb, D. A. (1984). *Experiential learning*. Englewood Cliffs, NJ: Prentice Hall.

Lieberman, A. (1992). Teacher leadership: What are we learning? In C. Livingston (Ed.), *Teachers as leaders: Evolving roles* (pp. 159–166). Washington, DC: National Education Association.

Little, J. W. (1988). Assessing the prospects for teacher leadership. In A. Lieberman (Ed.), *Building a professional culture in schools* (pp. 78–106). New York: Teachers College Press.

MacBeath, J. (2002). Democratic learning and school effectiveness: Are they by any chance related? In J. MacBeath & L. Moos (Eds.), *Democratic learning: The challenge to school effectiveness* (pp. 19-51). London: RoutledgeFalmer.

MacBeath, J., & Dempster, N. (2006). *Connecting leadership and learning: Principles for practice*. London: Routledge.

MacBeath, J., & Alexandrou, A. (2016). *A new brand of teacher leadership: Evaluation of the Florida Leadership Programme*. Cambridge: University of Cambridge.

Muijs, D., Kyriakides, L., van der Werf, G., Creemers, B., Timperley, H., & Earl, E. (2014). State of the art – teacher effectiveness and professional learning. *School Effectiveness and Improvement, 25*(2), 231–256.

National Commission on Excellence in Education. (1983). *A nation at risk: The imperative for educational reform*. Washington, DC: U.S. Government Printing Office.

Naylor, P., Gkolia, C., & Brundrett, M. (2006). Leading from the middle: An initial study of impact. *Management in Education, 20*(1), 11–16.

Organisation for Economic Co-operation and Development (OECD). (2005). *Teachers matter: Attracting, developing and retaining effective teachers.* Paris: OECD.

Organisation for Economic Co-operation and Development (OECD). (2009). *Creating effective teaching and learning environments: First results from TALIS.* Paris: OECD.

Organisation for Economic Co-operation and Development (OECD). (2014). *TALIS 2013 results. An international perspective on teaching and learning.* OECD Publishing. Retrieved from http://dx.doi.org/10.1787/9789264196261-en.

Phillips, D., & Ochs, K. (2003). Processes of policy borrowing in education: Some explanatory and analytical devices. *Comparative Education, 39*(4), 451–461.

Polanyi, M. (1966). *The tacit dimension.* London: Routledge and Kegan Paul.

Pont, B., Nusche, D., & Morman, H. (2008). *Improving school leadership, Volume 1: Policy and practice.* Paris: OECD.

Ramahi, H. (2016). Enabling teachers to lead change in one school in Palestine: A case study. *American Journal of Educational Research, 4*(2), 4–14.

Ramahi, H. (2017). Enabling the leadership of change in the Middle East and North Africa: Starting with teachers. In D. Frost (Ed.), *Empowering teachers as agents of change: A non-positional approach to teacher leadership* (pp. 111–117). Cambridge: LfL: the Cambridge Network.

Ramahi, H., & Eltemamy, A. (2014). *Introducing teacher leadership to the Middle East: Starting with Egypt and Palestine.* Paper presented within the symposium Changing Teacher Professionality through Support for Teacher Leadership in Europe and Beyond at ECER 2014, Porto, 1–5 September.

Roberts, A., & Woods, P. (2017). Principles for enhancing teachers' collaborative practice: Lessons from the HertsCam Network. In D. Frost (Ed.), *Empowering teachers as agents of change: A non-positional approach to teacher leadership* (pp. 154–160). Cambridge: LfL: the Cambridge Network.

Robinson, V., Hohepa, M., & Lloyd, C. (2009). *School leadership and student outcomes: Identifying what works and why. Best evidence synthesis iteration [BES].* Wellington, NZ: Ministry of Education.

Sachs, J. (2003). Teacher professional standards: Controlling or developing teaching? *Teachers and Teaching: Theory and Practice, 9*(2), 175–186.

Sari, M. (2006). Teacher as a researcher: Evaluation of teachers' perceptions on scientific research. *Educational Sciences: Theory and Practice, 6*(3), 880.

Scheerens, J. (2010). *Teachers' professional development: Europe in international comparison. An analysis of teachers' professional development based on the OECD's Teaching and Learning International Survey (TALIS, 2014).* Luxembourg: Office for Official Publications of the European Union.

Schleicher, A. (2016). *Teaching excellence through professional learning and policy reform: Lessons from around the world, International Summit on the Teaching Profession.* Paris: OECD Publishing.

Schön, D. (1983). *The reflective practitioner: How professionals think in action.* New York: Basic Books.

Simpson, B. (2016). Where's the agency in leadership as practice? In J. Raelin (Ed.), *Leadership as practice: Theory and application* (pp. 159–178). London: Routledge.

Steiner-Khamsi, G. (Ed.) (2004). *The global politics of educational borrowing and lending.* New York: Teachers College Press.

Steiner-Khamsi, G., Silova, I., & Johnson, E. (2006). Neo-liberalism liberally applied: Educational policy borrowing in Central Asia. In J. Ozga, T. Popkewitz, & T. Seddon (Eds.), *Education research and policy: Steering the knowledge-based economy* (pp. 217–245). New York: Routledge.

Supovitz, J. (2014). *Building a lattice for school leadership: The top-to-bottom rethinking of leadership development in England and what it might mean for American education.* Research Report

(#RR-83). Philadelphia: Consortium for Policy Research in Education, University of Pennsylvania.

Supovitz, J. A. (2015). *Building a lattice for school leadership: Lessons from England.* CPRE Policy Briefs. University of Pennsylvania Scholarly Commons. Retrieved from http://repository.upenn.edu/cpre_policybriefs/7

Teacher Leadership Exploratory Consortium. (2011). *Teacher leader model standards.* USA: Teacher Leadership Consortium.

Timperley, H., Wilson, A., Barrar, H., & Fung, I. (2007). *Teacher professional learning and development: Best evidence synthesis iteration.* Wellington, NZ: New Zealand Ministry of Education.

Tschannen-Moran, M., & Barr, M. (2004). Fostering student learning: The relationship of collective teacher efficacy and student achievement. *Leadership and Policy in Schools, 3*(3), 189–209.

UNESCO. (2014). *Teaching and learning: Achieving quality for all.* Paris: UNESCO.

Wenger, E. (1998). *Communities of practice: Learning, meaning and identity.* Cambridge: Cambridge University Press.

Vranješević, J., & Čelebičić, I. (2014). Improving the participation of ethnic minority families in schools through teacher leadership. In D. Frost (Ed.), *Transforming education through teacher leadership* (pp. 94–105). Cambridge: Leadership for Learning, University of Cambridge Faculty of Education.

York-Barr, J., & Duke, K. (2004). What do we know about teacher leadership? Findings from two decades of scholarship. *Review of Educational Research, 74*(3), 255–316.

Yukl, G. (2010). *Leadership in organizations* (6th ed.). Englewood Cliffs, NJ: Prentice Hall.

8

CHALLENGING POLICY, SCHOOL, AND CLASSROOM PRACTICE

In this final chapter, we revisit the key issues we have explored, the challenges they present to our own thinking, and what we have learnt since our previous publication nearly a decade ago. In reviewing the seminal ideas which underpin leadership for learning (LfL), we consider the nature of challenges to policymaking in the seven countries of the *Carpe Vitam* Project and beyond. What are the implications for members of the profession, for parents, members of the community, and others with the best educational interests of students at heart? We begin with the concept of repurposing.

> Repurposing is essentially a form of recycling. Instead of throwing an item away, an individual or business finds a new use for it.

Among the many new terms that have entered the vocabulary in the last decade or so is "repurposing". Included in its numerous definitions is "finding a new purpose" for practices or ideas that have outlived their usefulness or relevance. In relation to education, this is sometimes described as "reschooling", contrasting with the more radical notion of de-schooling, and offering a more realistic and pragmatic approach. It recognises the massive capital investment in schools and in the accompanying infrastructure, but also suggests that there is significant latitude for doing things differently.

However, it is always more comfortable to fall back on old familiar ways, to look wistfully back rather than dangerously forward. At what point does it become apparent that curriculum and assessment are no longer fit for purpose, or serve the wrong purpose? What does it take to raise awareness of collateral damage to children's welfare and education? How much evidence is required to acknowledge the demoralising impact of current policy on the teaching profession? In England after two decades of mounting evidence of systemic dysfunction, in July 2017 the

Chief Inspector publicly lamented the pressures on children as young as 9 and 10, rehearsing for tests year after doleful year.

Yet how viable is a radically different approach to curriculum, assessment, and professional autonomy? Is it essentially a Quixotic gesture to tilt at policy "windmills", failing to recognise their durability and their essential recycling function? Was the following vision for education in Singapore two decades ago little more than wishful thinking?

> What is critical is that we fire in our students a passion for learning, instead of studying for the sake of getting good grades in their examinations. Their knowledge will be fragile, no matter how many As they get. ... It is the capacity to learn that will define excellence in the future, not simply what young people achieve in school.
>
> *(Goh Chock Tong [Prime Minister of Singapore], 1997)*

However valid an aspiration, an essential prerequisite is to understand the systemic constraints which bind school leaders and teachers to legislated and legitimated practice. There is an art to composing "good" policy, making it sound like common sense, appearing to be a perfectly logical way for those who are tasked with its enactment. The appeal to common sense has been a constant over many years and in many jurisdictions. But the language of policy is never neutral. A close reading of any policy document requires a critical pause, to stop and consider the language, the choice of words, phrases, and metaphors infused with cultural assumptions, views, values, and ideologies that, by their nature, advantage some and disadvantage others. Education, as it becomes established more firmly in the marketplace, is seen as a marketable commodity together with the language of "service delivery".

Without a serious challenge, the ideologies that drive policy into practice soon become commonplace, as we have seen with the embracing of accountability realised, with inherent logic through high-stakes testing accepted, and the promotion of a managerialist rationale normalised. The central question for all stakeholders (systems, leaders, teachers, families, students, and communities) to ask in a challenge to policy, school, and classroom practice is, whose interest does it serve? Instead of looking to the cost–benefit relationship of accountability regimes, we might more fruitfully consider the cost–benefit ratio of failing to challenge the status quo of policy and its endorsement of practice. More specifically, in failing to challenge a test-driven curriculum, what are the costs for children in the short and longer term?

In their book *Leading from the Emerging Future*, Scharmer and Kaufer (2013) describe this as a system which, by its very design, is incapable of learning.

> Structural disconnects produce systems that are designed to *not* learn. The systems operate through *delayed* or *broken feedback loops* that prevent decision-makers from experiencing and personally feeling the impact of their decisions. In our current complex global systems, decision-makers often affect large groups of people with their actions but never see, feel, or become aware of

their actions' consequences. Without feedback, or with delayed feedback, there is no learning. As a result, institutions tend to change too little and too late.

(p. 8)

School leaders need to be able to read between the lines of a policy to determine how they are being positioned and what actions they need to take in response to an increasingly marketised and managerialist policy landscape. Ironically, while the nature of learners has diversified, professional discretion in meeting that diversity has contracted; the terminology of "implementing" is an indicator of the role in which teachers are cast.

What we have argued in this book

In Chapter 1, we alluded to the indispensable value of "connoisseurship", a high-level and complex skill equipping us to challenge policy because it stems from a deep understanding of the way a student learns and the way that learning changes over time. A grasp of the complex, developmental nature of learning leads to what this implies for revisiting and transforming teachers' own practice. This is the essential foundation of professional integrity, thinking differently about learning and teaching, and continuing to work on the issues that enhance professionality and the practice of leadership.

What the Delors Report (UNESCO, 1996) describes as the "treasure within" remains, in too many instances, tragically undiscovered. As it suggests and we argue explicitly, the treasures of the profession require (a) the reaffirmation of professional integrity, (b) thinking differently about learning and teaching, (c) enhancing professionality, and (d) redefining leadership as activity or practice. None of these are, however, viable in isolation. They come as a package, starting with the information, the impulse, and the resources to think differently, to draw on this to reaffirm what it means to be a professional and to have the integrity to follow where that leads, returning constantly to the **activity** of learning and leading. The integral relationship among these draws its strength from what we understand as *leadership for learning*. This is a form of words, now increasingly commonplace but masking a concept that reaches deep into transformational practice. For example, we may pass lightly over moral purpose without deep reflection and discussion of what it means and in what ways it challenges practice and its underpinning in policy. When much of national and international policy is tested against this single criterion, it falls lamentably short, begging consequent dissent and consequent advocacy.

A leadership for learning platform for dissent and advocacy

Principled dissent and advocacy does, however, require confidence in the platform from which a challenge may be articulated. Central to such a platform are the concepts and practices of leadership for learning, supported and sustained by four major endeavours which we have restated above and elaborated in Chapters 4, 5, 6, and 7, with the relationship now illustrated in Figure 8.1.

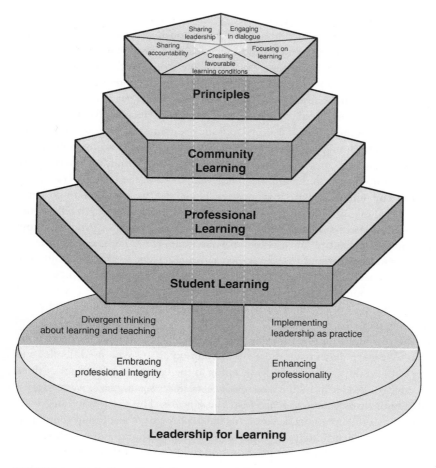

FIGURE 8.1 A platform for challenges to policy, school, and classroom practice

Figure 8.1 depicts the four fields of endeavour in relation to the LfL narrative central to long overdue challenges to particular aspects of educational policy, school, and classroom practice. The figure summarises much of what we suggest it takes to act in advocacy or dissenting modes. In what follows, we provide a brief description of the major elements of the figure before moving later to a more substantial summary of the key points in each of the four fields of endeavour.

The central tiers of the figure shown lifted above the circular base, repeat the concepts from the original LfL diagram illustrated in Chapter 3 (see Figure 3.1). The figure shows how leadership for learning is layered across students, teachers, the school, and wider community, always conscious of action consistent with the five principles at the peak of the diagram – maintaining a focus on learning, sharing leadership, engaging in dialogue, sharing accountability, and creating favourable conditions for learning.

The base supporting the central tiers of the figure holds the four distinct but related fields of endeavour – embracing professional integrity, enhancing professionality, implementing leadership as practice, and divergent thinking about learning and teaching. These four fields contribute to the justification of the LfL principles that inform an essential narrative in advancing the interests of students in the present policy environment. These five principles, which have been applied and confirmed in different international projects over the last decade, give us the confidence to position them as foundational to policy reaction and critique. To put this another way, LfL should be innate to principals and teachers – it should be in the educator's genes, so to speak – and in others such as parents, family, and community members with interests in the growth and development of the next generation.

In the top left quadrant at the base of Figure 8.1, we show the importance of divergent thinking about learning and teaching. If, as much research tells us, the spontaneity of learning is stifled by regimentation and conformity, and we know that learning is enhanced when choice is present, interest is high, and experience is shared with insiders and outsiders, then encouragement to "think outside the square" becomes obligatory. Broadening LfL requires not only the agency of the young but a genuine commitment to deep personal, collective, and networked learning with the full engagement of the whole school, parents, family, and community members.

In the top right quadrant, we include action on leadership as practice, a position we have taken drawing on the work of Simpson (2016) who used Bentley and Dewey's (1949) three-part typology on action as the basis for explanations of three perspectives on leadership – the *leader-practitioner, leadership as a set of practices*, often distributed or shared, and *leadership in the flow of practice*. This three-way categorisation provides a theoretical explanation for different forms of leadership action that will always be evident in schools. What we emphasise in our argument, though, is that the *trans-actions* which take place amongst colleagues as they attend to their professional responsibilities act as powerful motivators for professional learning and for enriched pedagogy.

The bottom left quadrant shows that this central commitment to LfL needs to be buttressed by people with a strong sense of professional integrity. Principals and teachers should embrace an unshakeable commitment to all of the following: the educator's moral purpose; the rights of the child; a broad educational experience for the young; a concern for their capabilities to function in the social and cultural circumstances of their birthplace; and the redistribution, recognition, representation, and parity of participation tenets of social justice. As we have said, professional discretion is abused and professionalism is violated when any decision made by teachers or school leaders fails to represent these integrity norms authentically. Taking a challenge up to policy when it is deemed necessary, requires principals and teachers who are unapologetic about their primary calling, their duty to refresh politicians and policymakers' memories about the moral purpose of education, the breadth of learning so necessary in the modern age, and the inclusivity essential in a shrinking global village.

Finally, in the bottom right quadrant of the figure we see enhancing professionality. This, we have argued, is a really important undertaking for principals and teachers in schools. After all, it is well known that teachers are the most significant influence on students' learning inside the school gates, so the quality of what they do and their dedication to it are critical ingredients in enhancing learning. Understanding that they are leaders themselves and that creating opportunities for their further development requires schools with networked collectives and critical friends to enter into frank dialogue about practice. When this occurs, individual and collective development become simultaneous with school development.

The four fields of endeavour – key points

Here we summarise key points in each of the four fields of endeavour which underpin our commitment to leadership for learning.

Professional integrity

First, we argue that in a highly politicised global arena, with arbitrary benchmarks and competitive league tables, it is difficult to detect where moral principles lie. Where these are observed, it is by teachers who have a deep professional commitment to their students' intellectual and ethical development. Leading and teaching with moral purpose, and making values-based decisions, require "flying below the radar". This is, however, a pragmatic rather than a principled stand which would argue for greater visibility and, while risky and potentially courting disaster, would also act as a model for change. When others know about a principled model for change and understand its persuasive rationale, support is likely to be more forthcoming.

This is much more likely to occur when there is the involvement of a critical friend, referred to in Chapter 4, holding together professional integrity and moral purpose. Professional integrity, we argued, is tested by decision-making which is explicit, enduring, and widely understood, but much more easily realised when disagreement and challenge is embedded within a confirming relationship. In citing the UN Convention on the Rights of the Child, which we refer to as aspirational, the Articles help in defining what may constitute an ethos for professional integrity and how it may be expressed and defended.

Enhanced professionality

Second, we highlight some of the key points related to enhanced professionality. This, we have argued, rests on a commitment from principals and teachers, but equally, it is a pressing concern for parents and members of the wider community. While it may seem no more than common sense, a substantive body of research, as we have said, confirms that teachers are the most significant influence on students' learning within the school gates. However, this is not always the case for all schools as an equally substantive body of research on the peer effect (also known as the compositional effect or school mix) reveals that in very challenging social circumstances, the powerful influence of disaffected classmates can undermine motivation and commitment and run counter to the best efforts of teachers (Mortimore, 1998; Thrupp, 1999).

As most parents already know, who their children will go to school *with* is a particularly salient criterion in choosing a school. While the power of the compositional effect has been shown to be one of the strongest determinants of achievement, it is mediated by the strength of cultural capital within the family. The weaker the social and intellectual capital in the family, the stronger the influence of peers, which tends to find its level as the lowest common denominator. Conventional measures, it is argued, tell us little about the nature of relationships within the peer group, a critical mass of motivation or disinclination, engagement or disengagement, a precarious balance, which may constitute a tipping point into either order or anarchy or be harnessed successfully by some individual teachers but not by others.

In Judith Harris's award-winning book *The Nurture Assumption* (1998), with its subtitle, *Why Children Turn Out the Way They Do*, she ascribes the dominant forces in childhood and adolescence to the "significant others" who shape values and character often more insidiously and powerfully than parents and teachers. She takes to task conventional assumptions about relative effects, her findings adding depth and texture to the compositional effect by revealing what quantitative studies stop short of measuring – the power of the connections between how peer group affiliations and expectations play out in school and classroom life, on the one hand, and how they play out in the street and neighbourhood culture, on the other.

Understanding what effective teachers do in relation to peer groups and in differing socioeconomic settings is key to enhancing professionality, in turn hugely determined by the nature of leadership that is able to create a growth-promoting school ethos. Where there are networked collectives, able to enter into frank and challenging discussions about practice, individual and collective development become coterminus with school development. When this occurs, advocacy and voice are expressed in ways which transcend the tokenism that is both current and constraining. Advocacy is not merely about teachers fighting for better conditions for themselves; rather, it is about advocating for education and for pedagogy. This entails making the case for better practice directly to parents and being able to give a robust account to policymakers, shifting the balance of power in favour of the profession. This is not an argument for a lack of accountability, rather for strengthening it in meaningful ways. It is not about denying the democratic right to hold schools and teachers to account but rather to do so in ways which engage in, and enhance, the quality of dialogue and enrich pedagogy. Such a focus on accountability would find a highly receptive response among principals who have an enhanced sense of their own agency and moral purpose and are constantly striving for improvement. These are school leaders most likely to engage in academic scholarship, most likely to engage in consultation, to listen to the voice of students, parents, and other stakeholders, sensitive and responsive to the needs, expectations, and perspectives of those constituencies.

When a researcher in the International Teacher Leadership Project visited an elementary school in Veliko Tarnovo, Bulgaria, the children and their teacher offered a gift to their visitor. It was a postcard with pictures that the children had painted, together with photos of the teachers and the slogan "We are not waiting for Superman!" It was a reference to the 2010 movie of that title which portrayed the public education system as broken and the unions as preventing the dismissal of poorly performing teachers. In the United States, in particular, it provoked a wide-ranging, and often heated, debate. In a three-way debate following a viewing of the film, the California Teacher of the Year, together with Rick Hanushek and Linda Darling-Hammond, discussed the issues it raised and some that it failed to address. While not entirely absolving the unions, Darling-Hammond pointed to a range of systemic factors including salaries, recruitment, working conditions, and professional development. She described some of the features of the highly unionised Finnish system in which teachers benefited from

> two or three years of graduate-level teacher education completely at government expense with a salary while you train ... you get a decent salary but wonderful working conditions, mentoring from your first day in the classroom ... about 15 to 20 hours a week where you are collaborating with your peers on the development of curriculum and assessments, developing the context within which students will be engaged and the kind of problem-solving curriculum that they have, and the kids will come to school fed, housed and healthy because it ... is built into the infrastructure, so to get a good teacher in every classroom you've got to make investments.
>
> (*Hanushek.net, 2017*)

In that very engaging and high-quality debate, less was said about leadership as more widely shared, as collegial, or as spontaneously engaged.

Leadership as practice

Third, we speak to some of the key points in taking action on leadership as practice, arguing that shared leadership should be one of the default positions in schools, complemented by spontaneous forms of leadership amongst colleagues seeking solutions to the problems of teaching and learning as they are encountered – in the flow of practice, so to speak. While acknowledging that positional leadership is a given in school systems and necessary for the management of human and material resources, we also expressed hope for a form of leadership which is exercised by collectives as they grapple with the issues of the day or address historically intractable problems. More effective networking among teachers and enhanced scope for collegial initiatives would also go a long way towards enhancing professionality. As we concluded in Chapter 5, the most obvious challenge to policy is to mitigate the ubiquitous influence of the heroic *leader-practitioner* while simultaneously increasing the influence of teachers who hold no formal positions but have an unrealised leadership potential.

Divergent thinking about learning and teaching

Finally, we have drawn particular attention to the importance of divergent thinking about learning and teaching. This is relevant in a number of ways. It is most obviously germane in relation to learning and its contested connections with teaching. It is clearly relevant to the context in which learning and teaching take place, and the structures which permit or inhibit that. Divergent thinking is affected by the latitude for spontaneity, choice and initiative, and freedom from regimentation and conformity. This returns us to the central issue of curriculum and assessment which may stifle such initiatives, but only where teachers and senior school leaders allow it to do so. As we have argued, and illustrated through case studies, learning is enhanced when experience is shared with people with expertise in the wider community as well as inside the school itself. Broadening the leadership of learning requires not only the enhanced agency of the young but a genuine professional commitment to deep personal and collective learning, networked and widely shared.

A "community of learners" approach to professional learning poses a significant challenge to standards-based professional learning programs by confirming the need for professionals to work from an ongoing sense of moral purpose and personal agency rather than under the direction of bureaucratic hierarchies. A potential leadership source that remains largely untapped is from the "bottom-up" where those in non-positional roles initiate leadership activities that are subsequently supported by positional leaders, such that it becomes an authentically shared undertaking in a particular context. This is referred to in Chapter 5 as "spontaneous agency" and "leadership in the flow of practice" which, we argue, is far less frequently found than other leadership perspectives.

We understand that none of the policy momentum and its embedded commitment to new public management and governance is likely to be wound back in the foreseeable future, so ensuring that performance standards, competition, efficiency, choice, and accountability remain as the cornerstones of measurable educational policy outcomes. However, the intent of the conceptual relationships illustrated in Figure 8.1 is to offer an alternative summary of what it takes to act with advocacy in the face of contemporary or emerging policy demands.

While such a creative and challenging stance is difficult to achieve in the shadow of what we have described as an insidious undermining of professional integrity, taking a challenge up to policy requires principals and teachers who are unapologetic about their primary calling, their duty to refresh politicians and policymakers' memories as to the moral purpose of education and the breadth of learning so necessary in the modern age and the inclusivity that is so essential in a shrinking global village.

Schools develop as professional learning communities (PLCs), as Pedder and Opfer (2013) have argued,

> through the cultivation of shared values and vision, shared and supportive leadership, norms of trust, respect, critical enquiry and collective learning. PLCs aim to promote improvements in students' learning by supporting change through teachers' learning that is not individual and fragmented but collaborative and embedded in their day-to-day routine work.
>
> *(p. 545)*

Continuing the struggle

Our judgement of the present environment implies a continuing struggle against competitive measures, intrinsic elements of new public management and new public governance. Critics have talked about the side effects of policy but more accurately, these are direct effects because they sit at the very centre of a policy, by design discriminating and by impact dehumanising. Consider systemic changes such as the following, all of which have occurred or have influenced policy over time in the name of reform:

- deeply embedded assumptions about "ability";
- system design and structures which discriminate on the basis of misconceptions;
- divisive and uninformed discourses on children as "academic" and "non-academic";
- forms of assessment which confuse formative and summative purposes;
- systemic factors such as streaming, ability grouping, and setting;
- overloaded curriculum and implicit hierarchies of "subjects";
- inadequate and ill-informed approaches to children with special needs;
- mainstreaming of children with special educational needs on economic or ideological grounds;
- ignorance, lack of attention to, and dismissiveness of research findings; and
- transfer of practice and policy borrowing.

Countering a reformist list such as this has commanded the energy of many in the profession over the years and using present international comparative indices as the best approach to policy should be no exception. What is good in one national context cannot be assumed to be so in another. We agree with Hodgson and Spours (2016) that an important distinction has to be made between policy borrowing and policy learning. The former, they describe as a highly political process, motivated by a desire by nation states to justify existing policy, to implement highly selective samples of "best practice" and to "transfer" policy across nations. The latter they describe as "processes that focus on modes of governance, curriculum, implementation and the conduct of policy itself across national boundaries; across time and involving different policy actors" (p. 514). They compare two contrasting approaches to policy learning – *restrictive* and *expansive*. *Restrictive* approaches are characterised by competition, centralisation, the identification and borrowing of best practice, and a culture of policy innovation. In contrast, *expansive* approaches are characterised by collaborative cultures, decentralised policy based on a partnership model, identification of common issues and "good practice" in comparable contexts, together with a reflective culture which understands the history of policy innovation within a specific context (Mowat, 2017).

The restricted policy environment has led to the concept of pedagogy being obscured and distorted. In 1981, Brian Simon posed the question: "Why no pedagogy in England?" – a question revisited in 2002 by Robin Alexander in relation to his major study of the state of primary education. He commented in a memorial lecture:

> Thus, the historical condition of unprincipled, fashion-led pragmatism, as Brian analysed it in "Why no pedagogy?" has lately reappeared, dusted and polished, as "what works" – an ostensibly novel criterion for judging not just classroom practice but a wide range of educational, social and economic policy as well.
>
> *(Alexander, 2010, closing paragraph)*

While Brian Simon went on to argue for a "science" of teaching, this is of limited use if it does not encourage the flourishing of professional discourse and dialogue in which teachers make and remake their pedagogy. It is this that has been under attack due to the incursion of performativity in recent years. A brief study of history illustrates how, from the late 1980s onwards, pedagogy has been forgotten while the broader purposes of education have been progressively narrowing. This is largely a result of national and international competition but is also owed to education having become increasingly politicised, the quality of learning becoming of less and less interest. The "scripting" and delineation of curriculum inevitably has brought with it a reduced capacity for principals and teachers to make professional and moral judgements. The discovery of accountability in the 1970s proved to be a double-edged sword. On the one hand, it drew attention to the debt that professional educators owed to children; on the other, it became consumed with its own power, feeding on itself so as to eventually dominate both policy and practice. As it grew, it required more and more and finer and finer discriminating comparative measures, having left behind its original critical and formative purpose. These were, in Fullan's (2010) words, "the wrong policy drivers" because they were both wrongly and narrowly conceived but, more worryingly, were allowed to drive policy with purblind conviction.

The political appeal was to "standards". Without a sense of accountability standards had, in many places, been allowed to fall, sometimes with dramatic effect. It was an easy target for a Thatcher-Reagan coalition to point to drastically underachieving schools, complacent or collusive local authorities and school districts, and to point the accusing finger at the root cause – progressivism and progressive teachers, more often than not a caricature, but sometimes worryingly close to the mark.

Yet, what comprises a standard and what the public rhetoric of standards actually means is simply assumed and not subject to critical scrutiny. In Chapter 1, we described the intolerance of dissent and challenge, yet argued that it is the ability to challenge what Alfred North Whitehead (1967) termed "inert ideas" which is the very hallmark of an educated individual. We argued that a good school would be one in which conflict is discussed, understood, and positively addressed. We emphasised the importance of, and the corruption of, accountability, what we owe to children and to one another – a collegial stewardship of the treasure within. It is here that we meet what is described in Chapter 2 as "the dilemma space", the juxtaposition of a cooperative commitment to educational principles on the one hand, with competitive, and unforgiving, service provision on the other. It requires what Hoyle and Wallace (2009) have referred to as "principled infidelity" – seeming to follow external policy diktat whilst pursuing critical commitment.

Inherited intelligence or hard work?

There has been a long-standing debate as to whether student achievement is mainly a product of inherited intelligence or hard work. Discussions following from the publication of PISA findings have led to comparisons between East and West, contrasting Singapore and France, for example. PISA didn't only test what 15-year-olds knew and could do with what they knew: it also asked students what they believed made them successful. "In many countries, students were quick to blame everyone but themselves", Schleicher wrote (2016), while in Singapore, students believed that if they tried hard they would succeed, and trusted their teachers to help them do so. Schleicher went on:

> [While] more than three-quarters of the students in France, an average performer on the PISA test, said the course material was simply too hard, two-thirds said the teacher did not get students interested in the material, and half said their teacher did not explain the concepts well or they were just unlucky.
>
> *(para. 7)*

There is nothing inevitable about underachievement or that deprivation is destiny, argues Schleicher (2017), pointing to remarkable achievements being made by children from deprived backgrounds. He points to the evidence:

> Education systems where disadvantaged students succeed are able to moderate social inequalities. They tend to attract the most talented teachers to the most challenging classrooms and the most capable school leaders to the most disadvantaged schools, which steers all students to high standards too.
>
> *(para 5)*

In these ideal conditions, it is very likely that the systemic gap between high and low achievers may be mitigated. It offers a challenging proposition for policy and school systems but would imply a number of systemic changes, addressing deeply embedded assumptions and attitudes to "ability": the commonly held myth that children are either academic or non-academic, resulting in self-fulfilling strategies such as streaming, ability grouping and setting, differential resourcing and selection. More enlightened ways of supporting children with special needs are required; these include social mix, aspiration, parental encouragement, belief systems and out-of-school support – indeed, a matrix of factors all of which play a key determining role.

Comparing French students with their Singaporean counterparts, for example, may fail to account for a whole complex of historical and cultural factors. French students may indeed have been justified in their challenges to their teachers, to the curriculum, and to testing regimes. In Geert Hofstede's (1983) comparisons of these countries on criteria such as "uncertainty avoidance", he shows that the extent to which the members of a culture feel threatened by ambiguous or unknown situations leads to creating beliefs and institutions that try to avoid them. On country index values in a range between eight and 112, Singapore scored eight, eschewing uncertainty as far as possible, as against 86 in France (more likely to admit or embrace uncertainty). While these data are only broadly indicative and open to challenge, such differences are freely acknowledged in Singapore where, as students have pointed out, their country is, after all, a dictatorship. We are left with the question, "To what extent do these comparisons and their cultural underpinnings tell us about the autonomy of learners?"

Autonomy and the dark side

Who could argue against autonomy, for individuals, for teachers, for schools? Yet there is an almost invisible element in this desire to stand alone, as an individual school, as an individual classroom, yet sitting uneasily with moral accountability, mutuality, and collaboration. The dark side of autonomy is that it enables governments to measure, and hold to account, the individual school, the individual head, the individual teacher, measured by the attainment of the individual student. This also allows international comparisons which start with each student's measured attainment, aggregated to school and system level. This may be meat and drink to statisticians and to the governments that employ them but a deeply worrying distraction from the essential purpose of educational systems.

It is important to contest the myth encapsulated in the headteacher's comment (quoted in Chapter 1), "this school is not a democracy". We might be prompted to ask, "and why not?" As the institutions most critical to the flourishing of democracy, how can democratic participation be learnt without the practice of it? While schools are organisations in which lines of communication enable effective decision-making and in which responsibilities are "distributed", these skills can only be learnt by participation, both by expressing and listening to disparate voices. Where senior leaders have the skills and understanding required for the husbandry of shared leadership, organisations can develop in ways that are consistent with democratic perspectives such as rights, responsibilities, reciprocity, and justice. In such organisations, everyone is able to experience an enhanced sense of personal and collective agency, essential to authentic learning. In Austria, Michael Schratz and Wilfred Schley, leading the *Carpe Vitam* Project conference in Innsbruck, drew heavily on the work of Otto Scharmer (2009) and his concept of "presencing" – stopping and listening to others, "co-sensing" through which co-evolving and co-creating take place. Scharmer and Käufer (2013) refer to the imperative for leadership to develop an understanding of the "inner field", the internal space where every activity's origin lies. This is consonant with Gregorzewski and Kovacs's (2017) explanation of Kwo's "kernel practice".

> Teachers today need to embrace a plethora of skills and knowledge to keep up with the changes that society reflects in the classroom. Hence, Kwo believes that continuous teacher learning is no longer merely an option, but a core trait of the craft. Especially in the most dynamic working environments that embrace innovations, changing the "kernel practice" ... must be closely connected to teacher learning. Since teachers are so precious in classroom procedures, they need to be allowed to "tinker" to better their practices and create possibilities for knowledge development and sharing.
>
> *(p. 207)*

The notion of tinkering is a more powerful one than we would generally associate with that concept, but change, however small, may set in train a dynamic akin to introducing new DNA into the cellular system, causing deep changes in the tissues that they compose and reproduce (Poekert, Alexandrou, & Shannon, 2016). So, apparently small and local interactions can lead to large global change, a new emergent system, a reformed community of practice. "Understanding leadership development as an instance of emergence allows us to treat it with the appropriate appreciation of uncertainty, complexity and unpredictability" (p. 329).

Uncertainty and unpredictably are an anathema to systems which rely on the certainty of sequential curricula and it is difficult to envisage how schools might work without them. We are, however, so inured to curriculum as we know it, that it is difficult to envisage how it might be different or in what ways it is currently dysfunctional. As Mary James has argued (2017), the structures of grades, scales, and attainment levels have accustomed us to regard progression as step by step and linear, with curriculum tied inexorably into stage-related assessments. A more rational and productive focus might be on how well people exercise agency in their use of the resources or tools (intellectual, human, material) to formulate problems, work productively, and evaluate their efforts. Work assignments with students having access to source materials would afford a better approach to assessing achievement because it is the way that resources are used that is of most significance. If theories of learning and assessment were developed more closely with each other, we might be able to rethink how this more rational alignment would more adequately serve the goals of education. Learning outcomes would then be captured and reported through various forms of recording, including narrative accounts and audio and visual media together with the use of portfolios which have an important role here. Evaluation would need to be more holistic and qualitative, not atomised and quantified as in most current measurement approaches. There are clearly challenges here for teachers and school leaders in understanding and developing the skills not only to practise assessment but also to be able to offer a coherent critique of assessment policy, and to be able explain it to, perhaps sceptical, parents.

The inertia of change

How successful have schools been over the years in engaging parents in genuine dialogue about the need, shape, and direction of change? How to frame the argument that what was good enough for parents two or three decades ago is no longer of equal priority? How to argue that there was an inherent flaw in assessing on a 100-point assessment scale? Why was 51% a pass and 80% regarded as the very apex of achievement? What could be wrong with exams which tested what we knew and didn't know, or at least what we were able to retrieve in that soulless exam hall in the hour or two allowed?

As the Danish theorist Illeris (2007) has written, these conventions of schooling are deeply embedded in practice which extends over decades if not centuries. We have learnt from our parents and from their parents that the essence of the school educational experience is:

- to be able to sit for extended periods;
- to direct attention primarily to the teacher;
- to speak only when encouraged to do so by the teacher;
- to feign interest long after interest has dissipated;
- to endure a high degree of conformity;
- to perform well in competition with peers;
- to be adaptive to different forms of authority and differing latitudes for behaviour;
- to learn to ignore one's own primary desires and needs; and
- to accept that school learning is a peculiar form of learning which has very little application outside school.

To what extent do those issues open the way for discussion with students? To what extent does "education" stop short of debates as to its essential purpose, its relationship to school, to curriculum, to assessment, to authority? Bourdieu's (1977) critique of "categories of thought" refers to a process through which the power structures of society are accepted and internalised – in perhaps hyperbolic language, "symbolic violence". There are echoes here of Paul Goodman's *Growing up Absurd* (1960) in which he argues that learning to accept the ritual conventions of the classroom constitutes the deeper purposes of schooling regimes: "And so we go on pretending that there is a correspondence between what is taught and what is learnt even though we have learnt that this is not the case, right back from our earliest school experience" (Illeris, 2007, p. 237). Students are exhorted to be responsible for their learning but, as Illeris goes on to ask, "who wants to take responsibility for something they have no control over?" (p. 204). He further argues that such is the weight of convention that it is almost impossible to challenge.

> It is far more convenient to add to an existing scheme than to perform the necessary demolition, organisation and restructuring. ...We don't simply give up on positions we have struggled to maintain and which we at any rate have become accustomed to building on.
>
> *(p. 43)*

And so, we continue to build and to consolidate on foundations so shaky in conception and so unassailable in convention. This is a gift to politicians whose blandishments exploit that conservative inertia, appealing to parental "common sense" and the worst of all arguments, "It never did me any harm".

There is, unfortunately, a substantive and deeply worrying body of evidence as to the harm done to children and young people by inappropriate and ill-conceived curriculum and assessment. In the *Carpe Vitam* initiative, which provided the antidote and the impetus for this volume, we devoted 4 years to building and refining a set of principles which, a decade later, have not only travelled widely in the world but remain largely uncontested. While we have discussed the policy inertia and constraints on school leaders and teachers, we also argue that these can be countered by the maintenance of an unswerving focus on professional integrity, seeing leadership as practice, thinking differently about learning and teaching, and continuing to work on the issues that enhance professionality and reframe accountability.

> It is a shift from an *ego*-system awareness that cares about the well-being of oneself to an *eco*-system awareness that cares about the well-being of all, including oneself. When operating with ego-system awareness, we are driven by the concerns and intentions of our *small ego* self. When operating with eco-system awareness, we are driven by the concerns and intentions of our emerging or *essential* self – that is, by a concern that is informed by the well-being of the whole.
>
> *(Scharmer & Kaufer, 2013, p. 2)*

Conclusion

While the purpose of the *Carpe Vitam* Project was not to launch a policy offensive, the further we ventured into practice in seven very different cultural contexts, the more striking became the disconnect between our seminal principles and the nature of day-to-day practice. There was a cumulative body of evidence as to the way much of present-day educational policy detracts from and devalues the fundamental purpose of education – learning for all, no matter their social circumstances. In this last chapter, we have challenged some deeply embedded cultural assumptions, the frailty of comparative data, and the inert ideas which continue to sustain them. With reference to OECD data and the conclusions derived from them, we have questioned the extent to which these tell the story of exemplary schooling or which might, more justifiably, be explained by wider cultural factors.

We have argued for reasoned dissent. We have argued for the ability and capacity to challenge national, local, and school policy and practice. And we have argued that when there is professional discourse, a quality of ongoing dialogue in which teachers lead the making and remaking of their pedagogy, there is a bulwark against a performativity agenda and an embrace of principled pedagogy.

References

Alexander, R. (2002). *Brian Simon and pedagogy*. Contribution to the celebration of the life and work of Brian Simon (1915–2002), University of Leicester, 8 June 2002. Retrieved from http://www.robinalexander.org.uk/wp-content/uploads/2014/05/Simon-memorial.pdf

Alexander, R. (2010). Legacies, policies and prospects: One year on from the Cambridge Primary Review (The 2010 Brian Simon Memorial Lecture). *Forum, 53*(1), 71–92.

Bourdieu, P. (1977). *Outline of a theory of practice*. Cambridge, MA: Cambridge University Press.

Dewey, J., & Bentley, A. (1949). *Knowing and the known*. Boston, MA: Beacon Press.

Fullan, M. (2010). *All systems go: The change imperative for whole system reform*. Thousand Oaks, CA: Corwin Press.

Goh Chok Tong. (1997). Speech presented at the opening of the 7th international conference on thinking, Suntec City Convention Centre.

Goodman, P. (1960). *Growing up absurd: Problems of youth in the organized society*. New York: Random House.

Gregorzewski, M., & Kovacs, H. (2017). A mix that works for school development: School leadership and knowledge sharing. In L. Rasiński, T. Tóth, & J. Wagner (Eds.), *European perspectives in transformative education, Part II: Transformative education in the European context* (pp. 204–215). Wrocław: University of Lower Silesia Press.

Hanushek.net. (2017). *A Conversation on "Waiting for Superman"* [video]. Retrieved from http://hanushek.stanford.edu/opinions/conversation-waiting-superman

Harris, J. (1998). *The nurture assumption: Why children turn out the way they do*. New York: The Free Press.

Hodgson, A., & Spours, K. (2016). Restrictive and expansive policy learning – Challenges and strategies for knowledge exchange in upper secondary education across the four countries of the UK. *Journal of Education Policy, 31*(5), 511–525.

Hofstede, G. (1983). *Culture's consequences: International differences in work-related values*. London: Sage.

Hoyle, E., & Wallace, M. (2009). Leadership for professional practice. In S. Gewirtz, P. Mahoney, I. Hextall, & A. Cribb (Eds.), *Changing teacher professionalism: International trends, challenges and ways forward* (pp. 204–214). London: Routledge.

Illeris, K. (2007). *How we learn: Learning and non-learning in school and beyond*. London: Routledge.

James, M. (2017). (Re)viewing assessment: Changing lenses to refocus on learning. *Assessment in Education: Principles, Policy & Practice, 24*(3), 404–414.

Mortimore, P. (1998). *The road to improvement: Reflections on school effectiveness*, Lisse, the Netherlands: Swets & Zeitlinger.

Mowat, J. G. (2017). Closing the attainment gap – A realistic proposition or an elusive pipe-dream? *Journal of Education Policy* [online]. http://dx.doi.org/10.1080/02680939.2 017.1352033

Pedder, D., & Opfer, D. (2013). Professional learning orientations: Patterns of dissonance and alignment between teachers' values and practices. *Research Papers in Education, 28*(5), 539–570.

Poekert, P., Alexandrou, A., & Shannon, D. (2016). How teachers become leaders: An internationally validated theoretical model of teacher leadership development. *Research in Post-Compulsory Education, 21*(4), 307–329.

Scharmer, O. (2009). *Theory U: Leading from the future as it emerges – the social technology of presencing*. San Francisco, CA: Berrett-Koehler.

Scharmer, O., & Käufer, K. (2013). *Leading from the emerging future: From eco system to eco system economics*. San Francisco, CA: Berrett-Koehler.

Schleicher, A. (2016). *Are the Chinese cheating in PISA or are we cheating ourselves?* Retrieved from ecdeducationtoday.blogspot.co.uk/2013/12/are-chinese-cheating-in-pisa-or-are-we.html

Schleicher, A. (2017). Debunking education myths. *Teacher.* Retrieved from https://www. teachermagazine.com.au/articles/debunking-education-myths

Simpson, B. (2016). Where's the agency in leadership-as-practice? In J. A. Raelin (Ed.), *Leadership-as-practice: Theory and application* (pp. 159–178). London, Oxon: Routledge. Thrupp, M. (1999). *Schools making a difference: Let's be realistic.* Buckingham: Open University Press.

UNESCO. (1996). *The treasure within* (The Delors Report). Report to UNESCO of the International Commission on Education for the Twenty First Century. UNESCO Publishing.

Whitehead, A. N. (1967). *Adventures of ideas.* London: Cambridge University Press.

INDEX

accountability: examined in *Carpe Vitam* project 28–29, 40–41; managerialism in 6–7; as policy driver 17, 60, 63, 164–165; principles of 12, 47–49, 53, 160–161

adult learning 17, 44–45

adult learning partners 75–77, 79, 103

agency: in *Carpe Vitam* project 27–28; defined 127; in teacher professionalism 95, 114, 147–149

assessments 167–168

Australia: Building Education Revolution (BER) 43; education policy 23, 28, 32–33, 49, 50, 60, 62, 66; PALLIC project 74–80; parental choice in 30–31; The Smith Family (TSF) 118, 130; Tough Times Primary School 101–105; *see also Carpe Vitam* Project

Australian Indigenous education 74–80

Austria: in *Carpe Vitam* Project 39; education expenditures 26; home education in 29; leadership learning in 27, 98–101; *see also Carpe Vitam* Project

authority: and classroom behaviour 124; of knowledge 122; and leadership 103–105, 137; responses to external 15

autonomy of schools 18, 23–24, 90, 133, 166

Carpe Vitam countries 24–25, 26–35, 39; *see also* Australia; Austria; Denmark; England; Greece; Norway; United States

Carpe Vitam Project: background 1, 38–41; framing values 58, 81; principles 42–49, 169–170

children: learning methods 115; in low socio-economic status families 101–102; UN Rights of 63–67, 81, 159; *see also* students

Children's University (CU) 125–126

collaborative team coaching (CTC) 100–101

collective leadership 16, 18, 91–92, 94, 96, 147–148, 160

communities: disadvantaged 7–8, 14, 30–31, 101–102, 145; engagement and activities in 115–118, 124–126, 130; as learning subject 128–129; in PALLIC project 75–77, 78; professional learning and leadership 139–145, 162–163

competitive service delivery 21–24, 29, 30

compliance: as policy driver 18–19; and professionalism 11, 12, 14–15, 63, 99, 148

conflict management 10–11, 15–16

connoisseurship 4, 17, 156

continuing professional development (CPD) 135, 148

critical friendship 42, 58, 75, 80–81, 159

cultural recognition: of Australian Indigenous capital 62, 76, 77, 78; as social justice 66, 67, 68–69

curriculum: breadth of 50, 61–63, 82, 125, 128, 130; in *Carpe Vitam* countries 32, 161; evaluations of 68–69, 78–80; scripting of 59, 164; and testing 14, 18, 60, 110, 122–123, 167

decision-making: and feedback 155–156; four-dimensional grid 13; and moral

purpose 60, 61, 81–82; in PALLIC program 76, 79
democracy: and policy experiences 8–9, 23, 25, 28, 34; semi-permanent disagreement 35, 61
democratic values: in LfL framework 42, 54, 58; and professional integrity 67, 68, 81–83; in schools 166; in teacher leadership 141, 143, 146
Denmark: education policy 28–29, 32; parental choice 31; teacher experiences in 34; *see also Carpe Vitam* Project
deprofessionalisation 11–12, 18
dialogue 45–47, 51, 105, 147
dilemma space 2, 15–16, 165
dissent 1, 2, 10–11, 18–19, 32, 35, 156–157
distributive leadership 90–96, 104–106
divergent thinking 158, 162–163

education: administration policies 21–24; costs and funding 26; management vs. leadership 100–101; as moral development 59; and opportunities 68, 121; power structures 8–9; research focus 13; rights to 29, 66; success factors 133–134, 135, 148; *see also* school management
educators: experiences of 64–65; in leadership for learning platform 156–159; and policy challenges 81–83, 162, 164; *see also* headteachers; principals; teachers
England: education policy 7, 11, 23, 32, 110, 154–155; parental choice 29, 30; school experiences 8, 9–10, 60, 137; teacher recruitment and retention 26, 33–34; *see also Carpe Vitam* Project; United Kingdom

feedback: institutional 155–156; student 52–53
financial crisis of 2007–2008 25–26
Florida Teacher Leader Fellowship Program 138–141

Ghana: *Carpe Vitam* principles in 41; educator experiences in 43, 64–65; Leadership for Learning program 70–74
grassroots leadership 106, 138
Greece: curriculum reform 32; education policy 27–28

headteachers: accountability and discretion of 47–49, 63, 83, 93, 147; experiences of 6, 15, 33–34, 43, 44–45, 64–65, 70–74,

81; global terms for 5; individualism of 9–10, 17; and teacher power distance 8–9, 18; *see also* educators; principals
Hertscam Network 138, 141–147
home education 29–30, 31
Hong Kong: Other Learning Experiences initiative 125; student feedback in 48, 52–53

Indigenous education in PALLIC project 74–80
Indigenous Leadership Partners (Australia) 75–77
individualism: in leadership 3, 9–10, 17, 89, 90, 97; and trust 48–49
inter-actions 89, 90, 92, 93, 97, 100, 104
International Teacher Leadership (ITL) initiative 143, 145, 161

justice: definitions of 65; *see also* social justice

knowledge: modes of knowing 118–121; professional 136; students 14, 49, 50, 68, 76–77; transmission 129–130

language: oral development 101–105; of policy management 5–6, 22–23, 29; *see also* literacy
leader-practitioners 89, 90, 104, 105, 106
leaders *see* school leaders
leadership: *Carpe Vitam* countries 27–29; characterisations for *Carpe Vitam* 40–41, 87–88; as distributive 90–96; in flow of practice 96–98, 105–106, 161–162; individualism in 9–10, 17; practice perspectives 3, 89, 158; sharing of 47–49, 102–106; training for 130–138, 141–147; *see also* non-positional leadership; positional leadership
Leadership Academy (Austria) 98–101
Leadership for Learning Blueprint (LfLB) 75–76
leadership for learning (LfL): Austria 98–101; background 2, 37–38, 87–88; Ghana program 70–74; Hertscam Network 138, 141–147; platform for challenges 156–159; principles 41–49; and teacher professionality 149; in teacher training 136–138
learning: as educator 104–105; nature of 17, 115; as performance 109–112; and policy environment 5; as school priority 42–44; through story 127–129; *see also* curriculum; knowledge

learning environments: conditions for
3, 44–45, 50–51, 54, 82; in-school and
out-of-school 122–125, 130–131; for
teacher training 140, 148
Learning School, The 112–114
LfL: The Cambridge Network 37–38
LfL see Leadership for Learning (LfL)
literacy 49–50, 116; see also Principals
as Literacy Leaders with Indigenous
Communities (PALLIC) Project

managerialism 6–7, 24–25, 155–156
marketisation 55, 155–156
Melbourne Declaration (2008) 62, 66
mentorship 130, 147
mindsets: changes 99, 106, 115; for growth
124–125; on intelligence 121–122
moral purpose: educator experiences with
74–75, 76–78, 100–101, 138, 141–142,
144; and leadership 160, 162; in LfL
framework 42, 58, 158; and professional
integrity 59, 61, 63–67, 81–82, 147, 156

National Assessment Program in Literacy
and Numeracy (NAPLAN) 28, 62, 75
NCLB see No Child Left Behind (NCLB)
policy
networking collectives 99–100,
144–145, 160
New Public Governance (NPG) 22, 23, 35
New Public Management (NPM) 22, 23,
34, 35, 59
NGOs (non-governmental agencies) 118
No Child Left Behind (NCLB) policy
13–14, 32
non-positional leadership 142–143,
145–146, 147, 162; see also positional
leadership
Norway: education expenditures 26;
education policy 23, 28–29, 32;
mentorship in 147; parental choice 31;
see also Carpe Vitam Project
NPG see New Public Governance (NPG)
NPM see New Public Management (NPM)

oral language development project 101–105
Organisation for Economic Co-operation
and Development (OECD): on
accountability 12, 53; on education
investment 26; influences of 23, 25, 28;
on parent choice 30; on school as eco
system 124
Other Learning Experiences
(Hong Kong) 125
Outward Bound 124–125

PA see Public Administration (PA)
Pakistan experiences with LfL 47
Palestine Teachers Leading the Way
Program 146–147
PALLIC Project see Principals as Literacy
Leaders with Indigenous Communities
(PALLIC) Project
parental choice 7, 29, 30–31, 160
parents: accountability of 7, 29–30, 33;
concerns of 62, 63; engagement with
115–118; experiences of 34, 50, 73,
76–77, 103; in Rights of the Child
66–67
parity of participation 68, 69, 73, 75–77,
82–83, 148
pedagogy: evaluations of 69, 79; moral
purpose and professionality in 144, 147,
160; politicisation of 164; student voices
in 52–53
peer effect 159–160
performance measurement: impacts and
effectiveness of 109–112, 166, 167–168;
learning passports 126; managerialism in
6–7; OECD reports on 53; see also testing
PISA see Programme for International
Student Assessment (PISA)
policy: discontinuities 31–32, 81–82, 99;
drivers 1, 17–18, 23, 24–25, 29, 130–131,
163–165; impacts 154–156; inertia
168–169; language of 5–6; reform 4, 19,
27–28; research challenges 13
positional leadership 91–93, 98, 105, 147–
148, 161, 162; see also non-positional
leadership
power: in Austrian education system 99,
100, 101; distance 1, 8–9, 18, 34, 147,
148; and grassroots leadership 104–105,
106; in leadership practice 89, 90, 92–93,
94, 95, 96, 98; structures 23–24, 116, 117
principals: accountability of 27–28, 50, 63,
137, 160; autonomy of 23–24, 92, 98,
106; experiences of 39, 41, 43, 44–45,
46–49, 102–105; global terms for 5; in
PALLIC Project 74–80; and parents
115–116; see also headteachers
Principals as Literacy Leaders with
Indigenous Communities (PALLIC)
Project 44, 74–80
problem-solving skills 129–130
professional development 4, 42, 43–44, 51,
54, 148–149
professional integrity: challenges and
defence 2–3, 11–12, 59–61, 63,
81–83, 156, 158, 159; elements 58–59;
evaluation questions 68–69; in PALLIC

project 74–75; and Rights of the Child 65–66, 66–67
professionalism: critical friendships in 80–81; and policy 19, 27; practice of 11–12, 106
professionality 4, 133, 134–135, 159–161
Programme for International Student Assessment (PISA) 14, 28, 49, 165
Public Administration (PA) 22
public schools 30–31
punishments 64–65

recognition of culture 67, 68, 73, 76–80
redistribution of justice 67, 68, 72, 74–80
representation of justice 67, 68, 73
repurposing 4, 154
reputation of schools 7, 29, 30
Rights of the Child 63–67, 81, 159

school leaders: accountability of 100, 167; deprofessionalisation of 11–12; experiences of 13, 27, 32, 34; global terms for 5; *see also* headteachers; principals
school management 5–7, 12
schools and schooling: Children's University (CU) 125–126; conventions and reframing 16–17, 99, 130–131, 168–169; engagement with parents 115–117; focus and priorities of 43–44; learning as abstraction in 123–124; as professional learning communities 162–163; social mix in 7–8, 30–31; The Learning School 112–114; Tough Times Primary School 101–105
Scotland: schooling 15, 26, 53, 62–63, 127; *see also* United Kingdom
self-actions 89, 90, 100, 104, 105
semi-permanent disagreement 1, 35, 61
Singapore schooling 5, 13, 155, 166
skills: critique and dissent 10, 168; oral language 101–102, 103; school management 48; student success 50, 60, 66, 110, 113, 125, 128, 166
social justice 66–68, 77, 82–83
social mix 7–8, 30–31, 51, 160
special needs 64, 121–122, 166
standards: school performance 41, 109–110, 164–165; teacher quality 32–33, 133–134, 138–139
stories for learning 127–129
Storyline 127–128
student learning 17, 42, 66

students: abilities of 165–166; conflict management skills 10–11; experiences of 48, 126; impacted by testing 14; influence in pedagogy 52–53; as leaders 44–45; and peer effect 159–160; supportive conditions for 50–51
Sweden 23, 31, 147

teacher leadership development: Hertscam Network 138, 141–147; University of Florida 138–141; *see also* professional development
teachers: deprofessionalisation of 11–12; experiences of 16, 60, 64–65, 94–95, 102–105, 111–112, 146; and positional power 9, 34, 147–149; recruitment and salaries 26, 32–34, 52–53
technology investment 17–18
testing: impacts and effectiveness of 14, 18, 28, 32, 60, 61–62; international results 23
TIMSS *see* Trends in International Mathematics and Science Study (TIMSS)
trans-actions 89, 96, 98, 158
Trends in International Mathematics and Science Study (TIMSS) 14, 28
trust: and leadership 48–49, 99, 101; in schools 50–51
2007-2008 financial crisis 25–26

UN Convention on the Rights of the Child 63–67, 81
United Kingdom: Children's University 125–126; education expenditures 26; school types 29; teacher experiences in 32, 34; testing and curriculum 62
United States: bussing policy 7–8; education cuts 26; New Public Governance in 22; school types 29; teacher experiences in 32, 33; University of Florida teacher training program 138–141
University of Florida Teacher Leader Fellowship Program 138–141

vocabulary development 101–104

Western Balkans International Leadership Initiative 145–146

young people: attitudes 129; conflict and inquiry skills 10–11; experiences of 112–114; *see also* students